Early Reviews f

MW00617170

"It was fascinating to go along on this journey with Candace and her child. Meeting parents with trans children, either in person or through this book, is life changing and exceedingly helpful for the parents and child. Comprehensive. Authentic. Compelling. A must read for all new parents!"

—**PAM GARRAMONE**, *Executive Program Director, Greater Boston PFLAG (Parents, Families, and Friends of LGBTQ People)*

"Candace Waldron has written a book for everyone! *My Daughter He* should be required reading not only for parents and family members of trans children, but for teachers, counselors, and school administrators. In fact, all of us will benefit from the information in these pages. Besides being an education, it's a story that keeps you on the edge of your seat. I couldn't put it down. All my love to the brave young man, Kai."

—**BETTY DEGENERES**, *Ellen's mother, is a national LGBT rights advocate and the author of Love, Ellen: A Mother/Daughter Journey and Just a Mom*

"In *My Daughter He*, Candace Waldron bravely delves into the new frontier of autobiographical writing by parents of transgender children. By sharing her own transition journey and that of her trans son, including issues around safety, schools, and mental health, Waldron has created an informative and comforting resource for other families."

—**RACHEL PEPPER**, *therapist and gender specialist living and practicing in Oakland, CA, coauthor of The Transgender Child: A Handbook for Families and Professionals and editor of Transitions of the Heart: Stories of Love, Struggle, and Acceptance by Mothers of Transgender and Gender Variant Children*

"A groundbreaking resource for parents and educators that blends the emotional journey of parents with strategies for transitioning and the urgent need for safe schools."

—**JEFF PERROTTI**, *founder and director of Massachusetts' Safe Schools Program for LGBTQ students and coauthor of When the Drama Club Is Not Enough: Lessons from the Safe Schools Program for Gay and Lesbian Students*

"In *My Daughter He*, Candace Waldron takes us on a remarkable journey revealing the deepest inner chambers of her own experience as a mother shepherding her daughter, Kendra, from a burgeoning recognition that Kendra was not the gender everyone thought her to be, to the blossoming of her young adult transgender son, Kai. With honesty, fortitude, and openness to sharing the good, the bad, and the ugly, she teaches us the simple but so complicated truth about our gender-creative, transgender children: It is not for us to say, but for us to listen to what they are telling us about who they are. Once we hear what they are saying, we have only one job: to help them get to be that person. With no sugarcoating, *My Daughter He* gives us a window into exactly how this can be done. This book is a must for anyone who wants support for or insight into the path that must be taken, by parent, child, and everyone around them, if our transgender youth and young adults are going to have the full opportunity to be the wonderful people they are."

—**DIANE EHRENSAFT, PHD**, *Director of Mental Health, Child and Adolescent Gender Center, University of California, San Francisco, and author of Gender Born, Gender Made: Raising Healthy Gender-Nonconforming Children*

"*My Daughter He* is guaranteed not only to open your mind to aspects of gender you never considered but also to give you an in-depth emotional analysis of what it is to be transgender or the parent of a gender nonconforming child. The author is able to build an intimate narrative that truly involves and moves the reader beyond its format of a personal, step-by-step, self-help guide for the parents of transgender children. You will embrace the rainbow of gender and the beauty of humanity as never before. After all, as Waldron says: 'In many ways gender is the last frontier of our human capacity to embrace diversity.'"

—**JOHN BOETTJER**, *newsletter of Gay Social Network of Southwest Florida, July 2014*

My Daughter He

Transitioning With Our Transgender Children

CANDACE WALDRON

STONE CIRCLE PRESS

My Daughter He:
Transitioning With Our Transgender Children

www.CandaceWaldron.com

Published by Stone Circle Press
Rockport, MA 01966

Library of Congress Control Number: 2014932458

ISBN 978-0-9914474-0-4
eBook 978-0-9914474-1-1

Cover photo: Kendra age 2, by Candace Waldron
Book design by Shannon Bodie, BookWiseDesign.com
Edited by Ellen Szabo

Manufactured in the United States of America.
First edition, October 2014

10 9 8 7 6 5 4 3 2 1

To my mother, Maryetta Grace Prior Waldron,
whose unconditional love for children
extended beyond her own family.

Acknowledgments

Friends, family, and allies grasped my hand along this journey just as Kendra used to hold me tight on our walks in the woods. On the other end of the phone, beside me in the woods, over a cup of tea, or held in my mind until we had a chance to catch up, their presence made the difference.

Knowing there are people we can count on helps blunt the piercing edges of life. Like midwives, the women who coached this book into the world are my oldest and dearest friends. Joanna Duda, Lisa Dodson, Char Wendel, and Carol Szatkowski were also my insightful, honest, compassionate, and probing editors. Writing is a solitary experience, especially a book as personal as this, and without guidance I would have become lost in the wilderness. These dear friends knew how to bring me back to the path that has become this book and hopefully a useful resource for other parents.

Life sometimes surprises, bringing people to us just when we need them. Ellen Szabo sent a letter for an entirely different reason and over coffee I learned she was a writing coach. After reading an early manuscript for this book, she encouraged me when I might have quit. I have relied upon her skillful editing ever since. Shannon Bodie at BookWise has been a critical resource and a delight to work with. Publishing a first book is daunting and I have consulted with Shannon on everything from design and marketing to paper and binding. Without her creativity and publishing expertise, this book might have remained a Word document. Thanks are also due to Palma Odano for her keen attention to detail and line edit precision.

Family forms our very first circle of support. I was blessed with Sandy, Donna, and Debbie, my three amazing sisters, who always created a loving, accepting circle for my children no matter their differences. Their willingness to learn about gender identity along with me and seamlessly change names and pronouns in their families without skipping a beat kept our circle whole.

Grandparents hold an outer circle, with their perspective of history, change, and time. Iyine Montout John, Tony's mother, gave Kai her blessing before she passed. Her acceptance, spanning generation, culture, country, and religion, gave him hope. Roz, my aunt, was a blessing for me, being the mother I needed after my mother passed. Her spirituality, advice, sense of humor, love, and care for my children continues to this day. And I am thankful for my Dad's loyalty, love, and gentle acceptance even when he admits he doesn't understand.

I am especially thankful for my daughter, Denali. Her wisdom, loyalty, strength of character, determination, and sense of humor amaze me. She brightens my life with adventure, love, and joy. I am grateful to Tony, my husband and life-partner, for his generosity of spirit, courageous insights, often different from my own and wiser, and his exuberant embrace of life. We made it through some very difficult days and his optimism held out hope better times would come. And they have!

I am grateful for Kai's love, strength, steadfastness, and courage and that he survived my misunderstandings and mistakes. I am thankful for the many lessons I learned on this shared journey of transformation.

And I am thankful for the love and courage of all parents and family members who stand by and support their gender noncon-forming and transgender children, teen, and adult kin on their journey toward authentic self-expression to welcome and embrace a daughter or son in honesty, humanity, and joy.

Together we create an ever-widening circle of friends, family, and allies.

Contents

Introduction

Children change their parents. *My Daughter He: Transitioning With Our Transgender Children* is the story of how my gender nonconforming child pushed me to grow in ways I never knew I needed. Children who are gender nonconforming are those whose behavior, speech, or dress defy culturally prescribed gender norms. They march to the beat of their own inner drum often from the moment of birth, and no amount of persuasion, parental role modeling, or peer pressure can dissuade them from their unique expressions of gender. Transgender children are those whose gender identity does not match their anatomy.

Parents face a transformative journey when their child doesn't conform to gender norms. Loving support for our child is weighted against the judging eyes of others, fears for our child's safety, and questions about our own competence as parents. If your child is gender nonconforming you may be asking where this will lead. If your child or teen has said they wish they were another gender, you may wonder why it's so gut wrenching to hear that the gender of their perfect body is wrong.

My Daughter He: Transitioning With Our Transgender Children is written to help guide you through your own change process so that you can be your best to support your child. The goal of this book is to share the story of how I traversed the difficult terrain that you might face today. With the advantage of hindsight I know more now than I did when my journey began. My daughter was gender nonconforming since early childhood, but it wasn't until she hit puberty and her bright spirit dimmed that I began to understand her inner pain and embarked on my own process of transformation. *My Daughter He* recounts the lengthy road I took to find the resources and guidance to understand my child's gender nonconformity and support her gender transition. It also explores my journey through fear, resistance, and sorrow over losing my daughter, until I finally reached peace, acceptance, and gratitude for my son. In my search for understanding, I have read widely in the field, bringing together much of what I wish I'd known at the start. Drawing on this research and recollecting my own experience, I reflect on the many questions, choices, and decisions you may face on your path.

If you feel overwhelmed with a confusing mix of emotions, you are not alone. Every parent with a gender nonconforming or transgender child has wrestled with a range of difficult emotions. You may be relieved to finally know what's at the root of your child's sadness while experiencing your own fears, questions, and feelings of loss. You may wonder how you and your family will get through this. You may feel unprepared and unsure of your next steps. Other parents have lived through this experience and their children are now happy and healthy. Some parents are living through it right now. Your love for your child and your desire for his or her happiness will lead the way.

I hope that *My Daughter He: Transitioning With Our Transgender Children* will be a valuable resource for you. It is the book I wish I'd had a decade ago when my journey began. I might have responded differently had I been more informed and prepared. I wrote this book to pass on some of my hard-learned lessons and hope they help you as you face your own extraordinary, challenging, and potentially transformative journey with your unique and creative child. In addition to my own story, extensive research, and reflections, the appendices contain a glossary of terms, a list of references, and websites for support, advocacy, and medical care.

While there is still much to be done, never before has society been more receptive to the needs of transgender children and teens. Never before have there been more resources and medical options. And never before has our need for information been greater as we parents confront the responsibility of making transition decisions on behalf of our children. Decisions we make today will have a lifelong impact on our children and many of us worry we might get it wrong.

Terminology

I have chosen to use *transgender* throughout this book since it is the current, preferred, inclusive term for individuals whose gender identity and expression or behavior differs from conventional expectations for their anatomical sex. *Gender identity* refers to a person's inner sense of self as male, female, both, neither, or somewhere in between. *Gender expression* (or *presentation*) refers to the way a person communicates their gender to others through name, clothing, mannerisms, body language, speech patterns, voice, hairstyle, and behavior. The dictionary defines *trans* as meaning "across, on the other side, change, or beyond" so you can think of transgender people as transcending gender and the socially constructed limits we place around it. Transgender children are not confined by the dictates of society for how they think of themselves and present themselves in the world. They color outside the lines of gender expectations and in doing so they transgress social norms. While transgender children are similar to one another in their nonconformity, their internal motivation may vary from one another and evolve over time.

One child's gender nonconformity may be an expression of their difference from prescribed gender roles and expectations while another child's may be an early indication of internal feelings of dissonance between mind and body concerning gender. In other words, some transgender children are comfortable in their bodies while others are not. For some children, feelings of dissonance can increase with age creating discomfort and anxiety; what medical and mental health professionals term *gender dysphoria*.

A transgender person who eventually seeks medical treatment (hormone therapy and/or medical procedures) to bring their body into conformity with their gender identity is technically termed *transsexual*. This term is seldom used today because it assumes only two polarized genders: girl or boy; woman or man; whereas transgender makes room for a rainbow of other possibilities inclusive of transsexuals. *Gender transitioning* is the term used for the multi-step process of moving from living as one gender to another. *Social transitioning*, which is reversible, includes changing one's name, pronoun, dress, body language, speech, and hairstyle. Gender transitioning may also include physical changes such as hormone therapy and medical procedures to modify one's body to conform to one's gender identity. For a complete glossary of other terms see Appendix A.

Transitions

Our job as parents of a gender nonconforming child is to help them help us understand what their gender nonconformity means and how best to create a path for them in a gender confining world. A parent's journey begins well before a child's birth since our own conscious and unconscious expectations impact our ability to perform this critical task. Our own capacity for growth and change determines how well we will do. As with all journeys, the place from which we begin determines the distance we must travel.

I considered myself an open-minded and progressive person so I was not overly concerned with my daughter's early gender nonconformity. I interpreted it in ways I could embrace and even celebrate. It was not until I finally realized her desire to become a boy that I balked. Unlike some parents who take their child's desire to transition in stride, I was tenaciously attached to the birth gender of my child. I loved having a daughter and was reluctant to let her go. I had to embark on a painful journey within that led to my own gradual transformation and eventual acceptance. Looking back I see now that I traveled through several phases of awareness, pulled along, sometimes kicking and (silently) screaming, by my son's own journey of emergence. In an effort to describe these phases of my journey I have arranged them chronologically by chapter:

At times the path felt like an ever-deepening spiral or labyrinth as I became more aware of myself, and my child. I circled back to earlier places, jumped ahead to imagine the future, and then regained my footing in the present. It was hardly a linear route. There was hopeful forward motion and progress even when I found myself doubling back to revisit an old trail. No part of the journey, however painful or frightening, lasted forever.

Each of the seven chapters is organized into three sections:

Recollections of my own experiences with my child who grew from a gender nonconforming daughter, to a transgender teen living as both girl and boy, to eventually transitioning to become my son.

Research by professionals in academia, medicine, and psychology, as well as memoirs of people who've transitioned, and advocates working for transgender human rights.

Reflections on the journey I took, weaving together what I learned from my reading and what I experienced as a parent, will hopefully lend insights for your own journey with your gender nonconforming or transgender child or teen.

Journaling is one of the ways I observe and make sense of my life. It helps me pay attention to the voice inside that witnesses rather than acts. It's one way to digest life's experiences in an effort to gain

perspective and understanding. Journaling was also an attempt
to slow time and hold onto precious moments with my child so I
took care to record events and snippets of conversation over the
years. These journals proved critical in piecing together the shared
history and tandem stories that appear in this book. It is also how I
reconstructed the sections of dialogue, most of which was done by
memory with help from quotes I recorded at the time.

As my daughter's desire to transition mounted, journaling
was also my refuge and outlet for unearthing painful feelings and
examining their roots. Writing through tears I unraveled the tangled
knot of emotions to make sense of the source and neutralize the
power of these overwhelming feelings. Once they were recorded in
stark black and white, as daybreak dispels fears in the dark, I felt the
weight of them lift. Writing was an outlet for my feelings, freeing me
to be present for my child and supportive of his journey, instead of
being mired in my own ruminations.

Transitions are difficult, sometimes fraught with complications.
When a child challenges a parent's understanding about a matter as
basic as gender, and refuses to dress or act in ways consistent with
social norms, or discloses that they feel themselves to be a different
gender than the one assumed and assigned at birth, everyone close
to that child is affected. And if the child or teen then wants to transition their outward appearance to more closely reflect their inner
sense of self, their parents, siblings, and extended family members
must also transition. These family members must change their
assumptions, opening their minds and their hearts as they get to
know and accept the new form that their loved one has taken. They
must also let go of the child or teen they've known. In childbirth
the transition phase is when the mother's cervix opens and her body
requires her active participation in pushing the baby toward birth.
If you are a parent of a transgender child, you are called upon once
again for openness and active participation as you help your child
birth him- or herself.

Pronouns

Pronouns make or break a transgender person's sense of self, helping them feel recognized and seen or isolated and invisible. My use of pronouns throughout this book is intentional. Because there is no gender neutral singular pronoun in English, I have chosen to use "they" with singular nouns such as child. Despite being grammatically clumsy, it is preferable to forcing a limited choice between "he" or "she" for those who are gender nonconforming. When writing about my child's years from birth to age eighteen, I use the name we gave her at birth, Kendra, and the pronoun "she" because that is how I knew her and how others saw her. From sixteen to eighteen Kendra was trying on what it felt like to emerge in the world as "he," congruent with how he had always felt inside. From eighteen to twenty we knew Kendra identified as male but was still working on a name change. Peers from school still knew him as female while strangers readily identified him as male. This was an androgynous period when we were still saying "Kendra" while moving between masculine and feminine pronouns depending on the context. When writing about the years from age twenty onward I use the name he chose for himself, Kai, and the pronoun "he" as others were now getting to know him.

He would say that he was always male but since this is the story of how I came to learn that truth, the change in pronouns was a central and painful passage in my journey. I had a relationship with Kendra, my daughter, and I had to develop a relationship with Kai, my son. Using "he" when speaking about the person I had always known as "she" felt distancing and estranged. I felt I was referring to a totally different person; certainly not to someone as close to me as my own child. The intentional and gradual change in pronouns in the story that follows is a more accurate portrayal of my own process of letting go of Kendra and getting to know and accept Kai. It invites the reader to experience the boy emerging from the girl in somewhat the way that I did.

Family Members

We all have our own story that only we can tell. The experience of having a gender nonconforming or transgender family member can impact each person in a family in different and unique ways. This is my story. I purposely do not attempt to tell the story of my daughter Denali, or my husband, Tony. We each have our own reflections and perspectives about how Kai's gender identity altered the terrain of a sister's relationship with her sibling, a father's relationship with his child, and the very fabric of our lives. This book leaves those stories for them to tell if they so choose. I do not attempt to tell Kai's story except as his journey of awareness impacts my own. In my telling, I draw on the experiences of my family only in general ways to reflect on some of the challenges that can arise between parents and siblings when a child is transgender. This is the story of one mother with permission and approval from my son.

Race

Race and gender define us. In a culture obsessed with marketing, they are our packaging. When meeting us, others make judgments based on these two characteristics before we even speak. In addition to being transgender, my son is biracial so as a white, gender conforming woman raising a mixed race child in a white community, I was beyond my depth on two critical counts. I had no direct experience with how frequently, palpably, and powerfully race bias is communicated through looks, comments, behaviors, and attitudes. Kai had felt it since he was little and as perceptive as he was, nothing went unnoticed.

Race, like gender, is a social construct developed in relationship to others to establish who belongs and who does not; who has power and who does not. Those of us in the racial majority cannot appreciate the impact race has on social acceptance until we travel to a country where we are in the minority. For a child of color, developing racial identity in America means coming to terms with the signals that others send about whether or not you count and belong. It means reading cues to learn whom you can trust and where you are safe, rather than assuming access is equal. Being multiracial adds another layer of complexity since neither the white nor the black community may fully claim you as its own.

The emerging sense that he was also a gender minority further threatened Kai's hopes of ever belonging; of finding one's kin. Few of Kai's peers understood or showed interest in learning the agility and tenacity it takes to navigate in the cross currents of race and gender. Few of the adults in our lives, whether friends or professionals, have charted these multilayered waters either.

I often felt lost in my efforts to support and guide Kai, having empathy, often anger over injustices, but little wisdom or lived experience to offer. Years of diversity training at work, my husband, and insightful friends and colleagues who taught me through words, example, and courageous confrontation about my own privilege and blinders, helped make me a more conscious white person willing to examine how oppression operates. It takes a village to raise our children and the people of color, and the gay, lesbian, gender nonconforming people in my life were critical resources in helping me be a better parent.

Labels

Labels by those who are not transgender (also called cisgender people, *cis* meaning on the same side and *trans* meaning on the other side) have historically been used to describe the transgender experience. Most have been negative, hurtful, and uninformed. Just as men have historically described and diagnosed women and whites have labeled and objectified people of color, cisgender people have put themselves forth as experts on transgender issues. This has contributed to the widespread impression that being transgender is disordered, deviant, aberrant, and pathological simply because it is not the experience of the majority of people.

To know a transgender person from infancy as we parents do is to dispel that myth. Our children are like other children, except for the disconnect they feel between the gender assumed and assigned at birth based on their anatomy, and the gender they feel inside. There are so many positive words we can use to describe our gender nonconforming children that I encourage you to explore some of the possibilities: gender creative,[1] expansive, fluid, ingenious, transcendent, expansive, imaginative, unique, distinctive, original, exceptional, inventive, resourceful, artistic, fearless, innovative, insightful, and gifted, to name a few. The next time you discuss your child's unique understanding or expression of gender, whether with a healthcare provider, teacher, babysitter, family member, neighbor, or friend, try using some of these, make up your own, or better yet, let your transgender child name their own experience of gender and let's begin altering and expanding the awareness of others.

Denali and Kendra

1

Anticipation and Attachment

A woman is taught to think first and only of her sons.
But to Morgaine . . . she was bound with a tie of the soul
which would never break. . . .
Was this why every priestess longed to bear a daughter,
who would follow in her footsteps
and never be lost to her?[2]

MARION ZIMMER BRADLEY, *THE MISTS OF AVALON*

RECOLLECTIONS

Learning Gender

I come from a family of women. My mother had a twin sister, my father had two sisters, and I had three sisters. I am a white, middle-class woman who grew up in Rochester, New York, not far from Buffalo where my mother grew up. My father spent most of his childhood in New England with a short stint in New Jersey. One of my most vivid early memories was when my mother and father took my older sister, Sandra, and me to see our baby sisters in the hospital. Because of their low birth weight, Debbie and Donna were kept in incubators for a month before they could come home. I was five and Sandra was seven. My father held Sandra's hand and my mother held mine. Children were not allowed to visit the hospital nursery, but we were excited to see our sisters and my father had no problem breaking rules he considered senseless. So up ahead were Sandra and my dad while my mother, having recently delivered twins and not at all comfortable with breaking hospital protocol, struggled behind with me in tow trying to catch up. It was the middle of January in Rochester, New York, a cold, gray, snowy day. My mother's boot heels clicked rhythmically on the shiny polished floor as my dad and Sandra pulled too far away to catch and then disappeared behind swinging hospital doors with large red letters clearly spelling out visiting rules. When my mother hesitated, we got caught.

On the exciting day when I finally got to see my baby sisters, the sun shone brightly on snow so crisp it squeaked under foot. Our old Desoto had a huge back seat long and wide enough for a grown man to stretch out and sleep. Sandra and I sat in the middle, our short legs straddling the center floor hump with a bassinette snuggly positioned at our sides between each one of us and the doors. The babies were bundled against the cold in pink and white snowsuits, and slept soundly all the way home. I stared in awe at the tiny face next to me, hardly able to believe this was not a doll but a real, live baby I could touch. It was one of the happiest days of my young life and since there was one for each of us I wouldn't even have to share them with my bossy older sister.

In the fifties, fathers were not as involved in childcare as some are now, so when my mother worried aloud at dinner that night about how she was going to feed two babies in the middle of the night my father had just the answer. He would wake us up so we could help her! I was in kindergarten and Sandra was in second grade but we were up for the challenge. When my mother protested that he should help her, that we were too little and needed our sleep for school, we sided with our father. We were big enough to handle it and she could rely on us. So just as planned, around 2 a.m. Dad tapped each of us on the shoulder and told us to go help Mom with the twins. We dragged ourselves downstairs and each had one of the babies placed in our arms with a bottle. I don't remember whether I held Debbie or Donna but I do remember falling asleep and dropping the bottle. This time it was Mom gently tapping my shoulder: "Honey, go back to bed. You have school in the morning. I'll take the baby."

Dad never woke us up again since Mom, of course, turned out to be right. But we were recruited to help with our baby sisters from the moment they came home. Mom taught us how to change a cloth diaper, putting our hand under the corner just above each hip to be sure not to prick the baby with a diaper pin. She taught us how to hold our sisters by supporting their heavy heads and how to heat the bottle and test the temperature with a few drops on our wrist before ever putting it in the baby's mouth. We rocked, walked, fed, changed, bathed, read to, and played with our little sisters endlessly. So as I grew up, caring for a baby felt natural and instinctive.

Raising a gender nonconforming child causes a parent to reflect on their own gender identity and how it developed. I was attracted to all things feminine. Nail polish, jewelry, purses, shoes, and frills fascinated me. My favorite color was pink and I loved twirling in skirts that flew out around my knees. So while I was always gender conforming, I was not pleased with the confining gender role for girls at the time. My heroine was Annie Oakley and I had her complete outfit—black velvet vest with silver fringe, skirt, boots, hat, holster, and gun. I felt like I could do anything in it, including riding a horse standing on the saddle and throwing a lasso just like her.

Girls still had to wear skirts and dresses to school and we dressed up in hats and white gloves for special occasions at church. But we happily wore pants and shorts the rest of the time. Sandy and I mostly played with the neighborhood girls who outnumbered the boys but every so often the two brothers who lived behind us came over to play. When I was about five and Stephen might have been four he wanted to try on a dress so I gave him my red and green plaid one with buttons in the front and a white collar. It fit him perfectly. He liked it so much he even walked home in it through our backyard carrying his own clothes in a paper bag. Sandy and I remembered that moment for how unusual it was. We knew it was fine for girls to wear pants but we were certain boys weren't supposed to wear dresses. We expected some commotion over this bold act of his but it was just as surprising when there was only silence. I still wonder what happened to Stephen when he got home since we seldom saw him after that. Maybe he was not allowed to play with girls any more.

Gender expression and roles are modeled and encouraged by parents and society. But for those who color outside the lines, these norms feel forced and policed and the punishment for infractions is most often shame. From a very early age, every message sent about gender indicates whether we are "in" or "out" of our gender group; whether we belong. Not belonging can devastate a child's self-esteem.

I modeled my gender role after my mother but unlike her and my sister Sandy, I was not interested in traditional women's work like cooking and sewing. When given a choice, I much preferred helping my father with his wood working hobbies. I was fortunate that my parents valued education as highly for their daughters as if we'd been sons, but my father held notions common for his time about what professions were appropriate for his daughters. An engineer himself, he encouraged us to pursue math and science in high school to prepare for college. But then he'd voice concerns such as whether or not we'd grow tall enough and have the right figures to become airline stewardesses even though none of us were considering that career. And it was my dad who could sit in his chair and read while the five of us prepared dinner, set the table, washed dishes, folded laundry, and kept the house running smoothly. All four daughters were learning the meaning of the saying "A man works from sun to sun but a woman's work is never done." Trained early to help my mother around the house, I felt guilty and selfish sitting down to read while my mother worked. It wasn't until my twenties that I realized how much I enjoyed books and the pursuit of ideas.

I came face-to-face with being excluded because of my gender from roles and responsibilities I enjoyed when I considered ordination to the ministry during my twenties. Now of course, women's ordination is possible in many faiths but it was not without a fight back then. There were professors and fellow seminary students that believed women are not created in the image of God in the same way that men are. Ultimately ordination was not something I pursued but it was a powerfully negative and unforgettable experience to be barred from something because my body did not conform to the prerequisites that others demanded.

As I sorted out what I wanted in life, my early childcare duties satiated any longings for children of my own. But by my mid-thirties all my reasons for not having children felt like excuses when my mother was diagnosed with pancreatic cancer and then learned it had returned two years later. She loved being a mom and was excellent at it. She always said I'd make a great mother and wanted me to open myself up to the experience. I knew it pained her to think I might forego it. She felt children could bring me the happiness I sought. She said she knew this about me because I was intuitive in caring for my little sisters.

My mother's illness pushed me off the fence. In some ways I wanted to please her. Once a first grade teacher, she was always happy around young children. She enjoyed telling funny quotes from her grandchildren and never missed the TV show, "Kids Say the Darnedest Things,'" sharing over dinner what the kids said that day. I wanted to bring light and laughter into her life during this dark and scary time. I also saw how children brought my sister Sandy and my mother closer. Sandy's children became the focus of their relationship as they shared stories, childcare tasks, safety concerns, and parenting ideas. Mom always had a stash of fun children's activities or some health tip on hand. Children were her joy and full-time job even though she no longer got paid for it. Sandy and Mom, who had been at odds for years, finally had something in common.

In many ways, the most compelling motivation for my belated decision to have children was the fear of being alone in the world. I'd always been keenly aware of my intense, embarrassing attachment to my mother. As a child I loved nothing more than to stay at home with her, and I resisted and hated anything that forced me out into the world. From kindergarten through third grade there were many days I walked to school brushing away tears, longing for the safety of home rather than the commotion and challenge of school. Every Sunday night when the theme song for "Lassie" played at 7:30 p.m., I felt a rock lodge itself in my throat. The end of the weekend was like the end of the world as I choked back my anxiety over Mondays and school. It wasn't only that I hated school. Mostly I missed my mother. I avoided sleepovers at friends' houses and summer camp for the same reason. While the culture demanded that I go out into the world, I longed to be by my mother's side.

The looming death of a loved one is a stark reminder of what little time we have. My mother's battle with cancer from age sixty-two to sixty-six was a wake up call. I didn't have forever to make decisions about my future, and as I prepared to lose the most significant person in my life, I felt an urgency about starting my own family. I had been dating Tony for several years, and we decided to get married and buy a house.

Tony

Tony was born in Trinidad and came to the United States with his dad when he was sixteen years old so he'd have more options for his future. It was a cold first day of June when they landed in Boston. Leaving a sunny, lush, mountainous Caribbean island for a congested, northeastern city shrouded in gray for half the year is a step in the right direction only in the mind of an adult. To an adolescent boy who left home, school, mom, friends, and extended family, the reasons for leaving were lost on him those first few years. The multiculturalism and inclusivity Tony grew up with in Trinidad in no way prepared him for what he encountered being a Black male immigrant teen living in New England in the '70s.

The chasm that opened in his heart between what he left and where he landed; between what he dreamed of and where he lived; was spanned in part by his art. Tony bridged the spiritual and emotional gulf by teaching himself to paint. In his senior year of high school, he was recruited by the U.S. Air Force with the promise of seeing the world and becoming a pilot. In boot camp he learned he needed a college degree to be trained as a pilot. The most he could do during his four-year stint was to work on fighter jets and travel as much as possible. Once discharged, he moved back to Massachusetts to work his way through college, which is how he happened to be renovating my apartment the summer we met.

I'd moved to Massachusetts to attend theological seminary and was divorcing my first husband after a too-early marriage at nineteen. Tony and I began as friends, with shared interests in dancing, travel, nature, camping, and politics. Neither of us was in a rush to be tied down. It wasn't until five years after meeting and my mother's diagnosis of cancer that we started dating and eventually decided to marry.

Our parents and families were mostly accepting of our marriage although my mother worried that multiracial children had a harder time feeling accepted. She was firmly committed to social justice and we were the only children on the block who had black dolls as well as white. Our church was involved in civil rights and my mother taught reading to inner city adults. My father's family was different. His father was superintendent of schools when my dad was young, and one day, after hearing my dad had walked home with an African American boy in his class, my grandfather told him never to do that again for fear it would jeopardize his job. Whenever my sister Sandra or I dated African American boys in high school we knew not to tell Grandma, our dad's mother. Tony's family had concerns of their own about Tony marrying a white American with no understanding or experience of their country, culture, and food. Tony's mom, Iyine, still lived in Trinidad and we flew her up for the wedding. I'm sure she saw our marriage as a sign that Tony was never coming back home to live.

Tony dreamed of living where mountains meet the ocean, just like his homeland. The closest place to us—but without the mountains—was in a scenic coastal town in Massachusetts with many striking views for painting. The real estate market was peaking and we would be lucky to find something we could afford. The broker warned us about the house we were about to see—on a noisy main road and in need of everything. We saw through the window into the backyard as we approached. As if in a trance, we walked through the kitchen, out the back door, and fell instantly in love with the half acre, hillside garden paradise that became our yard. The house was a never-ending renovation project that would sorely test our work styles, patience, budget, and marriage. But it was ours.

Losing My Mother

My mother used to say she was too nosy to die; that seeing what her children and grandchildren were up to was what gave her the strength to keep going. But when the cancer returned she'd already outlived the odds with pancreatic cancer. Mom wanted to die at home and we wanted to be with her as much as possible. My sister Debbie came back with her three small children from Bolivia, where she lived with her husband, to help my dad. My other sisters, Sandy and Donna, and I rotated weekends to help Debbie and Dad who had their hands full with Debbie's children ages five, three, and a newborn as well as my mom.

During one of my weekends in Rochester, I realized I'd missed my period. It was before pregnancy tests were available in drug stores so I searched the phonebook for a clinic. My mother was in the hospital for tests and my dad was with her so I stepped out unnoticed. The test was positive. I'd hoped to tell Tony the news over a romantic candlelight dinner. But I also wanted to tell my mom while I was still in Rochester so I called Tony and told him over the phone. He was surprised and kept saying, "Are you sure?

There's no way there could be a mistake is there?" He didn't want to get his hopes up only to be disappointed. I asked if he'd mind if I told my family. He said of course not.

I got back to the hospital anxious to share my news, and found a hospice nurse meeting with Mom and Dad explaining that their goal was to keep the dying person as comfortable and pain free as possible, and to support the family. It seemed disrespectful to share such happy news at so sad a time—as if joy might trivialize grief or death steal life from me. When I finally told them, Mom of course already knew. She'd always had an uncanny, exasperating intuition. Just two months earlier, after our wedding, she'd asked if we were going to try to have a baby right away. When I said yes she said she'd wait to die until after the baby was born. Now she thought she might die that night. It was obvious everything had changed. I stayed at the hospital just in case and we brought her home the next day so she'd be surrounded by family. A hospice nurse came Tuesday through Friday, and Sandy, Donna, and I worked out a schedule to cover the weekends.

When I bent to kiss her goodnight the first night home we cried.

"This is the hard part," she said, "saying goodbye. I'm so glad you're having a baby. I want you to have a healthy pregnancy and I don't want to wear you out. Sometimes I think I will see your baby and then I feel my bones under my skin and I don't know. I want your pregnancy to be peaceful and I don't want you having to come here every weekend."

"I'd love for you to see my baby Mom. I wish I hadn't waited so long. But I can't see you living like this for another eight months." I told her how much my baby was going to miss out by never knowing or visiting her, or getting just the right gift she always managed to find for each grandchild.

I asked what she'd like to say to my baby. "That you're a great person. I want your baby to know how lucky they are to have you for their mother." Then she laughed and added, "Who knows, maybe I'll come back and you can be my mother." This was an amazing compliment coming from a woman who hadn't always felt loved by her own mother.

She didn't want her three little grandchildren to remember her as weak, dying, and scary but as healthy, fun, and young at heart so the day before she died Debbie and I bathed her and at her request we all watched "The Lady and the Tramp," and ate hot fudge sundaes, two of her all-time favorites.

In life she'd always been hard to catch, too busy to stop, making it difficult to cuddle or converse but now we were more physical with her than she normally allowed. We said things aloud and in silence we'd always meant to say but had been too shy, or embarrassed to say. One night toward the end was the worst. There was fear in her eyes as she struggled to breathe and we waited anxiously for oxygen to arrive. We held her hands, her gaze, and her pain, hoping to calm her and feeling helpless. Another time I even lay down in her bed to help her relax by imagining sitting near a mountain stream listening to birds sing. And as if by magic or the strength of thought, a blue jay came to her bedroom window and looked right at us. Like a spirit from the other side, beckoning and welcoming her, to escort her on her journey: a sassy, beautiful bird—blue as her eyes and spunky as her spirit, and as persistent as death itself.

All four daughters and my Dad were at her bedside that final night and even after speech left her, we knew she heard us as she squeezed our hands. She took a breath and then stopped breathing and though we knew it was coming, we couldn't believe our mother was dead. We sobbed. I sat alone with her as dawn broke. So much was the same. Her pink bedroom slippers were still tucked under the bed where she always kept them. And yet everything had changed. It felt unreal, impossible. What do you do when your mother dies, especially when she was your champion, the one who believed in you like no other? Mommy! I wanted to call out. Where are you? I miss you already! I felt alone, afraid, abandoned, as if grief and sadness might flatten and kill me. What else could possibly matter now? And then I thought of my baby. This life, this living connection to my mother, our last gift of hope might be a bridge from the saddest day of my life to one of my happiest.

Friends came out in large number for my mother's memorial service. She'd told us what hymns she wanted and who should sing them and everyone was given a chance to say something. I was glad for the bond of siblings—especially sisters. We were a strong support for one another throughout this vigil. We had to fill in for Mom now, for each other. Even in our thirties, we all felt too young to lose her.

Winter of Waiting

Returning to everyday life after being death's escort is jarring. As a family of five now instead of six, we were about to all go our separate ways. It had not even been a week yet and already I was apart and away from my sisters and father. I hoped that getting out of Mom and Dad's house with all those childhood memories, happy and sad, would help me get some distance from my grief. It didn't. On the plane ride home the business conversations and work plans I overheard left me feeling numb and detached, as if I now inhabited another planet that hovered somewhere apart from everyone. I could observe but I couldn't participate.

The promise of this birth kept me going during the deep fog of grief that closed in around me that winter. Like all expectant mothers, I wanted a healthy baby and deep down I also wanted a girl to keep the circle of mother-daughter love alive. It was one last way to stay connected to Mom; to love and honor her. I loved having sisters. We had all just gotten one another through a major life loss and I wanted to give the support of sisters to my own children. Even my father had only sisters, so girls were what I was accustomed to. I also grew up watching the differences between women and men in relationships. My mother stayed connected to her sister, her mother, and her daughters. My father needed to be reminded by my mother to call his own mother and he seldom called his sisters. I liked the connection of women and I wanted my children to stay connected to me even when they were grown. My own bias was that daughters would stay more attached and in touch than sons. Tony's family shared the same pattern of female connection. His mother and grandmother were very close, with his mom living next door to his grandmother and caring for her until her death. Both of our families, and what I read about male/female relational differences, seemed to confirm my bias. Daughters were the way to go for someone who feared abandonment. As I tried on the idea of a son, I got excited about that as well but my longing for a girl was stronger.

Spring, the season of new birth, had always been Mom's favorite and it was now my talisman for survival. Grief comes in waves I discovered. Some days felt almost normal, like I could lock up the sadness in a box, opening it only when I wanted to gaze at some memory, ease some longing. But other times it came from nowhere knocking me off my feet and reducing me to uncontrollable tears just when I thought I was all cried out. Sunny days were the hardest, seeming to mock my melancholy. It was the steely gray sea, the wind that rattled windows and long foreboding shadows that felt most supportive. Like a brooding ally, those days reflected my sadness. I'd go to the ocean seeking solace. One day there was a young couple, a child, and grandparents. My own child would never experience my mom as Grandma. I felt the stab of envy for women whose mothers could come to help them after childbirth. I'd never know that kind of support. I became impatient when women complained about their mothers even though I'd had plenty of those complaints when I was younger and my mother was living.

I worried about how this tiny being could survive when I was feeling so bereft. I did all the right things physically—got plenty of rest, ate well, took prenatal vitamins, avoided alcohol, never smoked, had regular prenatal checkups, exercised, including prenatal yoga and meditation for stress management, and talked and sang to the baby to bond early. But the only way to get over the grief was to walk through it and my baby had no choice but to accompany me. I worried about the stress and grief hormones my baby was swimming in. Could he or she hear or feel my sobs? What about the despondency that sometimes wrapped itself around me, or the sadness I felt whenever I saw children with their grandmothers? I tried to reassure the baby, telling her/him to hang in there, that it wouldn't always be this rough; that he or she was incredibly brave and resilient to make it this far. Life and death in one place, one time, one body. My sisters and I were all grieving differently but we tried to stay connected despite our distance. Dad visited for Thanksgiving and helped us with a kitchen renovation project and we all gathered at Sandy's house for Christmas. I was lying on her couch Christmas Eve when I felt my baby's first kick. Now it was getting exciting!

Midway through the pregnancy Tony and I went on a two-week trip to Hawaii for a delayed honeymoon. It was a gorgeous, relaxing break from our long commutes, stressful jobs, house renovation project, and New England winter. Even in Hawaii, however, I felt the loss of my mother. It was here that her first symptoms occurred, just as she and my dad were starting to enjoy his retirement. She loved everything about Hawaii. The tropical breeze, abundant and fragrant flowers, vibrant and chattering birds, and majestic mountains helped lift my sadness. I hoped the baby could hear the roar of the formidable waves and the heat and light of the bright sun on my skin.

While there, I dreamed I brought my baby to a work conference and in the dream he was a boy. I suddenly realized I'd brought nothing for the baby—no bottle, no diaper, no wipes, no clothes. I decided Mom would have what I needed so I went over to my parents' house. She told me it was important to be prepared and have things ready. After giving the baby a bath (he was covered in leaves), I carried him into the classroom where I was an instructor. He pulled himself up on my hip and said: "Hello everyone. How are you doing?" He acted older than his years and very jovial. He repeated the question, so captivating the students that they were speechless. I woke up realizing that not only was I going to be on my own as a mother without my mother to guide me, but I could trust my own abilities. I knew I'd do better than this in real life.

It was the second dream I'd had of a talking baby boy. The first was a glimpse of a baby on a couch and he said to me: "Hi! Yes, I *am* a boy!" This probably came shortly after being given an ultrasound picture of the baby lying back sucking his or her thumb. My first impression of the photo was that I was having a boy. Then the midwife made this confusing statement, "I know you don't want to be told the sex of your baby but I can say you're going to be very happy." Did the midwife assume I wanted a girl because of my work in women's health or that I wanted the firstborn to be a boy?

At home we were busy working on our house and getting the baby's room ready. There was always something to be done after a long day of work as we scraped wallpaper, painted walls, and sanded floors. I was careful to test the walls for lead, wear a dust mask, and not inhale fumes for the sake of the baby. I wondered if there were there other toxins in this work I was unaware of.

One of the strongest constants throughout my pregnancy was this little baby's heartbeat. It amazed and comforted me during prenatal visits. The baby's heart was as strong and persistent as a herd of galloping horses! The determination to survive was nothing short of inspiring during days when I was grieving. I admired and marveled at the resilience, daring, and fight to live and thrive in this little spirit who was coming through me. I became more confident in the strength and endurance of our intertwined lives as well as in my ability to care for this being.

It's a Girl!

I'd expected the baby to be early partly because of the weight I'd gained—thirty-five pounds; a third of my normal weight—the stress of the pregnancy, long work hours, and the fear I wouldn't be ready. Now I was ready and waiting. Labor began in the parking lot of the local grocery store. I was delivering at a birth center, a small house opposite the hospital where midwives attended instead of doctors. Having a first pregnancy at thirty-six put me at high risk for a Caesarean and I wanted to have my baby as naturally as possible. The midwife on-call wanted to examine me so we left the house as soon as Tony got home. Contractions were two to three minutes apart and we had a thirty-minute drive without traffic. It looked like it might be a quick delivery. The midwife felt an unexpected bump and I was transferred to the hospital for an ultrasound. The baby was coming face first and the bump was the nose. Instead of tucking chin to chest and pushing out with the crown of the head this baby turned its head up, as if to see where it was heading. I wondered about this tiny, feisty being coming into the world so uniquely. It was a difficult position to deliver naturally and because of the possibility of complications, I was kept at the hospital instead of going back to the birth center.

For seventeen hours I rode waves of pain as the soft tissue of my baby's face struggled to dilate my cervix while Tony, the midwife, and the nurses stood by me. I pictured my mother in bed, and people hovering, watching, and powerless to help. I felt a deep sense of aloneness and wondered if Mom felt that too. These two thresholds—birth and death—were connected, the one preparation for the other. Women of old knew this. They were warriors in every sense, facing down their own death as they battled for the life of another. I thought of women and babies living before me and around the world that very day. Mothers and babies die like this, joined when it's essential to separate. I was lucky. Despite the pain, I could breathe through it, call for anesthesia or surgery for my release. Mom's own breath had failed her and no calls for help could restore it.

Little did I know that once fully dilated, the real work of labor begins. Without the help of the baby's bony skull, I'd have to do most of the work. Like a personal trainer, Linda Anne, the midwife, set the goal of every contraction moving the baby closer to birth.

With each excruciating push my eyes squeezed tight and groans erupted from a place deep inside. I sounded primal, wild, even to myself as if a raw, unbounded force flowed through me. The three of us—Linda Anne, Tony, and I were a team girded for battle. They timed contractions, coached, cajoled, and cheered me on. Their shouts joined my roars as if the combined strength of our voices could penetrate my body and pull this baby along.

Suddenly the room was filled with doctors, nurses, a warmer, aspirator, and countless other beeping machines. Only then did I realize something could be wrong. They aspirated my baby before it was even fully born. Then, with one final push a head finally appeared and the whole tiny body slipped out. I sobbed with relief. From a distance I heard Tony say, "Aw, it's a little girl." Exhausted from labor I'd forgotten how much the baby's sex once mattered. But when I heard Tony's tender pronouncement I was euphoric. But I worried why so many gloved hands were passing her to and fro massaging her limbs, clearing her lungs, and wiping her off. She began to curl her bottom lip and whimper and I felt an instinctive urge to grab and comfort her. I held her just long enough to kiss her sore, swollen face and bruised cheek before she was whisked out of my arms by a nurse to be weighed, washed, tested, even x-rayed I later learned.

That Saturday in May I felt like the luckiest person in the world! I was ecstatic and wanted to call everyone I knew. I wished I could show off my beautiful daughter to my mother. The first person I called was my big sister, Sandy. She was coming to help me.

When my friend Carol came to see her I had to ask the nurses to bring her to me. What was taking so long I wondered? I couldn't wait to hold her! She finally arrived all washed and wrapped in a blue and pink striped blanket and a little knitted newborn cap. She was snuggled tight on her side as they wheeled her to me. Even in that short time, the swelling in her face had gone down but her cheek was still purple, poor baby. She was even more beautiful than I remembered.

Carol asked her name. "Ariana," I said. We'd struggled mightily with names and finally rank-ordered our five favorites. Kendra was number one for me and fifth for Tony. Ariana was third for both of us so we compromised. Carol said: "Hmm, she doesn't look like an Ariana to me. I thought you were going to name her Kendra? She looks more like a Kendra don't you think Cand?" She was right. And Kendra meant knowledgeable, like one curious enough to pick their head up to see where they were going when the pangs of birth began.

When Tony came back I asked if he'd taken a nap since he too had been up all night. He said: "No way! I missed the baby and came back as soon as I could." He brought me a huge bouquet of purple flowers. Carol had left and I told him what she had said about the name. "After what you've been through, you can name her anything you want," he said. So Kendra it was.

I slept with Kendra swaddled next to me in bed that first night. I stared at her for a long time before finally falling asleep and woke up several times during the night to be sure she was real. Her tiny face captured my heart and I couldn't tear away my gaze. After nursing, she fell into a reverie of peace, fingers outstretched, rosebud lips pursed, and her head flung back like a cat. I guess I was bonding but it felt like falling in love—not only with her simple and innocent beauty but the fact that she was mine and I was hers. She was the mystery promise with the galloping heartbeat during those long, dark months of grief and waiting. This little warrior had battled her way into the world. And I was just as stubborn, since surgery would've made it easier for both of us. Her vulnerability and simple, unspoken request that I care for her awakened every mothering cell in my body. I wanted never to violate that trust. My mom had always hoped for this moment for me and now I knew why. Mothering was going to suit me if these first hours and feelings were any indication.

Initiation

Coming into our driveway three days later with our new baby, everything looked different. The leaves were greener and the azalea bush was decked out in shocking pink. Spring had popped. The yard was in its glory and sunlight shimmered through every window in the house. It was our one-year anniversary in this house and the ancient, gnarled apple tree snowed confetti blossoms as a welcome.

Bringing home a baby is sobering. Childbirth is an initiation into motherhood, a job that is physical, emotional, mental, and spiritual. This tiny, needy, vulnerable being that I didn't even know yet was attached to me for her very survival. No longer responsible just for myself, I was mother, caregiver, and sustainer of life for the next eighteen years, minimum. Fortunately my physical and emotional longing to be with this baby was in direct proportion to her need. Surprisingly I didn't resent the constant care. There was a stronger bond than I ever imagined. Whether by instinct, ardor, or both, newborns draw out feats of endurance, patience, strength, and love in parents.

She was a girl! At the time it felt like the most permanent of pronouncements; the only thing I knew for certain, or thought I knew, about my baby. Everything else was still a mystery but this I could count on for life just like millions of other parents before me.

Who Are You?

Getting to know a baby is fascinating. Every experience is brand new, so watching an infant can teach volumes about their personality. Do they like new faces or are they afraid of them? Do they sleep soundly or lightly? What excites or soothes them? Are they patient or impatient, easily startled or slow to react? Do they like new things or are they more comfortable with the familiar? Are they content to be held and rocked or anxious to get down and move around? Every day, every encounter, brings more information.

During the first few days and weeks as a new mother I spent many hours baby-watching. Kendra didn't like having her clothes off at first so I didn't undress her fully until she was four days old and then only under the covers and next to my warm body. I held her close so she could still hear my heartbeat. Her stretching arms, tiny fists, gurgling baby noises, and wonderful but inscrutable facial expressions gave me hours of pleasure. Tony especially enjoyed walking through the yard with her head in the palm of his hand, her body along his forearm, so she could see the flowers, trees, feel the breeze. Every so often he'd blurt out, "What a wonderful little girl!" or "I love this little baby." The outdoors calmed her when she was fussy. She stopped her tiny body from its heaves and sobs to listen to the chirping birds, watch the dappled light on leaves, feel spring air on her skin, and smell the ocean. She became relaxed and alert all at once.

She loved to cuddle and I couldn't get my fill of her—the smell of her head, the feel of her fine curly hair, the smooth satin of her brown skin. And her deep brown eyes—she had a confident, steady stare that she wouldn't let go, as if trying to read my soul. Before she could hold with her hands she held tight with her eyes. The first time she returned my smile we were leisurely swinging in the backyard hammock. It was exhilarating and unexpected. She knew me! Making her smile and laugh became one of my favorite activities.

I enjoyed a surprising freedom with my baby. I made up songs to sing for her; told her stories about what we were doing that day; turned everyday objects into toys for her entertainment. It was all just for her. Had anyone heard or seen me, I would've been embarrassed by my silliness. My five-year old inner child was reawakened and baby care became as playful and carefree as it had been with my baby sisters. It felt completely natural to me. A song came to me one day as I washed Kendra's face. She started to fuss and grimace and I realized I was being too fast, too rough. I remembered how my dad used to brush my teeth when I was little compared to how gently my mom did it. I was being dad-like so I slowed down. This was my first lesson from Kendra of just how differently we moved in the world. I would be repeatedly reminded to slow it down in the years to come.

I discovered I loved baby-pace and this child opened a locked door as she ushered me into an unhurried, quiet state. Kendra and I spent time doing only what we pleased and kept to no one's schedule. It was the perfect season and location—spring and summer near the ocean. We took long walks downtown, poked into stores filled with tourists, sat on the beach under an umbrella, Kendra sleeping and me reading or writing, hung out in the yard with the cat, smelled flowers in the garden, watched butterflies, visited our elderly neighbors who lit up with a baby, took long warm baths together before naptime. I did household chores while Kendra slept, so whenever she was up it was all fun. We spent as much time as possible outside while I kept work as far away as possible, bringing my focus back to our cocoon after intrusive phone calls from the office.

I had eleven weeks off for maternity leave. I wanted much more—forever really. The unexpected joy I experienced during this time made me rethink my future. The little girl inside me was tugging at my sleeve and I longed for more time to play, explore, be outside, daydream, walk, swim, write, create. In Kendra, I had a friend and companion once again to accompany me in these childish adventures. I dreaded being torn away from her, and from my own creative child that my love for her inspired, to return to the nine to five workweek.

Back to Work

By August I was back at work. It was the most wrenching adjustment of my life. I found a home daycare provider after several interviews. With no family nearby and Kendra an infant who still longed to be held and carried everywhere, I couldn't imagine her with lots of other children. In the short time I'd known her, it was already obvious she needed long stretches of quiet, alone time and disliked the noise and stimulation of too many people.

It felt like losing a limb when I handed her to a near stranger that first morning. Kendra and I had been physically attached and inseparable for a year by then. It was too soon and both of us felt it but try as I might, I hadn't figured out another solution. I cried all the way to the office. It was on that morning in early August that the first seeds of mother guilt were planted in the rich loam of my heart to flourish and bloom for years to come. Maybe it was the death of my mother that had altered my interior landscape, teaching the lesson of time's incessant march and the importance of cherishing fleeting moments. Precious time with my baby was spilling through my fingers and I felt powerless to change that so I made the most of what time we had.

I never knew how much I would love having someone need me so totally, or how good I'd be at being there for her. Yet everyday Kendra grew, she let go of me more. Suddenly she was no longer an infant bundled in my arms. One day, swaddling made her feel confined and restrained when once it felt safe and secure. Then she planted her feet in my lap and pushed to stand and squirm away. Mothering, like life, was about learning to let go.

RESEARCH

Sex Is in the Body; Gender Is in the Mind

The concept that sex and gender can diverge is as groundbreaking to our mainstream worldview as when our ancestors learned the earth was round. We think sex and gender are synonymous because we use the terms interchangeably but they actually refer to two different aspects of a person.

Sex is a biological term that refers to whether one's body is female, producing eggs; or male, producing sperm. Usually, but not always, female egg-producing bodies can be distinguished because they share physical characteristics such as having a vagina, uterus, ovaries, and milk-producing glands and carry two XX chromosomes.

Likewise, male sperm-producing bodies can usually be distinguished because they have a penis, testes, and carry an XY chromosome. But nature is more diverse than limiting bodies to only two types: male and female. The biological variations when it comes to sex include genetically male XY bodies that appear female at birth; genetically female XX bodies born without a vagina, uterus, or ovaries; and bodies with a combination of male and female genitals. These bodies are said to be *intersex* in that they share male and female genes and traits. Since intersex conditions are generally not spoken about outside of medical circles the general public is relatively unaware of them but they actually occur in about 1 out of 2,000 (1:2,000) births according to reliable estimates.[3]

Gender is cultural rather than biological. It is the way societies organize different kinds of bodies into separate categories based on sex. Males are boys who grow up to become men and females are girls who grow up to become women. Becoming a man or woman is achieved through a complex process of socialization in accordance with gender roles and expectations. The categories for gender differ across time and culture with some cultures having three or four gender categories and other cultures making room for people to change gender based on dreams or visions. In some cultures parents assign gender to a child for socioeconomic or spiritual reasons regardless of sex.[4] In most instances however gender is based on one's sex or the work roles one assumes in a specific society.[5]

Most of us are taught that sex determines gender. The majority of expectant mothers opt to be told the sex of their baby as soon as possible so they'll know how to reflect gender in the name, pink or blue clothing, decorating the baby's room, and preparing the siblings. The tried and true cultural rituals of childbirth march steadily along as though there is a guaranteed match between sex and gender. It's the first question people ask when they hear we are expecting. A blood test determines a baby's sex by the fourth or fifth month of pregnancy, with new tests under way to determine sex in the tenth week. As the technology improves the element of surprise will be removed all together. That is unless you have a child whose sex and gender develop along different paths. "It's a boy!" or "It's a girl!" are all we parents thought we knew when our baby was placed in our arms. We expected these pronouncements to be permanent and immutable because for most children sex predicts gender.

But sometimes the body's sex and the mind's gender take different developmental pathways for reasons that are still not understood.

When Is Gender Identity Formed?

Gender identity probably forms during the third trimester of pregnancy because it relies on the presence of sex hormone receptors in the brain that do not form until then. This seems to indicate that the external genitalia of the body differentiate before the brain.[6] According to author, biologist, and transgender woman Joan Roughgarden, "Gender identity, like other aspects of temperament, presumably awaits the third trimester, when the brain as a whole is growing."[7] In males, testosterone levels are usually high during three separate intervals: the second trimester of gestation when the genitals are developing; at birth; and again during puberty.

Based on observations of animals, Roughgarden believes that this increase of testosterone at birth may have to do with the organization of gender identity in the brain. Male canaries for example, learn their song from male "tutors," most often their fathers. Female canaries have a different song. But how does a male chick know to mimic its father rather than its mother? Roughgarden theorizes that the increased level of testosterone at birth may have to do with the creation of a cognitive lens in the brain that distinguishes who will be emulated from who will be merely observed.[8]

For some as yet unknown reason "transgender identity is then the acceptance of a tutor from the opposite sex."[9] Roughgarden summarizes her research by saying, "Combining the data for the early and late limits, gender identity appears to form sometime between three months before birth and twelve months after birth."[10] Because of failed attempts both anecdotally and in research studies, to change one's gender through child-rearing practices, gender identity must already be determined by several months after birth. This theory is confirmed by the experience of many parents of gender nonconforming and transgender children who report that their child's unique gender identity was already under way with little or no outside influence to account for it.

How Is Gender Identity Formed?

How gender identity is formed is still largely a mystery with theories vacillating from nature, to nurture, and then back to nature. The discovery of estrogen and testosterone at the end of the nineteenth century seemed to point to nature: hereditary or biological causes. Attempts to link gender identity to hormone levels were sought when internal secretions of these feminizing and masculizing hormones were first discovered. But when scientific proof for this failed, nurture theories came into focus: child rearing practices, parental attitudes, and societal influences were put forth.[11]

The focus on environmental causes for gender identity during the first half of the twentieth century coincided with the advent of Freud and the emerging field of human psychology. By the mid-1950's prominent researchers in human sexuality, most notably John Money at Johns Hopkins University, popularized the theory that newborns were psychosexually neutral so their gender could be shaped entirely by parents and society.

Historically parents of gender nonconforming children shouldered most of the blame for their child's suffering and social isolation. Fathers were labeled as absent or withholding; mothers were seen as depressed, indulgent, or ambivalent about their own gender; and gender roles at home were assumed to be blurred and ambiguous. The recommended treatment was to remove all gender nonconforming toys from the child despite how despondent she or he became, and to rigidly reinforce and reward only gender conforming behavior. Parental guilt drove parents to engage in long-term treatment for themselves and their child. Some children were institutionalized for years while others were subjected to electroshock therapy.[12] The ostensible goal was to conform the child's gender to their sex to prevent them from growing up to be transsexual, gay, or lesbian.

This prevailing viewpoint also led to the practice within pediatric medicine of assigning a gender at birth to infants with ambiguous genitalia (intersex infants) or those whose penises were unformed or injured. Most often biological males were assigned as girls based on surgical techniques available at the time. Parents were instructed to adhere to childrearing practices that conformed gender to the surgically assigned sex, obliterating past history of the infant as male and curtailing extended family connections if necessary to protect the new identity.[13] This misguided practice continued until case studies were published describing the anguish of these children, now adults, knowing their assigned gender was wrong despite what parents and doctors had told them for years.

The tide shifted back at the end of the twentieth century to neuro biological influences on gender based on case studies that showed gender identity to be less malleable than originally thought. As early as 1959 there was a minority voice in the debate over nature vs. nurture as the basis for gender identity development. Dr. Milton Diamond believed that evidence from biology, psychology, psychiatry, anthropology, and endocrinology, showed that gender identity was hardwired into the brain almost as early as conception[14] but it wasn't until nearly four decades later that his theory for the neurobiological basis of gender finally gained traction with a 1997 article in which Diamond stated:

> Gender identity and sexual orientation are largely inborn, a result of prenatal hormone exposure and other genetic influences on the brain and nervous system, which set

limits to the degree of cross-gender flexibility that any
person can comfortably display.[15]

Understanding transgender identity as within the realm of
biological diversity rather than viewing it as a defect or disease,
it is more productive to consider how it is adaptive rather than
dwelling on the biological unknowns of causality. Transgender
people themselves are beginning to articulate this and will continue
to do so as more break the silence that has historically surrounded
the experience. Their stories have already begun to inform and
transform many of the myths and misconceptions that are held
about gender.

But since parents ask *why* at the outset of having a gender
nonconforming or transgender child the following is a brief
overview of some recent theories. The biological influences under
consideration today that may have a bearing on gender identity
development are chromosomes, hormones, physiology, and environmental chemicals. Absent definitive answers, theories abound.
Researchers are looking at neurohormones in utero. A human fetus
differentiates male or female genitalia around the twelfth week of
gestation. The hypothalamus is considered the control center for
gender identity since it regulates endocrine or hormone function.
It differentiates in the fetal brain at approximately the sixteenth
week. It may be that if certain hormones are absent or out of
balance during this formative four-week period, gender identity in
the brain may not develop along the same pathway as genitalia.[16]

Another theory looks at chemical exposure in prescription drugs
and other environmental chemicals in utero that may affect fetal
brain chemistry.[17] Some of these chemicals are known to affect fetal
reproductive organs later in life. DES (diethylstilbestrol), a synthetic
estrogen, developed in 1938 and prescribed until 1971 supposedly
to prevent miscarriage for an estimated 4.8 million women in the
United States alone, crossed the placenta and damaged the reproductive system of the developing fetus.[18] In *Far from the Tree*, Andrew

Solomon notes that: "A 2002 survey of members of the DES Sons Network found an extraordinary 50 percent rate of transgenderism; this supports the hypothesis that gestational hormone levels can trigger cross-gender identity."[19]

DES was banned in the 1970s long before it was appropriately categorized as an endocrine disrupting chemical (EDC) but its permanent impact on developing fetuses should raise alarms about other chemicals in this category. EDCs are industrial and pharmaceutical chemicals that mimic naturally occurring hormones and they abound in our food, water, air, as well as in personal care, household products, and home pesticides. They affect "thyroid function, sexual development and behavior, metabolism, and nervous and immune system function."[20] They may be behind increasing incidents of breast and other cancers in women, endometriosis, miscarriage, tubal pregnancy, and reduced fertility. Fetal and infant health issues are also a concern as critical and complex processes take place in utero and during infancy. These chemicals may permanently impact developing and highly sensitive endocrine systems.[21] Since they are known to cause an increase in reproductive irregularities in amphibians, researchers wonder whether they may contribute to the rising number of genital anomalies in humans as well as atypical gender identity.[22]

A mother's own physical and mental health during pregnancy also has an unavoidable impact on the baby's health. Ever since admonitions about smoking and alcohol, and the imperatives of prenatal vitamins, expectant mothers worry about what else might be harmful or helpful that we don't yet suspect. Some believe severe emotional stress or trauma can alter the chemical environment of the womb thereby impacting the fetus. Studying such effects through hindsight makes this theory difficult to research.[23]

With the shift back to exploring biological causes for gender identity and a more limited role for the environment and childrearing practices, we parents are finally able to breathe a welcome sigh of relief. The past half-century has not been kind to parents of gender nonconforming and transgender children. The guilt and pain of believing that you are the unwitting cause of your child's suffering is a heavy burden to carry. A recent survey of 3,474 transgender adults found that the parents who rejected their children did so partly because they felt somehow responsible.[24] By correcting this myth with facts, parents will hopefully be able to avoid debilitating guilt and shame, and get on with supporting and accepting their unique children.

Who Decides Gender?

Most of us conjure images of a daughter or son even before we conceive or adopt a child. Gender is often the central theme in the stories we enact in our mind. We see ourselves with a girl or a boy and for some of us one gender feels like more of a fit than another. Parents are often unaware of the possibility that sex and gender can diverge, and are therefore unprepared when their child's gender does not conform to their anatomical sex.

Assigned gender is decided by others at one's birth based on genitalia. It is what parents and family are told by healthcare providers, what is listed on the birth certificate and birth announcements, what informs the name, and often the colors of a baby's clothing, blanket, and bedroom. It can also impact how often the baby is soothed, how they are spoken to, whether they are held facing their mother or the world, and what toys they will be given to play with.

Affirmed gender (or *gender identity*) is what a child feels inside about how closely he or she fits within a particular gender as defined by the society in which he or she resides. When there is a match between assigned gender and affirmed gender, gender is hardly an issue. A child may play at the edges of gender roles but their internal identity is not a concern. Most biological males are comfortable being socialized into becoming boys and men in their particular society, and most biological females are comfortable being socialized into becoming girls and women. But when a child's abiding internal sense that the gender to which they have been assigned at birth based on anatomical sex[25] and physical attributes, does not fit the gender they intrinsically feel inside, there are often early signs of conflict.

Affirmed gender remains a mystery until well after birth, when the child begins to form a mind of his or her own. Since it usually surfaces long after parents have formed their own clear ideas, images, and projections about who this child is, a child often faces an uphill battle to be heard and understood. Depending on the child's temperament, their ability to persuade adults and communicate their dissonance can range from subtle to urgent. A child's personality can influence his or her method of communication. A highly verbal, extroverted child may readily articulate their gender dissonance, where a child prone to physical methods of expression may act it out in play. Some children are clear and decisive at a very young age, while others move between genders and feel ambivalent about claiming one or the other.

Gender roles are the social expectations that have traditionally defined proper behavior for one's assigned gender. Gender roles can become gender stereotypes over time so that people who do not adhere to gender roles are seen as being inappropriate for their gender. The women's movement has challenged many of the traditional gender roles in our culture so that roles are not as confining as they once were. Few people today will directly tell a girl she cannot become a soldier or a boy he cannot be a stay-at home dad but a quick trip to the children's clothing section of any department store illustrates that gender stereotypes are alive and well in the ways we continue to socialize girls to be sexually available, and boys to be aggressive.

Young children watch those with whom they identify and learn how to behave and express themselves. Through modeling the behaviors, speech patterns, voice inflections, gestures, clothing, and facial expressions of those they emulate, children learn how to express their inner sense of gender. Some young children come right out and say, "I'm not a boy, I'm a girl." But for children who are not as verbal or who are less clear about their affirmed gender, a child's behavior, play, and preferred clothing are often the first ways parents and teachers notice that a child experiences some level of dissonance with their assigned gender.

REFLECTIONS

Our backgrounds, needs, and expectations, whether conscious or not, have a direct impact on how we respond to our children. I had a deeply buried inner child needing affection and attention. With Kendra in my arms, it was as though I relived being my five-year-old self, caring for my baby sisters, and rekindling the magic of childhood. Tony's and my presents for Kendra her first Christmas illustrate how a baby can awaken our inner child. I bought her a soft, brown, wide-eyed, stuffed doll with bouncy, curly hair that reminded me of her. It was a present I would have cherished when I was little. Whether by accident or on purpose Kendra ripped off the doll's head. Tony bought her a train. I envisioned a chunky, durable plastic train with two or three indestructible cars. He came home elated with an elaborate engine, electrical control switch, five or six cars with tiny parts that all needed to be assembled, glued, and painted, and enough track to encircle the living room. It was a train she could watch but was not allowed to touch. Over the years they assembled cars together and it became a tradition to set up the train under the tree. Tony had always wanted just such a train when he was a child.

My attachment to Kendra was strengthened because in meeting her needs I met my own. In caring for her I was taking care of myself. I had trouble seeing her as apart from my own lost little girl. When I clasped Kendra's hand for a walk in the woods there were two hands there; my daughter's and the little girl inside me that she reawakened. Eventually one wanted to let go. And as she did so, I fought to keep her lest both be lost to me. This inner child in me was particularly vulnerable and alone at the time of Kendra's birth having just lost my mother. Kendra came into my life after a pregnancy overshadowed by grief. My earliest expectation was that she would bring joy where there had been sorrow. She filled that expectation immediately, strengthening my attachment. But perhaps that encouraged me to think she would fill other expectations as well.

When we gaze upon our baby's pure, open face, and explore the source of the feelings that arise, we may notice that many are based on our own hopes and dreams. The images we have for what life will be like for these little beings are totally unknown and unbidden by them. I dreamed of being mother and daughter together for life with all the feelings of constancy, companionship, and affection that image evoked for me. I based it on my relationship with my own mother; my mother-in-law with her mother; and then embellished it just for us. I imagined that this mother-daughter bond could help fill the void now that my own mother was gone.

My preference for daughters was largely based on my fear of loss and abandonment since I assumed daughters stayed close while sons separated and left. I wonder whether my bond would have been different had Kendra been born male? Would my own assumptions and expectations about a son have changed my feelings of attachment? I might have felt more tentative, hesitant to get too close lest I feel bereft when he grew up and left me. I knew girls. I'd been surrounded by girls and women my whole life at home and at work. I feared I wouldn't know how to raise a boy. Boys were a puzzle, sometimes even a challenge to my feminist way of thinking. My work in women's health, sexual assault, and domestic violence prevention, made me acutely aware of all the ways we train boys to embrace aggression as the measure of their masculinity. I worried about having the right balance of love and vigilance to raise a gentle, conscious, confident boy. Of course I worried for my daughter too—her safety, self-esteem, and future—but I was less fearful she'd grow up and leave, eschew my values, or break my heart.

In order to prepare for the journey ahead it's helpful to consider some of your own expectations and assumptions—many of which existed even before your child arrived. Did you want a boy, a girl, or didn't it matter? Why? What experiences in your own background laid the foundation for how you first related to your baby?

Photo: Char Wendel

Tony, Candace, and Kendra

2

Awareness of Difference

These kids are making a statement with
their every move and word.[26]

NORMAN SPACK, MD

RECOLLECTIONS

Exploring the World

When Kendra started to walk she became fascinated with the flowers in our yard. She called them "yayas," one of her first words. A walk in the woods or on the beach was slow and tedious as she scrutinized everything she saw on the ground and resisted being rushed. She stopped to fill her fists and pockets with stones, berries, acorns, leaves, flowers, pinecones, sticks, chunks of moss and shells. Sue, her daycare provider, gave her a little basket purse to store her collections and she toddled with it swinging on her arm. She began talking early and had a great memory for an impressive vocabulary. She surprised us by tossing out words like "actually" and "absolutely" or putting together cute phrases like "I can't know member" ("I can't remember") or animatedly holding her hands out, palms up, and asking "Beev it?" ("Can you believe it?"). She recited the names of the three other children, all boys, in daycare; enjoyed looking for "teeboes" (tomatoes) to pick in the garden, loved all the Christmas "yites" (lights) and was always ready to "go 'cation" (vacation). Once while overhearing a news report about a two-year war she exclaimed: "What! Two-year olds at war?"

Kendra had a stubborn streak and once she decided something, she would not be convinced otherwise. She was a spirited child, never one to go along easily with the crowd and quick to let us know when she was frightened, anxious, or unhappy. She resisted being part of a group, and loved to be cuddled, rocked, and read to—all quiet, one-on-one activities. She hated loud noises, crowds, fire engine parades, and fireworks, so much so that we avoided many childhood amusements with large numbers of people including carnival in Trinidad and even Disney World until she was much older.

She was fascinated by colors, shapes, picture books, and enjoyed drawing. She loved all animals whether living or stuffed. Kendra never tired of being outdoors exploring and she noticed everything. She frequently saw things that escaped my notice, as when she pointed out a bird's nest at my dad's house when we were in my childhood bedroom looking out the window. She so loved mashing things in the yard that I bought her a mortar and pestle and knew where she was by the ching, ching, ching sound of her crushing. She especially loved painting with the various colors she made by crushing berries and more dangerously, how they tasted. Once she surprised me with a beach towel spread out on the crest of the hill in our backyard for a picnic that she had decorated with petals and fruits from the yard creating a feast of color.

A free spirit, Kendra loved nothing more than to run around naked—after a bath, before bed, when changing clothes, even at the beach. Most spacious and outdoor settings delighted her—the woods, beach, garden, ocean, quarry—just as indoor, congested, and busy settings such as shopping malls agitated and displeased her. She could tolerate the grocery store because the colors and shapes in the produce section fascinated her.

Kendra was a keen observer of animals. She loved going to the zoo to see new animals, study their behavior, and then imitate them.

Before she was two, a goat at a picnic tried to eat the leaves she had in her hand so she fed him every single one. When she got home she brought leaves in from outside and put them in the cat's dish thinking maybe cats liked leaves too. In the bathtub she practiced what she called, "kissing the water," as she drank like a cat.

Omen

When Kendra was about two, I carried her on my hip while browsing in a local gift shop that was holding psychic readings in the back room. The reader, wearing a black shirt with a gold astrological chart, came out and unexpectedly walked straight toward us.

"Is this your child?" she asked.

"Yes," I said, wondering whether she'd ask this if Kendra was white.

"You know she's different, right?"

"Yes," I said, realizing at that moment that I did know this without ever having said it before.

"You're going to worry about her," she said. "But she's going to be fine."

I was at a loss as to how to respond. I felt scared, wanting to defend myself against whatever she was implying. Did she see some dangerous future for Kendra? Should I find out more? I assured myself that all parents worry about their children. That must be what she meant. Of course I would worry. What parent doesn't? But I was still enjoying a bubble of bliss and love with my little girl. I hugged Kendra to me even tighter and left the store in an effort to put the whole experience behind me.

Whatever you think about psychic readings and astrology I found the whole event curious. When it happened, I wasn't open to any foreboding news about the future and preferred to take it as it came. But as the years progressed, there were times I wished I'd paid the twenty-five dollars for the full reading to know what she saw in my child at so young an age. A few years later, if the store were still in business, I might've gone back to this prescient woman for a consultation.

Racial Identity

Between ages two and three Kendra began to notice the different skin colors of people in her life. At first she asked why I was the only white person in our family. As she got older and became more aware of the outside world, the question changed. One night just before her third birthday she asked, "Why am I the only brown one here—me and Daddy?" We reminded her of other brown people in our family: her Grandpa; her two Grandmas; her aunts and uncles; her many cousins. She was right in that they were seldom "here," as in at our house since we usually traveled to them. We assured her there were many brown people in the world. She fell asleep with pictures of her cousins that night—both boys.

By three she was talking about the racism she experienced in how people looked at her and us, things children said to her and how it made her feel different, separate, less-than. One day when I picked her up from a friend's house she said in the car on the way home: "I hate white people. They cut up brown people and eat them for dinner." I wish I had asked her what prompted that statement. I reminded her of all the white people in our family and among our friends. She then revised her statement to "I hate stranger white people, not friends."

Living in a town with few people of color was a challenge. Because I am white and Tony grew up in Trinidad which is much more multiracial than where we lived, neither of us was adequately prepared to deal with the overt and subtle forms of racism Kendra encountered in a mostly white school and community. Years earlier an African American colleague of mine advised us to live in a more diverse community so that our racially mixed child would not feel singled out and isolated.

We read books, watched movies, listened to music, and exposed her to racially diverse people but we could not inoculate her from the bias of white, provincial New England. Once she was asked whether her skin was brown because she ate too many brownies. There was the time Sue, her daycare provider, in an effort to make Kendra feel included, pointed out the one manikin of color in the annual Christmas Village display in Boston. Efforts like this, while no doubt well meaning, had the opposite effect. Drawing attention to the ways a child is different, made a shy child like Kendra feel more self-conscious of her difference rather than proud of her uniqueness in a sea of sameness. The manikin was male just like her cousins.

Dress

As Kendra grew, there were signs she was on a path all her own. Almost as soon as she could walk she enjoyed toddling around in Tony's high top sneakers. Never did she put on my shoes. My encouragement for her to dress up for photos and family gatherings if for no other reason than to show off a dress from a relative, was usually met with tears and tantrums. Kendra made her contempt for dresses clear by the age of two when I put her in a dress her grandma gave her for a formal photo. Getting her to smile in that dress was a chore. At the time I chalked it up to the scratchy fabric of the puffy slip.

I vividly remember the day I finally understood the depth of this child's drive for self-expression against which I was no match. We'd invited several kids over for her three-year birthday party. She woke up early and dressed in mismatched, faded, and threadbare shorts and top. When I tried to convince her to change into a newer, matching shorts set, a battle ensued which threatened to ruin both of our moods minutes before the guests arrived. Kendra could be shy and withdrawn from her peers in her best frame of mind so I gave up the fight to save the party and the day. We were both going to lose otherwise.

Even then, when I asked myself why I was insisting she change clothes, I knew it was not for her sake or her friends who could have cared less what she was wearing. It was for me. I wanted to look good to the other mothers. I recalled that lesson many times in the ensuing years. My own fear of being judged by other mothers for how my child dressed or behaved was not the crucial issue. My child's health, happiness, and self-esteem were what mattered.

One of Kendra's first prayers was asking God to make her into a cat. Kendra not only loved animals, she loved *being* an animal. Over time she had a collection of face paints, masks, antlers, and tails to combine with animal pajamas I made, Halloween costumes, or outfits she improvised. She could quickly become any cat: leopard, jaguar, yellow-spotted cheetah, ocelot, or housecat. She was also a convincing bull, horse, or reindeer. She'd stalk, gallop, or trot through the house on her long limber arms and legs, bringing to life each animal's likeness with uncanny accuracy. When polishing our nails, she requested yellow turning her nails into claws. She seemed more at home in costume than in her own skin. Make-believe always involved animals, never people, and she implored others to get on all fours and join her. She cleverly covered her shyness when visiting my sisters by answering questions in character—with growls and paw swipes rather than words. When she got homesick and irritable on our first long vacation she said it was because she had no costumes so we packed some for vacations after that.

Kendra loved catching animals and became skillful at it. She begged to bring home her favorites including a baby shark and a baby seal from the aquarium. As she grew older she asked for every pet imaginable and rescued wounded animals. Whenever she went swimming, ferrying drowning insects to shore was imperative. She named a household spider even though spiders scared her and she hated their tiny webs when they crossed against her skin while walking in the woods. She created elaborate landscapes and jungle scenes throughout the house using furniture, plants, fruit, stuffed or plastic animals, pillows, blankets, and towels so there was always some nature scene at play. Animals were on windowsills, in plants or sinks eating leaves or clay balls of food. In addition to copying their movements, she memorized each species, where they lived and what they ate. Her favorites evolved over time. First dinosaurs fascinated her, then all the great cats—lions, tigers, cheetahs, leopards, and panthers—and later small reptiles.

When Kendra was four she said she didn't like the teacher at the dance class she'd just begun. "I just want to do my own thing when I dance," she said. "I don't want to be told what to do. And I want to be a cat, not a princess like she's always telling us to be." She refused to go back. One day she arranged a tea party that was attended by four wild cats—a lion, tiger, leopard, and jaguar. In the center of their seated circle was an orange hair elastic. When I asked what that was Kendra said: "See how powerful cats are? They make fire!"

At the time, we didn't interpret Kendra's desire to be an animal in the context of gender. But her persistent desire to be in costume, her longing for an animal disguise when we were away from home, as well as the confidence she exuded when she was dressed as an animal were signs she felt uncomfortable in her own skin. At the time I interpreted this as a make-believe cover for her shy, introverted nature. It never occurred to me that it reflected her longing for a gender-neutral presentation in the world. While she never directly said she wanted to be a boy, she clearly felt dressing and acting like a girl was incompatible with her sense of self.

Kendra started preschool when she was four. She cried every day for the first week, which was heartbreaking. I often went to work crying as well. The director of the preschool took Kendra under her wing and let her stay with her one-on-one for the first few days until she felt more at home. On the fifth day Kendra asked me to stay for a little bit then blew me a kiss, signaling she was ready for me to go.

Preschool

Alone
in the corner
of
aloneness
and
fear
waiting
for mom.
Preschool,
a
child's nightmare.

KENDRA, MIDDLE SCHOOL

For the Halloween party that year Kendra wanted to be a bull. We created her costume using black tights, Tony's large black turtleneck with shoulder pads sewn in, a mask with pink nostrils, and a headband with horns. When she looked at the horns and saw they were stuffed she said: "But Mommy, people are big. These are too soft. They can't push people around." When we first got to the party she clung to me as she had those first few days but all that changed when she put on her costume. She stuck out her chest, put her head down, enlarged her shoulders, dug hooves in the dust, and snorted. Then she started chasing people—mostly the boys—"thundering around" as she called it. She often hung at the fringes of play but in costume that day she was the center of activity and she didn't want to leave.

Kendra continued to wear the tail from her bull costume for months including all during Christmas at my sister Donna's house. It was around this time that she told me she wanted to change her name to DeRonco and she even made a nametag for herself. She didn't give a reason and she said it was okay if we forgot and called her Kendra. Other names followed such as Lightning Strike and Tardino. These all came to her during make-believe when she was a horse or bull. It didn't escape my notice that she was a Taurus, born in May. It did escape my notice that the names and costumes were all male.

I now know that gender nonconforming dress, play, and trying on new names, can all begin very young and persist for transgender children. Kendra not only dressed differently from her peers, her play was also different. She never wanted to play house or dress dolls. She could be very nurturing and intuitive about the needs of animals but dolls didn't evoke the same feelings. Her best friend in kindergarten loved Barbies. Kendra however, specified, "No Barbies please!" on her birthday party invitations that year. For her sixth birthday, she chose an invitation with a cowboy riding a horse swinging a lasso. This time I did notice the boy on horseback and thought it was an odd choice but since it was one of the few invitations with animals I chalked it up to that. The closest Kendra came to playing house was with the elaborate care she took in decorating and playing with a dollhouse given to her by her Great-Aunt Roz, my father's sister. She had a doll family with furniture and food in the kitchen and played miniature make-believe for a short time. She even decorated the house with Christmas lights one year.

Since she loved to gallop or stalk around the house on all fours dressed as a wild animal, few girls her age could be convinced to play make-believe this way. But she wasn't comfortable with boys either. She wasn't interested in sports and felt boys played too rough. Family and friends assumed she'd grow up to be a veterinarian given her passion and care for animals and her ability to imitate them so well. We never noticed how little she role-played adult women. Yet as much as adults admired her free spirit, curiosity, and connection to nature, finding friends became increasingly difficult because she shared few interests with other children.

In prior generations this disdain for feminine clothing, disinterest in dolls, and lack of maternal role modeling might have been cause for concern but with changing women's roles, we viewed this as within the range of normal. Had she been a boy with this level of nonconforming dress and play, alarms would have sounded sooner.

I did wonder about Kendra's fascination with cat costumes and tails when she showed no sign of giving them up. I asked Joanna, my psychologist friend, when I should start worrying about the tail. She said not until around eight. When eight came and went, she revised it to ten. Ten came and went and I stopped asking.

The more she ventured out into the world the more indicators there were of our child's deep and abiding difference from her peers. In kindergarten I bought her a dark green, floral print, velour pant set. It was comfortable and soft and the colors complimented her. I thought it the perfect outfit for my finicky child who fussed and fumed over scratchy tags, stiff material, and tight waists. One day she announced she would no longer wear it to school, "because Kevin doesn't like flowers." I interpreted this to mean that my daughter was already being influenced by a boy's opinion of her appearance and gave her a feminist lecture on how she should be able to wear whatever she wanted without caring what other people thought or said—especially five-year-old boys! She still never wore the outfit again and reflecting on the incident years later, I realized what she meant was that she wanted to dress *like* the boys not to be pleasing *to* them.

The next year in first grade they had red, white, and blue day. The only red, white, and blue clothing Kendra had was a dress from her Great-Aunt Roz—one that had hung unworn in the closet for months. After going through all her other clothes, I pulled out the dress. She tried it on that afternoon and twirling around, decided she would wear it the next day. I hid my surprise and my pleasure that maybe she was finally ready to dress more like the beautiful little girl she was. Knowing that the more I made of her unexpected decision to wear a dress the more likely she would be to change her mind, I acted nonchalant but deep down, I was elated.

When she came downstairs to breakfast the next morning, she had on a completely different outfit with no hint of red, white, and blue. When I asked what happened she said, "I feel shy in that dress." Looking back now, it was her six-year-old way of saying she felt shy being seen as a girl. The dress was the external expression of the internal dissonance. She was more comfortable rejecting the dress code for the day and honoring her own identity than she would have felt fitting in on the outside while betraying herself.

Flower Girl

When Kendra was seven my cousin Wendy, Roz's daughter, asked if she would be a flower girl in her wedding. I was thrilled to show off my beautiful daughter and knew she would look adorable. Wendy chose a rich blue velvet dress with a satin ribbon belt tied in the back and a white lace collar. She wanted me to get white lace stockings and matching white shoes. She ordered a blue and white ribbon for Kendra's hair and a white basket with blue, white, and pink flowers.

Kendra balked. First she refused to be in the wedding at all. Then she refused to wear the dress. She was moody and uncooperative shopping for the shoes and stockings. To make matters worse, there was a wedding and reception in Philadelphia where my cousin lived and then another reception weeks later in Rhode Island where her parents lived. This meant wearing the dress twice! We finally compromised. She'd wear pants under the dress for the wedding ceremony and change out of the dress immediately after photographs for both receptions. We outright bribed her with a gift of her choosing—a ceramic turtle for the garden.

Kendra had become legend for her unique preferences by then and no one in the family was surprised by her aversion to dresses. We were surprised by the depth of her conviction and insistence that pants were the essential antidote to the discomfort she'd feel in a dress—even if no one else saw them, she knew they were there. By then I was learning how to deal with her refusal to wear the clothes I bought her so it didn't feel like the personal rejection it once did. I did however feel she was cutting herself short, having a closed mind at such a young age. It surprised me how strongly she matched her will to mine and it was hard for me to hear that there was no room for compromise. She showed no mercy in her persistent and persuasive refusals to indulge my fantasies.

Though I grieved my own loss, I knew it was important to support her independence and self-expression, and I never bargained with her again after this wedding. I knew it had violated something in her that was growing stronger with age. I held onto the notion that this was a phase she would outgrow and I kept a watchful eye for any hopeful sign. As stubborn as she was I was careful never to let her know what I hoped for lest she redouble efforts to defy me. And the seeds of loss that had begun to germinate in me put down deeper roots with each passing year.

Maybe I'm Finally Becoming a Jaguar!

In the spring just before Wendy's wedding, we went on our first trip to Tony's homeland, Trinidad and Tobago. Tony and I were sleep-deprived by the time we got on the plane with all the preparation and packing but there was no sleeping during the flight because of our restless, curious, talkative child. When we arrived Kendra couldn't wait to jump into the warm Caribbean Sea. She was ecstatic whenever we were at the beach where she bodysurfed and jumped waves to her heart's content. The warm water was gentle, the surf thrilling, and she was able to stay in all day without tiring or getting cold.

Tony introduced us to his relatives as well as his favorite childhood places, foods, fruits, sights, and smells. We drank coconut water and ate boiled corn at the Savannah, tried more tropical fruits than we could name, viewed breathtaking vistas, smelled the humid and fragrant air, and visited the zoo with Tony's mother, Grandma Iyine. There Kendra saw several types of wild cats, as well as alligators, monkeys, turtles, and snakes. She saw her first ocelot and was excited to add that to her repertoire of animal aliases. She got sunspots on her face from the bright equatorial sun in Trinidad, which I worried would be permanent. When she looked in the mirror she exclaimed: "Oh good! Maybe I'm finally becoming a jaguar!" And of course she had a jaguar bathing suit that summer.

Kendra was like a wood nymph or nature sprite—artistic, creative, adventurous outdoors, sensitive, spiritual, and knowledgeable beyond her years about the natural world. She was always busy with her wide array of pets that over time included cats, birds, hermit crabs, tadpoles, frogs, toads, lizards, salamanders, fish, hamsters, turtles, an iguana, geckos, and snakes. Once when we were vacationing on a lake in New Hampshire she announced first thing in the morning that she planned to catch ten salamanders. My dad and Donna offered to help, showing her how to use buckets but with limited success. Before we knew it she was quickly scooping them up by hand. When she got older she explored a nearby pond with an inflatable raft, scooping turtles out with a net. She'd measure, draw or photograph them, and then let them go. She was forever creating books of her animal studies. She was nine when Disney's production of *The Jungle Book* came out and more than one friend or family member noted how much Mogli reminded them of Kendra.

RESEARCH

Early Clues

The biological building blocks for a child's gender identity have likely already been laid down before a child can speak so it's not unusual for a very young child to let their parents know when something doesn't seem right. Children as young as two and three years old may announce to parents and caretakers that they sense a keen difference between what they are told and what they feel inside. For some, a transgender identity is often clear by this age.[27]

Parents may assume that their child is simply confused about what anatomical parts go with what gender or that this is a phase.[28]

Some parents will be right since only about one quarter of children with gender identity disorder show cross-gender identity in adolescence.[29] Many children "try on" gender, or move between gender, and beyond gender, so it often takes time to sort out what a child is really experiencing and saying when they are very young. Other children show very few signs of gender nonconformity when young but then experience gender dysphoria during puberty or later.[30] What makes matters so complex for parents is trying to look into the future to know where a child will land along the gender spectrum as an adult based on their play, words, and dress when they are children. Making decisions for one's child without all the relevant information can be daunting since the stakes are so high.

Gender creative and transgender children may make statements like, "I'm going to be a boy when I grow up," or "God made a mistake with me," or "My heart is boy but my body is girl."[31] It's not unusual for young children to think that what they are today can change in the future. Small children are not as literal as adults. They understand transformation as having to do with the power of the mind, not bound by the body. A child's imagination is open to whatever changes are required for the self the child knows inside to emerge.[32] Understanding what a child is really saying with statements like this is critical. A child may be reacting to gender role stereotypes that don't fit them or they may be feeling their body doesn't match their gender. Because the vast majority of gender nonconforming children will not grow up to be transgender or transsexual,[33] it's hard to know what if any action should be taken at such an early stage. Words together with behaviors, over time, help lead the way.

According to Dr. Norman Spack, founder of the GeMS Clinic (Gender Management Service) at Children's Hospital in Boston, the following are some clear ways that children indicate their gender incongruity:

1. Bathroom behavior—a girl who insists on standing to pee
2. Aversion to bathing suits of their anatomical sex

3. Desiring underpants of their affirmed gender—girls in boxers; boys in floral bikinis

4. Playing with toys usually associated with the opposite gender.[34]

And transgender children are often drawn to trying on the clothes of the parent with whom they identify.[35] Even without being able to articulate in words the gender mismatch they feel inside, children with these types of behaviors are likely showing early signs of gender identity incongruence. If these feelings and behaviors remain strong over time and last into puberty, it's likely not a phase the child will outgrow.

Once a child has an internal sense of gender, they actively strive to socialize themselves accordingly by seeking cues for how to act much like a male canary chick learning his song from an adult male. This is true whether their sense of gender conforms to their anatomical sex or not. From three to four years old, children become aware of their own gender identity and physical differences. They start categorizing masculine and feminine gender roles and form stereotypes based on what they learn from the media, family members, and their social setting. They gravitate to members of their affirmed gender for play, which usually intensifies until about age twelve.[36]

Gender nonconforming boys are more obvious at younger ages since there is more social stigma for boys whose gender expression is feminine than for girls whose gender expression is masculine. Girls can hide their cross-gender identity more easily, often until puberty. Letting a child experiment with cross-gender clothing in the safety of their home can relieve some of the child's urgency and give parents time to consider the next steps.

Verbal assertions of gender, as well as play and art may often be clues. Your child may dress in clothes that reflect their inner gender; change their name during play or ask that their given name be changed; draw themselves as both genders or an ambiguous gender in pictures; take on make-believe roles during play that express their affirmed gender; throw tantrums if they cannot have the clothes or toys or other accessories connected with the gender they feel.[37]

While most children play with toys associated with either gender, transgender children often refuse toys associated with their assigned gender preferring only those toys associated with their affirmed gender. On a scale ranking gendered behavior with masculinity at one end and femininity at the other, transgender children tend to be two or three times more identified with their affirmed gender than children whose gender matches their anatomy. Cisgender boys range from three-and-a-half to five standard deviations in the direction of masculinity and girls toward femininity, while transgender children range from seven to twelve standard deviations *away* from their birth gender.[38] It's as if a child's cross-gender identification needs to be stronger in order assert their internal gender, counterbalancing the pressure they face to conform to an external norm that doesn't fit.

Whether or not a child is ready to socially alter their gender will likely be evidenced by the intensity of discomfort they feel with their bodies. Some children show a marked need to socially transition as young as four or five. Other children are more fluid or nuanced in their gender identity so parents may feel they have time to listen and observe. Still others are decidedly gender nonconforming but happy with their bodies. A child may struggle against gender roles and expression without actually questioning their gender identity.

Sometimes a parent's need for immediate answers can interfere with the child's need for time to explore and grow. A parent who is uncomfortable with a feminine boy or masculine girl may assume their child is transgender before the child is certain. Parents uncomfortable living with more questions than answers may find it difficult to watch and wait for their child's gender identity to become clear. But that is exactly what is required. Rushing in either direction by urging gender conformity or pushing gender transition will not be in the best interests of the child. Time will tell. Every child's internal sense of gender and the timing with which it unfolds is unique. Some know in preschool, some in high school, and others in adulthood.

Unlike other childhood medical conditions, children, not parents or professionals, first diagnose gender dysphoria. From most outward appearances, things may seem fine while your child struggles internally to make sense of their feelings. Hearing what your child says through words and actions, and creating an open and informed environment that welcomes communication and exploration, is crucial. Seeking help early from professionals experienced in working with gender nonconforming and transgender children can be critical for making the best decision and supporting the whole family because of the many feelings and questions that arise for parents and loved ones.

REFLECTIONS

Observe

Some children communicate their gender dysphoria directly in words. Others do so in play, art, music, or storytelling. Reflecting on the quote from Norman Spack that began this chapter, "These kids are making a statement with their every move and word," I realize I missed Kendra's abundant, clear, nonverbal statements. I now understand that Kendra's comfort as an animal was due to her desire for a gender-neutral or male gender expression.

Kendra creatively chose a species other than human as she playfully tried on being male. There was a feeling of freedom and abandon about her in costume that was not present without one. As a male animal she was bold in her movements, self-confident, and eager to engage in play with boys as well as girls. As a girl she was shy, anxious, and withdrawn. Her suggestion that we change her name was all part of her early experimentation with trying on a different gender. Of course now I wonder what her childhood would have been like had we understood sooner her desire to be in the right gender presentation full time. She probably would have been more relaxed, happy, and confident.

While we cannot control the inner experiences of our children, we may communicate our discomfort directly or indirectly when they do not conform to the gender norms we expect. Efforts to steer or force them into gender conformity may cause them to hide their conflicting feelings, censor their behavior, and stop exploring openly with us. This may result in our child's cross-gender identity going underground and becoming internalized with shame.[39] Negative self-images can start very young—as soon as our children are old enough to feel the sting of glares and scowls by others. By the time their peers taunt and tease them they've absorbed the message that something is wrong with them rather than the world.[40]

I never discouraged or forbade Kendra from dressing up in animal costumes but I never allowed myself to delve into what her play might actually mean. Feeling the need to protect the precious moments of childhood and enclose my daughter and me in a safe, impenetrable bubble of bliss, I was a master at letting into my consciousness only that which I could handle. I erected swift and effective defenses at any suggestion that all might not be well in our future, as I did when the astrologer in that tiny storefront suggested I would worry about this child.

Pay attention to what your eyes, ears, and observations tell you about your child's internal sense of gender. Be brave and honest. The sooner you begin your learning process—your own transition in awareness—the better prepared you will be to support your child wherever they eventually land on the gender spectrum. Observe your child's play and the gender roles they assume when you allow them a full range of options. Notice how they talk about themselves as it relates to gender. Write down what they tell you and record dates so you can see if there is consistency over time. How do they talk about their body? Are they pleased or dismayed about their appearance and body parts? What do they say about your body or their siblings' bodies? Notice how they express themselves with clothing, hair, shoes, or dress-up. What do they say about themselves when they are dressed in costume or playing make-believe? Do they select a cross-gender role or name? What toys do they prefer? Are they gender-neutral or nonconforming? Do they gravitate more to their brother or sister's toys than their own? Do they seem jealous of their sibling's gender or expression? Are they happy when others mistake them for the other gender? Notice how they draw themselves in pictures and what they don't do or say related to gender and roles.

Engage

I was terrified to engage with Kendra around gender because I held some erroneous notion that naming and discussing gender might encourage and solidify her nonconformity. Part of me already knew and wasn't ready to hear my child's truth. Unfortunately it was years later that I realized Kendra always played a male animal, and missing that clue, I also missed the opportunity to engage her in conversation about how she felt being an animal or being male instead of being a girl. I can only imagine how confusing it must have felt for Kendra as she dropped hints right and left—whether consciously or not—only to have them met with silence.

Our child's ability to express their feelings about gender can be predominantly influenced by us. The sooner we pick up on whatever clues they send and begin the conversation, the sooner they have permission to share their private and unconventional perspectives on gender. Letting your child know they can talk with you about their feelings concerning gender will assist you both. Your child will feel less isolated and alone and you will have more information about what he or she is thinking and feeling over time. This will be your best guide for how to help them long-term.

Gender, like the weather, is everywhere and yet we seldom notice or discuss it until it manifests as something out of the ordinary.

Children who are gender nonconforming know they are breaking the rules even when they don't understand why the rules exist. You can become your child's ally by cutting through their confusion and isolation about gender and opening yourself up to their questions and explorations. Appreciate and enjoy your child's creativity when it comes to gender. Try looking at the world through their fresh, young eyes and see what you've missed. Relax in the fun they have with gender. Allow yourself to laugh at their ability to play with gender and not take it as seriously as adults do. Know that gender for children can be fluid, magical, transient, and malleable. Let your child help you replace the fear you have about gender with the exploration they bring to it. Think back to your own childhood and how you felt about this mysterious social construct we call gender.

Safety Planning

Plan for the safety needs of your gender nonconforming or transgender child. Affirming their feelings and preferences while negotiating when and where they can wear cross-gender clothing or use a new name is crucial in ensuring their safety.[41] Supporting your child's sense of self while protecting them from ridicule and bullying requires walking a fine and movable line. As children grow, they begin to assert themselves about what they'll eat, when they'll sleep, when they'll pick up their toys, and other areas of their lives they feel ready to control. Just as you help them consider actions and consequences in these everyday areas of life, apply similar guidelines for gender expression. Help your child understand that others may not comprehend or accept their gender identity or expression. They are not to blame for the attitudes and behaviors of others, but you want them to stay safe. Set limits as needed to ensure the emotional and physical safety of young children. Help older children consider how best to stay safe while staying true to themselves. These are lessons that will serve them throughout their lives.

There will be times when you need to speak with daycare providers, school personnel, medical professionals, and others on behalf of your child. You will probably be surprised and relieved by how supportive some people are. You may also be surprised by how little most people know about gender identity development and the experience of being transgender. You may have had little knowledge or awareness yourself until your child began to educate you. You will probably find yourself educating others with what you are learning.

Some people may have questions that seem ignorant or insensitive when they are honestly intended to gain more information. Other people, however, may have judgmental and hurtful biases with no intention of changing their perspective. Prejudice is communicated in overt ways through words and actions as well as covert ways through body language and ostracism. If there is someone with this mindset who has decision-making power over how your child will be treated in school or any other setting, speak with their supervisor and move your child to a more supportive environment.

Learn what your state's policies are with regard to creating safe schools, and how bullying and intolerance is addressed at the local level. Find out whether school personnel are required to be trained in creating a safe and supportive environment for LGBTQ students and other minorities. If training is required, find out who does it, who attends, and how often it is held. If training is not required, advocate for professional education for all school staff. Connect with a local chapter of PFLAG (Parents, Families, and Friends of LGBTQ People) to meet other parents who can help you advocate for your child and others like him or her. See the Resources and Support section in Appendix C for websites with legal advice for advocating for the safety rights of our LGBTQ children.

Family Backgrounds

There are family, cultural, and religious perspectives that may impact gender development. I have wondered about the effect of Kendra's biracial identity on her gender identity. Did her close identification with Tony around race impact her gender identity? She obviously noticed that the two of them shared something that few others did in her immediate surroundings and she bonded with him. She didn't like being one of the only people of color because it made her stand out. Once when my sister Donna visited she took Kendra to a playground and came back infuriated. Kendra had tried to engage some other children but they just stared at her and then shunned her even after she made several overtures. Donna stormed in the door, saying not only had we moved to an all-white community, it was an all-blonde community. She lived in the Washington, D.C., area so she found the demographics where we lived striking in their homogeneity.

Had there been more women of color in Kendra's life on a regular basis might her gender identity have formed differently? Unfortunately she didn't spend enough time when she was young with either grandmother on Tony's side of the family to form an attachment. When she was older, Kendra herself wondered if this was a factor in her being transgender by stating, "I suppose a theory could be that since my dad and I were both minorities, I closely associated with him." From the research cited in Chapter One it's clear that the building blocks of gender identity are laid down long before we even meet our children. Kendra's emerging racial identity might have impacted her gender identity but it's unlikely to have been decisive. I too felt the impact of the multiracial composition of our family. We already stood out in our community and having a gender nonconforming child made it even more difficult to blend in. Perhaps I would have been a more outspoken advocate for Kendra had I not already felt like an outsider.

Cultural and religious traditions can also influence perspectives on gender identity and sexual orientation. Comments and behaviors of acceptance or judgment signal to children how safe it is to ask questions and explore their feelings about gender. Reflect on your own background, experiences, and environment. What has influenced your feelings and responses to your gender nonconforming or transgender child?

Questioning Our Parenting

My first feelings about Kendra's gender nonconformity were embarrassment and dismay over how adamant and obstinate my child was and how powerless I was in my attempts to change that. I longed to see my little girl wear the dresses her women relatives sent her if even just for a photograph. There can a secret narcissism for some mothers in showing off our daughters in ruffles and lace. Kendra would have none of it and I worried the women in our family of my mother's generation faulted me. Why didn't I demand obedience? What was wrong with me? If I couldn't get my daughter to comply with something as easy as wearing a dress, what other limits was I incapable of setting?

A child's gender nonconformity can call into question our feelings of competence as parents—especially first-time parents. I wished I could ask my mother's advice. She often had a straightforward, effective solution like the time my sister Donna had difficulty sleeping because she had nightmares about fire. My mom went out and bought her a fire extinguisher to keep beside her bed. I searched to no avail for a solution that simple.

There is a long tradition in the mental health field of blaming and diagnosing parents when boys act like girls and girls like boys. Traditional norms hold that mothers teach daughters how to dress, do their hair, and care for dolls while fathers teach sons how to throw a ball, ride a bike, and not to cry when they fall. When children refuse to learn gender-specific developmental milestones, it is we parents who are judged as failures.

Parents of gender nonconforming children can become targets of attack from all sides: professionals in medicine, education, social service, religion, the general public, even members of our own families. Some question our motives for allowing nonconforming gender expression, others question our sanity, and all question our parenting. It's no surprise then that many of us feel ashamed about our inability to properly coach our child thereby protecting them from a lifetime of ridicule. The parent with the same assigned gender may feel a particular burden.

We can internalize these judgments by feeling guilty that we somehow contributed to the problem by giving our child mixed messages about gender. Historically, mothers of feminine sons were accused of being over protective or smothering in their love while fathers were blamed for emotional distance or being absent from the home, giving mothers too much control. Instead of being supported in our parenting we have traditionally been viewed as perpetrators of our child's gender dysphoria often by the very professionals from whom we seek help. This guilt is compounded by the fact that gender nonconforming and transgender children often face a hostile world. We parents might blame ourselves for creating a lifetime of danger and risk for our child.

Guilt and blame are paralyzing emotions. They block growth and forward motion. Trying to ascribe cause, when there is as yet so little actually known about how gender identity develops, only consumes energy best used elsewhere. I spent some early weeks attributing Kendra's gender nonconformity to the prenatal hormones she was bathed in for nine months, tainted I was certain, by my grief over the loss of my mother. Then there was the prolonged natural birth I might have done without, opting instead for a quick Cesarean section. I felt guilty for what I missed, ignored, or denied; for how long it took me to notice the clues that my child was struggling with gender identity.

We do ourselves a favor when we resist the temptation to ascribe cause. Who knows why our unique children are who they are? It's nothing we did or didn't do so why does it matter? What matters instead is figuring out how to navigate the uncharted waters of supporting our child's drive to express her or his inner self while preparing for the fact that this may cause estrangement or worse from others. This can be especially challenging during adolescence when belonging is as essential to our child's health and wellness as the air they breathe.

Self-Talk

Seeing how different our children are can be frightening so we may try to avoid what we see or name it something else. Because of the pain and fear these feelings evoke, some of us seek refuge in denial. We tell ourselves it's just a phase; it will pass; it's no big deal. I took pride in all the ways Kendra was her own person. I admired her courage in defying social norms and her commitment to self-expression and though I sometimes found it threatening or concerning, I interpreted it in ways I could embrace. I imagined her a nascent feminist; becoming a self-assured woman unconcerned with externals and the trappings of feminine fashion; at home with herself and in her own body; a strong woman; a role model; a visionary and leader. I saw her with traits I honored and admired in adult women.

Thoughts of what this might mean included: "It's a phase she'll outgrow; she'll always be her own person; I'll never have to worry she'll succumb to peer presssure"; or "She'll be a lesbian," but never "She's really a boy." I saw my little girl as unique, stubborn, independent, and nonconforming. I couldn't have known then that she would one day long for a different body, a boy's body. Unbeknownst to me, Kendra was also noticing her difference from peers and asking her own questions about what exactly this meant about her, her friends, the present, and the future.

Your Other Children

Notice how your children relate to one another. Older children can influence younger children because of their age. Extroverted children can have more control in a family because they are better communicators. Gender conforming children can hold center stage because they have the confidence of peer support and being in the majority. All of these dynamics can contribute to how well siblings respect, accept, and support one another when there are differences. Mitigating sibling rivalry by attempting to give each child equal attention and influence in a family is challenging enough, and a transgender or gender nonconforming child can easily tip the balance.

Helping both your gender conforming and nonconforming children learn to respect and accept one another's gender expression and differences without teasing, censoring, or attempting to change the other is critical. For example, does your older, gender nonconforming child set the stage for your younger children making them feel apologetic or ashamed of their gender conformity? Does your gender conforming child overtly or covertly tease or bully a nonconforming sibling? Does your extroverted, gender nonconforming child soak up all the family's attention? Or are they withdrawn, isolated, and depressed, so that your gender conforming children feel overly protective, responsible, or anxious for their well-being?

As with any special needs child, it is easy to spend more time and attention on the unique needs of your gender nonconforming or transgender child, sometimes, though unintentionally, at the expense of your other children. Telling all your children that you love them and spending time with each child, can help assure them that they are loved and important, and their needs will be met.

3

Asking Questions

As Free as a Child

I am not a responsible adult
I am a kid
that still likes
trying to break the laws of gravity,
trying to walk on water,
trying to start a snowball fight.

I do not like to clean my room.
I like getting dirty
and standing outside when it is raining.

I like playing tag.
I like swimming and
diving under to see who can lift the largest rock
from the bottom of the pond.

But these days must end sometime.
I wish I could be careless and free forever.

KENDRA, AGE 12

RECOLLECTIONS

Gender Presentation

Even though boys can't wear dresses while girls can wear pants, Kendra was well aware at the ripe old age of five that girl pants and boy pants were worlds apart. I don't remember how old she was when we started clothes shopping in the boy's department. She was probably eight or nine. The fact that it never made it into my journal means it didn't really concern me, which is one of the differences for parents of girls who are gender nonconforming vs. boys. Jaws drop when boys want to dress like girls but reactions like this don't occur until puberty when girls want to dress like boys.

It made perfect sense why the clothes in the girl's department felt foreign to Kendra's sense of self. The pink, form fitting cuts, white Disney faces, spaghetti straps, sequins, and sparkles, were from a different world than the one she inhabited. There was simply no way she'd wear any of it and I couldn't blame her. Every so often we tried more gender-neutral places like Sears but those clothes weren't youthful, so boy's clothes worked best. The pants were baggy, comfortable, and fun with plenty of pockets for collecting things and zippers that turned pant legs into shorts and quickly back into pants again as the weather and hiking conditions demanded. The shirts were harder to sort through if fighting and weapons didn't appeal but often there were simple T-shirts with active animals in vibrant colors. Nothing for girls was as practical, durable, and versatile.

For years Kendra's long, shaggy mane of dark curly hair was her signature, a symbol of her untamable spirit. She sometimes tied it under her chin pretending to have a beard like Abraham Lincoln. I usually cut her hair but one day when she was about ten we ventured out for a professional trim. Business was slow so the hairdresser decided to style her hair after the cut. Using a curling iron she tamed the waves into ringlets telling Kendra how pretty she was and asking about boyfriends. I sensed a slow burn in Kendra and wondered why she didn't protest.

As soon as we made our exit, Kendra threw herself on the floor in the backseat of the car afraid someone might see her. She ranted. The lady was stupid; the hairstyle dumb; she hated boys; never wanted a boyfriend; and why did I take her there in the first place? I hadn't spoken during the incident despite suspecting she hated what was happening. I still harbored hope that Kendra would conform; that she would eventually dress, groom, and act like a girl. As unlikely as this was, based on everything I knew, I dreamed she would one day look into the mirror and be happy with what she saw.

As Kendra screamed in the car my heart sank. This was her emphatic, "No!" not only to the hairdo but also to me. "Stop waiting for me to come around to your image of me. Stop putting me in situations that deny who I am. Stop hoping that some seed will be planted that will grow me into your dream daughter." The force of her fury and defiance frightened me. Something deep in her had been violated that day but neither of us could name it.

Now I can. My wishful thinking that this was a phase she'd outgrow kept me always on the lookout for clues that the tide was about to turn. It kept me watchful for every opportunity to subtly expose her to more feminine ways of being. I was careful to keep these thoughts to myself lest she sense a lack of support. But I cannot deny my internal longing and hidden agenda. This misplaced hope interfered with my ability to support and protect Kendra in circumstances like this. It was two against one in that beauty salon and Kendra knew it. I might have stepped in; checked with Kendra to see if she wanted her hair styled; created an opening for her to say "No! That's not me." It would have signaled to Kendra it was okay to refuse; that I was on her side. Instead I stood back and let a stranger try to mold this unique, self-defined child into our image of girlness.

In the car I saw how angry and alone, how violated Kendra felt by the expected rituals of feminine preening that loomed on her horizon. Of all the people in her life, she wanted me, her mother, to understand and defend her. But I'd crossed over and joined all the other voices urging her to stifle her true self and conform to gender norms. I tried to make amends. I assured her we'd go right home so she could jump in the shower and get her hair back to normal. I drove the mile and a half as fast as I could trying to distance us from my own duplicity. I told her about the time my mother took me to her hairdresser and I came out looking like a forty-year-old sixth grader; how it took weeks for my hair to grow out. But this was much bigger than that and we both knew it. Kendra, ever gracious and forgiving back then, let me squirm away from my guilt. After her shower, we talked and laughed as though nothing earth-shattering had happened. But it was the first tiny fissure between us and it was about to expand.

Peers

I encouraged Kendra to try activities outside of school to help her discover new interests. She resisted every group activity imaginable, from Sunday school to sports. She even disliked the rinky-dink circus that came to town because of the scary clowns, the chained animals, and the noisy crowd. Coaxing Kendra to join a group of peers while she clung and begged me not to leave was embarrassing. At parties or events I stayed until she felt more comfortable, then waved goodbye for a stealthy retreat. Swimming was the one activity where my encouragement paid off and I was eventually exonerated for leaving her poolside in tears because she grew to love swimming. My desire that she walk confidently away from me with little more than a wave was for my own assurance that she was stable and self-confident. Had I been more attuned to her feelings of difference due to gender and race in addition to being naturally introverted, I might have sought smaller groupings of like-minded children for her to spend time with.

The summer before fourth grade I persuaded her to attend a two-week day camp when she learned a friend was going. "It's just like school only more fun right?" she asked the night before, trying to quell her last minute jitters. "It's just like recess all day right?" She wondered if she could draw and do anything she wanted. That helped her regroup after being with people all day. The next day Kendra stepped onto the Frog bus wearing her backwards, red Chicago Bulls hat, matching pants, and sweatshirt. She sat in front and waved goodbye. The bravery she mustered made me proud and sad that it should be so hard. Exciting simple outings for other children were daunting undertakings for her. I was the one in tears that day walking home from the bus stop. Kendra attended camp three out of ten days. The day she spent with her friend was the best; the day at the water park the worst, mostly because of the long, loud bus ride. Her last day that first week she got off the bus empty-handed— no backpack, sweatshirt, bathing suit, towel, lunchbox—nothing. She knew we'd go back to get her things so she showed me around. There were spooky signs on trees in the woods and kids told scary stories. Kendra was frightened of cemeteries, spirits, and death so the dark woods and macabre stories scared her. Now that I had seen the place myself, I got it. She didn't return the second week.

Unlike many gender nonconforming children, Kendra formed few friendships with opposite gender peers. She noticed that boys, not girls, did more of the things she enjoyed. She asked why boys made huge and elaborate sand castles and played in the woods more than girls. And she was more apt to challenge herself physically when she played with boys. But she was still more emotionally at home around girls. Maybe it was because she wasn't accepted as one of the boys. Had she presented as a boy she might have formed more friendships with boys.

Her shyness was compounded by being one of only a few children of color in the community. Anthony, a multiracial boy that lived nearby, was her friend for a while but she eventually complained that he played boys' games and was too rough. Every day from first grade through fifth she brought her lunch to school because she refused to stand in the lunch line and walk across the cafeteria for fear the other children would stare at her. Maybe they did—I never really knew. It was her perception and therefore her reality. She was different and others noticed, which made her feel self-conscious and uncomfortable when blending in was important to her.

Tony and I tried to combat the racial isolation she felt by participating in Tony's local family gatherings, traveling to Trinidad, reading books, and watching movies where people of color were prominent but none of these impacted her day-to-day experiences. We countered some of the gender stereotypes she was observing by pointing out the ways girls and women were involved in the world. Again, books, movies, and conversations were a good start in addition to her seeing how gender stereotypes were broken every day in our own family. Tony shopped and cooked; I managed the finances; we both pursued our careers; we both enjoyed camping, swimming, gardening, biking, and we worked together on home renovation projects.

Kendra sought friends who loved animals and enjoyed playing outdoors. She was elated when, in first grade, she found just such a friend. They walked hand in hand in the Halloween parade to the nearby nursing home, Kendra dressed as a cheetah and her friend as a princess. When this girl moved, Kendra reported that once again she had no friends. She started a cats club that had a rivalry with girls who loved dogs. Kendra considered dog lovers followers, willing to please, and conform; while cat lovers were independent, creative, and self-defined. Other cat loving girls were happy to take her lead. Eventually she decided not to confine herself to just one group of friends.

Every summer we looked forward to a week away at my Aunt Roz and Uncle Dave's beach house. Our friends Lisa and John joined us for a few days most summers with their daughter Clara, who was one year younger than Kendra. The two of them had a special bond. Each was as zany and imaginative as the other. They loved creating funny costumes, playing on the deck in their bathing suits when it rained and hanging out together in the tiny playroom hideaway. They were happy, carefree, and confident. As they got a little older we let them paddle the canoe themselves when the tide was low and we could wade out to them. They especially loved skinny-dipping in the fresh water pond nearby. Once, just as they'd gotten their suits off, a boy came to swim with goggles. They panicked, certain he could see them through the murky water so I walked out with their suits and they struggled into them while swimming and giggling. When Clara left that summer Kendra cried and wouldn't go anywhere they'd been because everything reminded her of Clara. She badly needed a best friend, someone she could rely on and have fun with. Her confidence was buoyed, however, having handled the canoe on her own and when we returned home she was more self-assured in the pool we often visited. She loved running off the side, her long lanky legs looking like she could pedal across the water to the other side. She was becoming more physical with new determination and delight on her face.

Parties

Birthday parties were especially challenging. Kendra came home disappointed when extroverted friends invited large numbers of kids to a party. For her, loud gatherings were exhausting when she looked forward to one-on-one time with her friend. Her ambivalence about parties increased rather than decreased over time. She'd get excited about going, imagine having fun, choose the perfect gift, and then refuse to go in when we got to the door. The other girls didn't understand her behavior and sometimes feelings got hurt when she wouldn't stay. She seldom did sleepovers and found girl talk and interests boring. And yet her sensitive spirit and lack of interest in sports didn't make her a natural with boys either.

Most of Kendra's birthday parties were at our house. One year Curious Creatures came with a variety of unusual animals including a cute little hedgehog and giant albino snake that wrapped around the children's shoulders. For her tenth birthday we loaded up the car with four girlfriends and drove to a community farm. They made their own movie of the day's activities: feeding baby goats from a bottle, handfuls of grass to the cows, chasing butterflies, playing on the playground, and feeding birds from their hands. They sang at the top of their lungs, whether they knew the words or not, all the way home and said it was the best party ever. At home there was pizza, running through the yard, and a communal bath that included comparing breasts. After ice cream and cake it was time to watch their movie. The dizzying speed and crazy angles made it hilarious so they relived their favorite parts over and over, laughing until their sides ached. Kendra never tired of them despite the party lasting nearly twenty-four hours. These girlfriends seemed totally free with one another. Their sense of adventure, passion for animals, outrage over fenced-in places, and exuberance over their own creativity was inspiring. They were at home in their bodies. I loved their wild abandon and hoped they could keep it during the years ahead. It was at times like these, despite her boy's pants and baggy shirts, Kendra seemed all girl.

Age 6

School

Kendra asked to be home-schooled at the end of fourth grade. When she was younger she was able to bridge friendships with girls from various groups, even including a few boys, but the older she got the more challenging she found peer relationships. There were girl cliques she couldn't navigate and she felt isolated and alone. Gender identity was the backdrop but it hadn't come into focus yet. Again, had she been a boy, her gender nonconformity would have sent out alarms by now.

Home-schooling was not an option since Tony and I both worked, nor did we think avoiding peers altogether a good solution, so we started searching for a new, smaller school for sixth grade. While visiting the school we chose, students were friendly, even vying for her to sit with them at lunch. When asked what would have happened to a guest at her current school she said, "They'd let you sit by yourself and ignore you at first. Then they'd start laughing at you for sitting all alone." She was skeptical of so much friendliness at the new school and wondered if she could trust it. Other reasons for the change included strong academic curriculum, a longer school day, first name basis with teachers and plenty of teacher-student interaction due to small class size. A more diverse student body and faculty would have been perfect but that involved a long commute. There were two other students of color in Kendra's class of eighteen so that was an improvement over where she had been. All students were required to participate in sports, theater, art, and music in addition to core academic classes so by normalizing electives students were forced to try new experiences. An especially appealing feature for Kendra was its rustic campus. Students got to go outside since their classes were in different buildings.

But no sooner had Kendra been accepted, we learned that every Monday was "dress day" where girls were required to wear skirts or dresses, and boys, dress pants and collared shirts. It was nearly a deal breaker. My solution was to make culottes and a matching vest out of leopard print velour. The first Monday Kendra's tutor/advisor told her the outfit didn't conform to the dress code. Kendra went into a tirade since she was already having doubts about the place by then. Fortunately the school gave in and Kendra wore that outfit every single Monday for the four years the school imposed dress day. By the time she reached high school, they wisely dropped the restrictive tradition.

The first day of school was predictably difficult for Kendra who was not a fan of change. It felt like every other first—resisting and refusing on her part; negotiation, persistence, deep breathing, and exasperation on mine. By the time we arrived her class was already sitting outside in a circle. We walked out into the yard and Kendra, to my horror, took one look at the circle and walked right past it, across the yard, and sat under a tree near the driveway. I followed after Kendra, not sure what I'd do when I caught up with her, when her tutor/advisor rescued me and told me she'd take it from there. Grateful and relieved, I waved goodbye and slunk toward my car.

Separations tore at me. Would they ever get easier? What would help Kendra feel she belonged somewhere? As tears started to flow, a mother I knew called to me. "It gets easier," she said. "She'll be fine here." That helped. I struggled to see the road as I drove to the office making a quick costume change between scenes, from mother brought to her knees, to woman in charge at work.

When I picked Kendra up she was happy. She was with a girl who became her first new friend. On the ride home I asked when she finally joined the circle.

"Oh, I never did," she said.

"You didn't?" I asked. "What happened? I thought your tutor was going to take you to the circle."

"She was, but we talked for a while and then she asked the circle to move to where I was. It was nicer out on the grass anyway," she said.

That left a great first impression. What could've been an embarrassing first day was handled very tactfully I thought. Kendra didn't seem to feel the least bit embarrassed by the incident.

In mid-October the school sponsored a Grandparents' Day and my dad and his sister, Roz, attended. It was a crisp fall morning and the school was festooned with maroon and yellow chrysanthemums, bright orange pumpkins on hay bales, and autumn leaves decorating windowsills. Despite the festive ambiance, Kendra was aloof and withdrawn when I arrived with her guests. I was disappointed she didn't show more warmth and enthusiasm toward her Grandpa and Great Aunt since both had traveled some distance to join her on this special day. Guests were invited to participate in discussion groups with a faculty advisor and students ranging from sixth grade through twelfth. Kendra wore her oversized, yellow and navy down jacket into the classroom and slumped in her seat, drawing her head turtle-like, into its high collar. She nearly disappeared, quietly and effectively avoiding any connection to her surroundings. Roz noticed this and suggested therapy but my dad disagreed. He likely saw himself in Kendra, his social skills much like hers. In fairness to her, she'd missed more than half of the meetings with her tutorial those first few weeks of school due to illness. Plus she was one of the youngest students in the group. I knew it was going to take more than a couple of weeks for Kendra to become comfortable speaking her mind in a group she hardly knew. But I hadn't expected her to become invisible.

Elementary school

Refusal

Long before puberty struck Kendra, I wrote a poem for her about the passage to womanhood. Even though I fully anticipated the crisis this would evoke for her, I never connected it to gender identity. By rooting the experience in nature I hoped it might lessen the blow. She was still running topless on the beach in boy's shorts when I wrote it. She and I both longed for a magical world where time stopped so she could remain her wonderfully wild, androgynous self. I feared the bondage she'd feel covering her free heart with clothing. I hoped that by the time puberty hit, she would've outgrown her disdain for all things female.

Menarche, for Kendra

Your lithe, sleek brown body
    carefree, strong, sufficient
    unself-conscious, unashamed
a vehicle for action and expression
    your own to use and move
    to rest and dress however you wish
On a journey toward an abyss, perhaps
    an uncharted pathway
    it's whatever you decide

As if by magic, when the time is right
    your body and the sun and moon take a turn
    budding nipples like the first growth from the
        smooth land
Life blood like the waters of the earth
    ebbs and flows and you are called by earth herself
    to embody her to hold her image

A tall order for a young girl
  one you can grow into if you will
Though the impulse all around you is to run—
  now even your body seems against you

Yet in truth if you let her
  your body is your one true guide
  your first and only lover
Trust in her attend to her
  learn her language and
  together find your path
Revile her ignore her clues and
  batter yourself or permit this of others
  chasing mirages of you
Beware distractions
  mirrors, scales, boys
  clothes, hair, skin
What sense is pulling up a seedling to smell the flower?
  this cocoon time is for inward looking
  nature spirits and animal guides

Join the animals who like you
  know the season for building, breeding, birthing
  as well for storing, resting, letting die what has passed

Participate and celebrate the turning of the wheel
  welcome to the sacred journey
  from the magic of childhood
  to the mysteries of womanhood
The heavens move to bless you
  a reflection of beloved earth herself
The animals call you sister
  and embrace you as their own

CANDACE, 1998

We stood on opposite sides of this shore; me beckoning for her to cross, waiting to enfold her in the protective circle of women with kindred spirits; Kendra balking, unable to cross but knowing she couldn't stay where she was. I longed to coax her, hoping to make the passage palatable. I considered making a jacket to wrap her in love and affirmation with memories from her past. Or give her a book of favorite poems and songs along with her own writings and drawings. I wanted to weave carefree threads of childhood into her emerging, unhappier adolescence. Maybe a handheld mirror with leopard or tiger stripes to help her take in her own beauty; look into her own wildness and love what she saw. I'd attended several coming of age celebrations with friends and their daughters and dreamed of sharing a similar experience with Kendra in some quiet but meaningful way, mother and daughter. But I slowly gave up my hope of any such ceremony.

I was not prepared for how devastated and hopeless Kendra felt when puberty finally arrived. She would not ever celebrate the body that so misrepresented and betrayed her. But where exactly did that leave her? My own woman-affirming, girl-empowering stance, once a means of protection now became a barricade between us, a symbol for each of our difference. Not yet in a land of her own, but decidedly unable to follow me, Kendra began to turn her back, refusing to speak, in silent retreat to find her own path. It was a painful and unexpected fork in our journey.

I knew Kendra was silently struggling and spent time with her hoping she might share her thoughts and worries. I interpreted her struggle as one of self-esteem, common in prepubescent girls, so I explored role models and expanded gender roles. Since she was not getting any female consciousness-raising from school or elsewhere I read extensively on how to raise a conscious, confident, resilient daughter. Kendra showed no interest in talking about girls' or women's issues and was drawing further inward. I wondered about counseling but wasn't sure who would be a suitable therapist or how to get Kendra to talk to a stranger. The physical changes of puberty were likely on her mind but whenever I tried talking about it she stormed out of the room saying the whole topic was gross and disgusting and she didn't want to discuss it now or ever. I told myself it was just her emerging sense of privacy about her body, but with no indication Kendra would ever make peace with the journey her body was traveling, I began to worry.

On our second family trip to Trinidad, Kendra began to pass as a boy. Trinidadians are often more forward in conversation than Americans, saying things like, "Girl, you put on some size since last time!" Kendra loved coconut water so we always went to the Savannah in Port of Spain. As the vendor cut off the top of a coconut with her machete she asked, "Is this a boy or a girl?" pointing to Kendra. "A girl," I replied. "She has a boy face," she said. Then at the airport on our way home the security guard asked, "Male or female?" as he herded us into gender-specific lines to be patted down. "Female," I said when he pointed to Kendra and he put her in the male line anyway. Tony and I shook our heads. What we didn't know was how happy Kendra felt about incidents like these. They gave her hope. She also loved whacking open coconuts with a machete on that trip so Tony bought her one of her own.

Acting

As shy as Kendra was in life, she discovered she loved acting on stage because, she said, she wasn't playing herself. I didn't fully understand what she meant at the time, but now I realize how hard it was becoming for her to continue playing the role of girl every day, and she was getting a lot of acting practice. In theater productions she enjoyed being with others in a creative, imaginary, outside of herself way, working together on a shared goal, anticipating opening night.

> *A dream that I had for this year was to get a lead role or get an award or just be good at something and enjoy it. I got to be Puck in our play . . . What more could I want!*

> *Being Puck was a great experience. It's not like being any other character in a play.*
>
> *The experience was somewhat magical and unexplainable. It was like a dream.*
>
> *I wasn't even nervous. If I could always be like that. . . .*

Kendra, age 13

The summer Kendra was fourteen she was under pressure to decide whether or not to go on a four-week class trip out of the country in the fall. Naturally Kendra was reluctant to go, but school personnel made it seem like a big mistake to miss it. Tony loved travel. He would have jumped at the opportunity when he was her age so he couldn't understand why Kendra didn't want to go. I understood her reservations since that was how she approached everything new, so I was as torn as she was. Kendra insisted she wasn't ready to be away from home for so long. She'd had a two-week trip with Tony that spring and was homesick by the end. She also didn't feel close with her class and didn't trust the faculty and chaperones to support her if she got homesick. These were all solid and perceptive reasons.

But we thought this experience might help her bond with her class and worried if she didn't go, it would only isolate her more. The school had numerous field trips, concerts, plays, athletic events, art shows, and sleepovers and Kendra had seemed to be right in the middle of things. By thirteen, however, maintaining friendships was becoming harder since she shared few interests with her peers. She'd agree to join in various events, but when the time came, she balked. Rather than hurting feelings by saying no, she just didn't show up, and invites dwindled. The older she got, the harder it was for her to fit in. Loneliness wrapped itself around her, and family couldn't take the place of friends. Increasingly, she filled this void by tending to her many pets. Under pressure from peers, her parents, and school, Kendra ultimately decided to go on the school trip.

The summer leading up to the trip Kendra seemed to be jettisoning her past to grow up and apart. None of what she'd considered fun interested her anymore and she grew difficult to be around, sullen and isolated in her own world of rap music. For years she loved caring for her pet iguana, Iggy, creating new habitats, walking with him on her shoulder, finding places for him to bask in the sun. In August Kendra left Iggy on the deck railing to get him food and he jumped off and ran away. Kendra never even looked for him. In fact, she seemed relieved to be free of him. As quickly as Iggy disappeared, my trusting daughter did too. Kendra was severing the bonds of her childhood, first with one of her beloved pets, then with me. Like Iggy, she was preparing to take a leap and never look back. Unlike Kendra, I was not prepared to let go so easily but that summer day was the harbinger of Kendra leaving behind her attachments of childhood.

Betrayal

It was also the summer Kendra got her period—her body's ultimate betrayal. I realize now that until then, she'd held onto the hope that by sheer mental force she could forever forestall the inevitable. But any fantasy she would magically turn into a boy—or at least stay an androgynous youth and not become a woman—was gone. While her peers were acclimating to the physical changes they'd anticipated, maybe even happily awaited, my daughter's body filled her with dread. She struggled with this realization alone, angry, and afraid. Nothing about becoming a woman felt right to her. She never even told me when she got her period. I noticed she needed a bra when I found my sports bra missing. Whenever I brought up anything remotely related to her body's changes, she recoiled, repulsed by the subject, and by me for mentioning it. It felt less intrusive and conflictual to let her approach me when she was ready, but she never did.

Everything has changed. She is taller than me and so slender. Her face is hidden, distant, her thoughts and attentions no longer include me. She is most alive outside no matter what the setting so I take us to our favorite beach hoping to bridge this chasm. Our once fluid, elemental connection is now awkward. She hides behind her adolescent mask of indifference. She is fourteen today and this place replays scenes from earlier years: Kendra loping like a gazelle, frolicking at water's edge her lanky appendages dancing in every direction, her spirit loose, carefree and happy.

We sit in silence overlooking the rolling sea. I dream of rolling back time. Maybe that is why the beach is so redemptive. It reminds me of second chances, starting over, leaving no previous trace. How many mothers dream of this? If only we could take back those harsh words, that oversight, missed opportunity, or bad decision. Unlike feet on sand, a mother's mark seems so permanent, potentially damaging and we, unlike the strong eternal sea, so fragile and fleeting.

She fidgets with what she has gathered in her hands: the tiniest of stones, smooth like bird eggs, a fragrant leaf, a feather. Her connection to earth is her salvation and I take comfort in that. If that is all I do, place her in a setting where she now finds her own way, my job is part way done. As mother to this particular daughter at this particularly painful time, I place her in the presence of the universal mother—perceptible in this place of beauty.

The dog that greeted us earlier runs to a middle-aged couple walking languidly by water's edge. They call to him and he comes running. His body registers delight at the sight of them even as they grasp his collar and leash him. When was the last time this child ran to me arms outstretched, and gleeful I wonder? So many last times pass, unmarked, til years later.

Just as Kendra was coming face-to-face with the heartbreak that her body and mind were on a collision course over gender, she was going off with a group of her peers whose bodies were likely congruent with their hearts and minds. She'd be staying with strangers without the support of family and the safety of home. There was a Halloween party at school the week before the trip and true to form, Kendra told me the night before that she needed a costume. We managed to find a King Arthur costume last minute. She was surprised and elated to win second prize—for being a man—a king at that!

Lost

Kendra's irritability during the weeks leading up to the trip should've been clues for me that every bone in her body was telling her not to go. She became increasingly volatile, hostile, uncooperative, and withdrawn. She refused to waste time preparing so I did all the shopping and packing. At the last minute she'd insist on something urgent—like getting her hair cut—and became furious when it wasn't cut short enough. A glimmer of enthusiasm came when she got letters from her host family or imagined some of the outings planned and I grasped those shreds of eagerness and prodded her along.

"It hasn't hit me yet that I'm going to be gone for a month. I think I'll just take it one day at a time," she said as we drove to the airport. Her philosophical approach was impressive. She'd succeeded in getting herself ready, I thought. She was calm, cheerful, and funny as we listened to her favorite music. She gave me a heartfelt hug at the terminal and I knew that we both were learning to let go. My stomach was in knots over how she would fare as she fell in with her friends, her class. We were proud of her for taking this risk and she seemed up to it. When she looked back, it was not to assure herself she'd be okay it was to assure herself I'd be okay. It was in her eyes, the look on her face.

We heard from Kendra Saturday morning when she called to say they'd arrived safely. She was with friends and sounded tentative, like she couldn't really talk. She was happy with her room and relieved to be done traveling. We spoke on Sunday and again all seemed fine. On Wednesday I got a voicemail on my cell phone I couldn't make out. It was muffled and distant. Then it hit me. Kendra was speaking in a whisper. I played the message over a few times before realizing there were two! I was on the road and didn't even have her host family's number with me. What could've happened? She sounded urgent, pleading, and desperate. Then Tony called. She'd called him too and said she was homesick. She was not in danger—just sad, lonely, and missing us. He spoke with her for a while and told her he'd call me.

When I finally got her on the phone she sobbed: "I wasn't ready. I shouldn't have come. I got talked into it. I knew I wasn't ready." The sharp truth of her words pierced my heart. I knew she was right. She had tried to tell us. We did talk her into it and she was outnumbered from the start. And now she was across an ocean and I felt powerless to help her. What I didn't comprehend at the time was not only was she on her own in a strange country, she was feeling estranged from her body, isolated from peers, and alone in the world.

We spoke every day—at night when her host family was sleeping. "I need to come home. Please save me Mom. Get me out of here. I have no friends. There is no one I can talk to. I miss you and Dad and home. I miss my room, the food I like, Dad's cooking, pumpkin seeds," she said. "No one else is homesick. They all talk about how they don't miss their parents. I wasn't okay when you called, I was holding it in. I've never been away from home this long. I can't stay a whole month. I'm in a city and there's no yard, no nature, only one tree. I wanted to be in the country. I want to be home by Thanksgiving. I need to be home by Thanksgiving. It's a really important holiday. I've never felt so thankful before. Don't go Mom. I need to talk to you. It makes it better. Call me tomorrow."

The voice on the phone, sad, scared, strangled, and so far away, was shattering to hear. Kendra was proud. Vulnerability was something she worked hard to hide so this was a crushing defeat to feel so broken. I longed to reach through the phone and grab her to me and not let her go. I broke down the trip into manageable pieces thinking once she got closer to Thanksgiving she'd realize she could make it the whole way. I also explored airfare to either bring her home early or go there myself to see her. I was concerned about how she'd feel in either case since she was keeping up a stolid front in public.

She was more communicative and open on the phone than she ever was in person. She was afraid something would happen to me; that I might die before she saw me again. I assured her I was fine and would be waiting here for her when she got home. It felt like our bond was strengthening during our long nighttime phone calls. While I painted her room one night she told me she'd gotten lost and was missing for over two hours! Her host family was waiting for her at their veterinarian's office because they knew she was interested in seeing how they practiced veterinary medicine there. She'd been looking forward to that appointment for days but never made it. She'd gotten on the wrong bus and managed to find her way home just as her family was about to call us to say she was lost!

"How did you realize you were on the wrong bus?" I asked.

"There were fewer buildings and then some fields so I knew I was leaving the city instead of going across it," she said.

"Were you able to ask for directions?" I asked.

"Sort of. Marie's mom had written down their address so once I got back to where I took the wrong bus, I showed the address to the bus driver and he pointed to the right bus."

"It's great you were able to find your way back by yourself," I said. "Were you scared? Did you want to scream or cry like I do when I'm lost?"

"I wanted to but there were too many people on the bus. I just chewed on my bus pass and the cuff of my sweatshirt," she said.

"What shirt were you wearing?" I asked.

"The black one with cats," she said.

"I can't believe you were lost in a foreign country!" I said. "I am so sorry that happened to you honey and glad you found your way back. You've always been aware of your surroundings and have a good sense of direction so that came in handy."

"Yeah," she laughed.

"That's a big deal—finding your way around in a foreign country at only fourteen years old. Has anyone else in your class gotten lost?"

"Not this time but someone got lost even worse than I did a couple of years ago so now it's one of the stories they always tell," she said.

"Have you told your class about what happened?" I asked.

"Yeah, we all laugh about it now," she said.

"Thank God it's over. It's only funny when it's over. And thank God Marie's mom didn't have to call me to say you were missing! I would've freaked right out!"

Kendra learned she had strong survival instincts that would help her in life but still, every time I think of her lost and alone, in more ways than one, sitting on that bus chewing the cuff of her sleeve I could cry. My need to touch her, wrap my arms around her, and not let go for a long, long time grew with each day as her homecoming got closer. Finally, on December 5 in the middle of a blizzard we waited with other families at Terminal E in Boston for our children to arrive, grateful the flight wasn't cancelled.

Clearing customs took forever but then I finally saw her. When she came through the door I burst into tears, awash with joy and relief. But Kendra walked toward me distant, cold, and aloof. As other families enjoyed long, heartfelt embraces, kissing, jumping up and down and shrieking with delight, our daughter barely hugged or greeted us. She was detached and impassive, like we were picking her up from just another day at school. I told myself it was just her way of defending against feeling or showing any weakness or vulnerability. Of course she was happy to see us, to finally be home. She'd just show it later. But I later realized instead of me dying while she was gone, part of her died and never came home after that long separation.

Chasm

As promised, I'd cooked a complete Thanksgiving dinner that night and our friends Joanna and Mike joined us. I'd forgotten it was about two in the morning for Kendra. She was too tired to join us for the festive, welcome home meal and instead went straight to bed. She slept the whole next day. She continued sleeping for nearly a week getting up briefly to give us the presents she brought back, to eat, or pet her cat, Sage. She seemed anything but elated to be home. At the end of two weeks she finally began talking about some of her experiences. Spending a month with her classmates, half of them girls, seemed to widen the chasm between her peers and herself.

She pulled out a new pair of fitted girls' pants while unpacking, along with a feminine shirt. A far cry from her usual baggy, boy's clothes.

"Did you go clothes shopping?" I asked.

"Yeah, two friends decided to give me a makeover and convinced me to buy these," she said.

Again I caught myself hoping. Had she finally turned the corner I'd been wishing for?

"I hate them. I never even wore them. I wish I'd never wasted my money when there were other things I could've bought," she said tossing the clothes at me.

"Want me to put them in the donation bag?" I asked, as if my hopes had not just been dashed. I was careful not to betray that I, like her friends, was an accomplice in the desire to see her accommodate to her assigned gender. Kendra had indeed come to some newfound awareness on her trip. But trapped behind my own blinders I was unable to see that the change was in a direction diametrically opposed to the one I was still hoping for.

The ground beneath us opened, and Kendra disappeared when she was fourteen. She had coped on the trip by building a fortress to hide behind, so by the time she got home she was angry, distrusting, exhausted, and practiced in fragmentation. She retreated

deep inside herself, closed the door, and dissociated like a person
with post-traumatic stress disorder. What I did not know at the
time was according to psychologist and author Diane Ehrensaft,
"When children's gender creativity is squashed, that can become
burdensome enough to be labeled a childhood trauma."[42] Having to
be inauthentic for so long a period was a traumatizing experience.

Kendra barely emerged from her room that winter, sleeping
for hours. She found solace in seclusion and caring for her pets.
Her passion had turned from cats to reptiles—turtles, lizards, and
geckos. She filled her days researching habitats and health issues
while deciding which ones to collect and breed. As if building a
magical kingdom for herself and her menagerie, she transformed
a corner of her tiny bedroom into a tropical paradise with a hand-
painted mural, exotic plants, waterfall, and turtle pond. Too old to
hide in costumes, she now hid in her room.

RESEARCH

Gender Identity vs. Sexual Orientation

Does gender nonconformity indicate my child will grow up to be gay, lesbian, bisexual, or transgender?

Gender identity is different from sexual orientation though they
are often confused. Because a high percentage of gender nonconforming children will grow up to be gay, early signs of gender
nonconformity are often assumed to be clues to a child's eventual
sexual orientation. But gender nonconformity is not indicative of
sexual orientation. Many gender nonconforming children do not
grow up to be gay and many children who are gender conforming
do become gay.[43]

Sex, gender, and sexual orientation are three separate aspects
of a person. Confusion by parents, the general public, and even our
language can hinder our ability to name the issue at hand so that

we can seek timely and appropriate help. Sex is a biological category based on reproductive physiology. Gender is a psychosocial construct used to classify a person as male, female, both, or neither. Sexual orientation is a feeling of attraction to others—romantic, emotional, physical, and sexual—defined by the sex of the person to whom one is attracted. These aspects of a person come in chronological order, with sex being first based on the observation of one's anatomy at birth. Gender comes second, when a child begins to assert his or her own feelings, thoughts, and expressions for how they perceive their sense of self. As has been discussed, gender is often congruent with sex but sometimes not. Sexual orientation manifests later, around puberty when a person begins to feel attracted to others.

Gender nonconforming children are expressing their *selves*. Their nonconforming expression is about who they *are*, not who they *like*.[44] Their identity and style of expression comes first; sexual orientation comes later. Jumping to conclusions that boys who are effeminate and girls who are tomboys will be attracted to same sex partners when they grow up focuses on the future without attending to the present. Before a child feels attracted to others, they first need to feel at peace with themselves; at home in their bodies. Parents may mistakenly dismiss the dissonance a young child is expressing if they assume indications of gender dysphoria today point to sexual orientation tomorrow.

Diagnosis

Does my child have "gender identity disorder" or "gender dysphoria"?

In 1980 the American Psychiatric Association included "gender identity disorder" (GID) in its *Diagnostic and Statistical Manual of Mental Disorders* (*DSM*) for the first time, to name the "disturbance" of not fitting the gender norms assigned to a person based on their birth sex. For the past three decades a diagnosis of gender identity disorder has been required for transgender people to access medical and mental health services related to their gender dysphoria. The diagnosis was also required for cross-gender hormone treatment and/or sex reassignment surgery, as well as access to what little health insurance coverage there is for transgender health services.

In the 1990s the diagnosis was used as a method of early intervention, labeling children and teens that were gender variant, and then engaging them in treatment methods intended to prevent them from becoming lesbian, gay, bisexual, or transgender. Treatment included behavior modification methods that rewarded children for gender conforming behavior; the removal of all toys associated with the opposite gender; conversion or reparative therapies; institutionalization; and electroshock treatment. Despite the lack of evidence that these methods were successful in their intended outcome, they prevailed for decades. Some therapists practice them to this day regardless of their being considered unethical by experts in transgender health.[45]

In response to these abuses of the GID diagnosis and the stigma attached to labeling one's gender identity "disordered," pressure from numerous professional fields as well as from transgender people and their allies resulted in changes in the *DSM-5* released in May 2013. "Gender identity disorder" was replaced with "gender dysphoria," emphasizing the dissonance a person feels when body and mind are incongruent. The diagnostic criteria for gender dysphoria in the *DSM-5* are summarized as follows:

Gender Dysphoria in Children
Gender dysphoria in children consists of an evident mismatch between a child's assigned gender and their affirmed gender for at least six months resulting in considerable distress or a reduction in their ability to function socially, in school, or in other areas of their lives.

The desire to be the other gender or insisting they are the other gender (or an alternative gender) must be shown in at least six of the following ways:

1. Preferring clothes of the other gender.
2. Playing the other gender in make-believe.
3. Preferring toys, games, and activities associated with the other gender.
4. Preferring to play with children of the other gender.
5. Rejecting toys, games, and activities associated with their assigned gender.
6. Dislike for their sexual anatomy.
7. Wanting the anatomy and physical characteristics of their affirmed gender.

Gender Dysphoria in Adolescents and Adults

Gender dysphoria in adolescents and adults is an evident mismatch between a person's assigned gender and their affirmed gender for at least six months resulting in considerable distress or a reduction in their ability to function socially, academically, occupationally, or in other areas of their lives and evidenced by at least two of the following:

1. A mismatch between one's expressed gender and their primary and/or secondary sex characteristics (or anticipated characteristics for prepubescent teens).
2. A desire to change or prevent one's sex characteristics because of their incongruence with one's affirmed gender.
3. Wanting the sex characteristics of the other gender.
4. Wanting to be the other gender (or an alternative gender).
5. Wanting to be treated as the other gender (or an alternative gender).
6. Believing that one has the feelings and reactions associated with the other gender (or an alternative gender).[46]

Not all gender nonconforming children experience gender dysphoria. Some children are perfectly comfortable in their gender but just find the culturally prescribed dress and roles of their gender too confining. Other children experience emotional distress including anxiety and depression due to their physical sex characteristics and prefer clothes, toys, and peers of the other sex. Childhood gender dysphoria does not always continue into adulthood. The few follow-up studies that have been done indicate that only about one-quarter of children with gender dysphoria will continue to experience these feelings as adults, whereas the persistence for adolescents with gender dysphoria appears to be much higher.[47] Adolescence is a pivotal period during which some will experience an intensification of the gender dysphoria they felt as children, while others experience gender dysphoria for the first time as secondary sex characteristics develop.[48]

If your child or teen exhibits the feelings or behaviors described in the gender dysphoria diagnosis it is wise to seek the assistance of a gender specialist to help you consider the next steps, if any. It is critical to find the right therapist since inexperienced clinicians may mistake gender dysphoria for delusions or underlying psychiatric illness[49] and some still hold misinformed and outdated theories about treating children with gender dysphoria. The treatment of choice today, based on outcome studies, is to depathologize the condition and allow the child to live as the gender they experience. Gender dysphoria is applicable mainly to the early stages of awareness that one is transgender. Affirming one's self-defined gender and partly or completely transitioning socially or physically can significantly mitigate the emotional anguish.[50]

Standards of Care and Gender Counseling

If my child has gender dysphoria when do I need to do something?

Gender counseling for your child is critical in helping you both sort out your child's feelings. The sooner you find the right therapist with whom your child, you, and your partner, if appropriate, can relate, the better. A competent gender therapist can help you and your child clarify the physiological and psychological issues related to gender dysphoria and can guide you both in your decisions about reversible and/or irreversible treatment options to resolve your child's feelings of discomfort.

The *Standards of Care for the Health of Transsexual, Transgender, and Gender Nonconforming People* (SOC), were developed in 1979 by the Harry Benjamin International Gender Dysphoria Association (HBIGDA). That organization has become the World Professional Association for Transgender Health (WPATH) and the SOC are currently in their seventh edition. The SOC provide time frames and guidelines for patients seeking treatment for gender dysphoria that include psychotherapy prior to hormone treatment or surgery. Individual and family counseling is recommended to explore gender identity and presentation; address the impact of gender dysphoria; enhance social and peer support; improve body image; and promote resilience. To guide you in the process of finding a trained professional, the SOC includes competency requirements for mental health professionals working with transgender children and teens, their appropriate role, and the components of a psychological assessment.

The SOC outlines the competency requirements for mental health professionals working with transgender people. Those working with children must meet competency requirements for working with adults, and in addition to being trained in childhood and adolescent developmental psychopathology, they must be competent in diagnoses and treatment of ordinary problems of children and adolescents.

What is the role of mental health professionals working with children and adolescents with gender dysphoria? [51]

- Mental health professionals trained in gender identity can assess gender dysphoria in children and adolescents.
- Provide family counseling and psychotherapy to assist children and adolescents to explore their gender identity and alleviate distress related to gender dysphoria.

- Assess and treat coexisting mental health issues (or refer to another mental health professional).
- Refer adolescents for additional physical interventions such as puberty suppressing hormones to alleviate gender dysphoria.
- Educate and advocate on behalf of gender nonconforming children, adolescents, and their families in the community since they can experience harassment that puts them at risk for social isolation, depression, and other negative outcomes.
- Provide information and referral for support groups for parents of gender nonconforming and transgender children.

Assessment and intervention for children and adolescents is often provided within a multi-disciplinary gender identity or LBGTQ specialty health center. If such a service is not locally available, the mental health professional should work with a pediatric endocrinologist experienced working with transgender children and adolescents to facilitate assessment and provide consultation about physical interventions.

What are the guidelines for psychological assessment of children and adolescents with gender dysphoria?[52]

- Mental health professionals should not dismiss or express negativity toward gender nonconforming identities or feelings of gender dysphoria but acknowledge the concerns of children, adolescents, and their families; provide comprehensive assessment for gender dysphoria and any other mental health issues; and educate clients and families about treatment options. Acceptance and openness can bring considerable relief to children and adolescents with gender dysphoria, and their families.
- Assessment should explore emotional functioning, peer and other social relationships, school achievement, strengths and weaknesses of family functioning as well as unresolved issues in a child or youth's environment.

- Assessment for adolescents should inform youth and their families of the possibilities and limitations of treatment since accurate information may alter a youth's desire for specific treatment if their desire was based on unrealistic expectations.

Prevalence

What are the chances my child is transgender and if so will they transition to the other gender?

Of all the conditions parents consider when expecting a baby, having a transgender child is usually not on the list. Because transgender individuals are seldom visible in society, many assume it is a rare phenomenon. But it's more common than one might assume. The Williams Institute at UCLA estimates that 3 out of 1,000 (or 1 in 333) people in America are transgender; approximately 700,000 people nationally. Other estimates range from 1 out of 1,000 (1:1,000) to 5:1,000.[53] Determining the number of people who then go on to transition in some way is a complicated matter. Prevalence data from ten studies over thirty-nine years in eight countries range from 1:11,900 to 1:45,000 for male-to-female individuals (MTF) and 1:30,400 to 1:200,000 for female-to-male (FTM) individuals.[54]

Prevalence estimates were first derived from the number of patients seeking sex reassignment surgery at gender clinics in several European countries when surgical procedures were just beginning. As more transgender people emerge and therapeutic interventions improve, these numbers continue to grow with 1:45,000 male-to-female individuals in 1980; 1:26,000 in 1983; 1:18,000 in 1986 and 1:11,900 in 1990.[55] Prevalence rates continue to rise with clinics in the United Kingdom doubling their cases every five or six years, and a pediatric clinic in Canada reporting a four- to five-fold increase in child and adolescent referrals over a thirty-year period.[56]

But estimates based on sex reassignment surgery undercount those who identify as transgender; those who seek other help for their transgender identity; those on hormone therapy; those who socially transition; and those who opt out of genital surgery. Since those undergoing genital surgery are probably the smallest of the groups to be considered, current prevalence numbers represent the lower limit for the number of people who are transgender. One of the reasons for the lower prevalence rates of female-to-male individuals may well be the high cost of genital surgery along with less than satisfactory results. Many transgender men have only chest surgery and are therefore not included in estimates.[57] One study suggests a conservative but more accurate estimate ranging from 1:2,000 to 1:4,500 for male-to-female individuals and 1:5,500 to 1:8,000 for female-to-male individuals.[58]

Prevalence matters from a biological standpoint since frequency of occurrence determines whether a condition is considered within the range of natural diversity or a disease. A genetic defect occurs in the population in the range of 1:50,000 births; a disease is in the range of 1:5,000 births; whereas a transsexual identity occurs in approximately 1:1,000 births removing it "from the realm of genetic defects into the realm of natural, normal, though uncommon, forms of human variation."[59] It's instructive for parents and those working with children and teens to be aware of this prevalence data since it indicates more people experience gender dysphoria than we might imagine. Being aware of the possibility that a child might be transgender as they grow up can inform what we notice in children and how we respond. It might also inform how tightly we hold onto the assigned gender of our children since that may be mistaken.

Transsexual and transgender people have always existed and will continue to do so. Advances in surgical techniques as well as the development of hormone treatment have enabled those wishing to alter their bodies to align with their affirmed gender to do so in ways that were previously impossible. The Internet has greatly expanded access to information about emerging treatment and facilitated the formation of online support networks, which have reduced the secrecy and isolation that transgender people often experience and expanded access to services that alleviate the painful dissonance that is experienced when body and mind are not aligned. As demand for services increases, so too do the number and expertise of professionals experienced in providing treatment.

But even before these recent developments, some societies defined gender more broadly than ours. In some Native American tribes there is historical evidence of third and fourth genders based not solely on anatomical sex but on "individual and social factors, such as occupational preference, behavior and temperament, religious experiences, and so forth."[60] Males who were gifted in or preferred work normally done by women and women who were gifted in or preferred work normally done by men did not become the other gender but were considered third and fourth genders. Though not required or universal, the most common marker was dressing as the preferred gender.[61]

Alternative genders were sometimes adopted as the result of dreams or visions, spiritually sanctioning them and assuring individuals a place of belonging within the tribe. Today's LGBT communities have revived these historic roles with "two spirit" identities. Two spirit is an inclusive and expansive term, embracing both men and women and evoking the positive qualities, roles, and practices historically associated with native cultures before colonization. It draws on the past to help us imagine a future beyond the gender binary.[62]

Alternative genders existed historically in many countries and cultures and some even survive today in Polynesia, Pakistan, India, and Southeast Asia. Gender transformation in religious roles is cited in Borneo, the Philippines, Korea, Vietnam, and Cambodia.[63] When there are only two gender identities possible—man and woman—the feelings, insights, and talents of people outside the gender binary are hidden and constrained. Valuing each individual and making room for everyone can create a stronger, more diverse culture.

REFLECTIONS

Listen

The most difficult exercise in unlearning we as parents of transgender and gender nonconforming children might have is overcoming the long-held parental convention that we know what's best for our children. Even with the best intentions, parents sometimes get it wrong. Thinking we're doing what's best for a child, we might be doing what's worst.

As soon as I heard Kendra's voice on that first phone call from her school trip, I regretted persuading her to go. From the beginning she'd said she wasn't ready to be away from home for that long and she was right. But we urged her to listen to everyone else instead of herself. It was what I'd done from time to time in my own life, but had wanted to teach my daughter differently. Despite my intention to raise a strong, confident daughter, I had inadvertently tutored Kendra in self-betrayal. I hadn't withstood the pressure of spouse and school to protect my daughter and it was a painful but powerful lesson.

The sooner we realize that sometimes our children are the best judges of what they need, and when we form trusting, listening partnerships with them, the fewer mistakes we are likely to make. Rather than feeling embarrassed, apologetic, or vulnerable to peer pressure, I needed to be more attentive to what Kendra was saying. As parents, we often draw upon our own experiences to guide our children as they grow up. But I did not grow up as a gender nonconforming or transgender child and therefore had no personal experience to draw from. Tony and I love to travel. Growing up on an island, Tony watched airplanes come and go and dreamed about going new places himself. We both allowed our decision about what was best for Kendra to be influenced more by what we enjoy than by listening to what she knew about herself.

Our gender nonconforming and transgender children may be on a different developmental timeline than their peers and we need to adjust to that. Safe places where they feel unconditionally loved and supported being themselves are as crucial to their survival as air and water. Our children have special needs and it's our job to think those through, particularly because of the misunderstanding and judgment they sometimes perceive and receive in the world. I hadn't fully appreciated how bereft Kendra would feel when detached from the lifeline of home. By pushing Kendra out into the world when she needed the love and protection of home, we exacerbated the crisis of puberty causing her to feel distrustful and estranged from us at a time when she needed support.

Learn

All parents have questions. Parents of gender nonconforming or transgender child have questions that few parents or professionals have dealt with before. These questions vary depending on the age of your child and how long they have been gender nonconforming. For those of us with children like Kendra who have been nonconforming almost since birth, the most pressing question may be whether or not they'll outgrow it, and if not, what next? Parents with children or teens who become gender nonconforming at puberty have another set of questions. These may include why now; have they felt this way for a while but were unsure or afraid to tell; are they reacting to gender roles; feeling uncomfortable with their changing body? The more you know the better you'll be at helping your child, your family, and yourself.

To more fully understand what your child's behavior and perceptions mean, you may want to do some research. At this point in my journey I turned to books for solace, information, and understanding. They helped answer questions and quell the incessant litany of worries. In 2004, there was much less to read than there is today but just knowing I wasn't alone made all the difference. I felt encouraged to know there were people with insight and experience who could help. I appreciated their compassion since I feared how Kendra would be received in the world. Personal narratives of transgender people helped me understand their strength and resilience as well as their pain. It saddened me to know this might be Kendra's pain too, but their stories offered hope for the future.

When I was at this fact-finding stage I was still unable to speak about the possibility of my daughter being transgender without crying, so curling up alone with a book was more my style than seeking out other parents. And keeping any decision as far into the future as possible helped me cope with my own fear and sadness. New resources emerge every day as teens and parents add their voices and experiences. You can learn a great deal through books, memoirs, websites, blogs, groups, news articles, and research. See the Appendices in the back of this book for a partial list of resources and websites.

It's normal to feel frightened and confused about how best to help your gender nonconforming or transgender child. Even while part of me gathered information about the process of transitioning, another part of me looked for signs that this would not ultimately be Kendra's path. I felt comforted learning some children outgrow their gender nonconforming behavior and hoped that would be the case. From time to time my heart raced as I put down books to catch my breath when I read what might be ahead if Kendra didn't outgrow it. There is a lot to consider and some of it can be very emotional. I gathered as much information as I could handle at the moment. Some of your questions may be answered this way while others are more emotionally rooted and may take longer to sort out.

Notice if you have barriers to taking in new information. These will likely be the topics where, like me, you may need to stop reading for a while. You may hear a voice inside say, "This is interesting but it's not anything we'll have to experience." Notice the places where you distance yourself from what you are learning. These are the borders of acceptance beyond which you may not be ready to go. Your child may eventually bump up against these sharp edges—or might feel wounded by them already—so the sooner you know where your limits are the better. The good news is that you can move these walls over time so that what was once inconceivable gradually becomes acceptable. At this point in my journey, the wall for me was surgery. I could embrace gender nonconformity and androgyny, and could even tiptoe around hormone treatment, but I could not yet fathom surgery of any type.

Loving a gender nonconforming or transgender child or teen increases your motivation to let go of long-held but inaccurate information in order to better understand and support your child. Once you have made some progress in your own learning process, you will hopefully be able to encourage and inspire others in your family and circle of friends to engage in their own change process for the sake of the child in your midst. If you are parenting with a partner, keeping pace with each other in the learning process can be a challenge. You may want to devour everything at once yet your partner may feel overwhelmed by this approach and respond with resistance. For some, the very process of learning more can feel threatening if they have erected a fortress of denial around even considering their child might be transgender. You may have your own deeply buried questions gnawing on the margins of consciousness. Helping each other explore questions and fears and finding answers together while respecting each other's pace and learning style will ultimately help you to support your child.

Negotiating Parenting

Like cracks in a building on shifting sand, our parenting differences as a couple grew more pronounced with each passing year. I grew up watching my mother turn faithfully to her dog-eared edition of Dr. Benjamin Spock's *Baby and Child Care* book whenever she felt stumped by the behaviors or symptoms of one of her children. I studied psychology in college, pastoral care in theological seminary, and participated in Jungian analysis for more than a year during my twenties to gain self-awareness. Tony majored in chemistry, has a natural aptitude for math and science, and little cultural or personal experience of psychotherapy. When I cited books on parenting, Tony cited his upbringing. His approach was to ignore what was happening internally for Kendra and hold her responsible for respectful behavior at home while achieving academic milestones in the appropriate time frame. He considered my search for the cause of her mood swings, anger, defiance, and academic disinterest as coddling; a hindrance to her maturing into a responsible adult. I considered his perspective one-dimensional and unrealistic. He felt I was too protective of her and I felt he was too harsh.

When differences in perspective such as these begin to surface with the person you are parenting with, it's safe to assume they will be exacerbated as your child approaches puberty. Kendra had been gender nonconforming all along, but her explosive moods during adolescence are what created the most conflict in our marriage. We both felt frightened and overwhelmed. Tony was adamant about holding her accountable for her negative behavior. I saw her behavior as symptomatic of her pain and was interested in getting to root causes. We did best when we agreed both perspectives were needed instead of trying to get the other to see it our way.

If you and your partner are on opposite ends over how to handle your child's gender nonconformity it is important to seek help. If you remain divided, you add to the stress in your family and undermine your relationship with your partner as well as with your children. Children take sides when parents disagree. Trying on your partner's perspective can help open your eyes to what you might have missed. Finding some middle ground might help your partner explore his or her own blind spots. Creating a united front of love, respect for all family members, and consistent consequences for disrespect requires constant communication and negotiation. Getting the help you need so you and your partner have the knowledge, skills, and commitment to achieve this will support all of you during this stressful period.

The pressure on you to have answers and get it right can feel unrelenting. Your child may be moving too fast in one direction, your partner in the other, and social convention sending signals you're doing it all wrong—that you should just wait for it all to blow over and that children are too young to be credible when it comes to gender. Your child may vacillate, so just when you begin to have some clarity you find yourself back where you started with more questions than answers. For some, gender identity formation does not end at a point in time but is a fluid process that might extend over the course of one's childhood, adolescence, or into adulthood.[64]

Gender Specialist

A psychologist or mental health professional specializing in gender identity and experienced working with children and teens, can help your child, you, and your partner, if appropriate, sort out your child's immediate and longer-term needs. A trained therapist will build trust with your child and let her or him guide the process of discovery. They will view gender as an expression of self rather than a symptom. The role of the therapist is to listen to your child—using art, play, or words depending on your child's age—and help you hear their truth as far as they know it in the moment. In this supportive milieu, your child will feel free to explore their questions, conflicts, and feelings while building confidence and resilience.[65] The therapist is not there to fix your child, or mold their behavior using rewards, or question you about what might have happened to cause your child's gender nonconformity.[66] If the therapist begins moving in these directions, find a new one.

Depending on your child's age, the therapist may actually spend more time with you than with your child. In doing so, the therapist can help you gain a clearer picture of your child, address your questions and feelings, help you mourn the loss of the child you thought you had in order to accept the child you do have, address safety concerns, help you plan how to tell others, and explore treatment options and timing.[67] In instances where there is time, the therapist can help you experience a thoughtful journey with your child that includes hopes, fears, coping strategies, and affirmations rather than rushing toward transition.[68] This can enhance communication and your parent-child bond longterm as well as prevent unexpected issues from cropping up after gender transitioning. The therapist can also help you and your partner identify your own needs, those of your other children, and find family and community supports.

We were very late in finally getting to a trained, gender therapist. Had we found one sooner, we may have been spared some of the difficulties along our journey. An objective and supportive third party can often see aspects of us, and our relationships with loved ones, that we are too close to observe. Most parents are anything but objective. After all, we have known our child for several years, maybe even decades by now and have formed an attachment to their assigned gender. We can be so habituated to how we've known and related to our child that even when they are in boy clothes we see the girl and vice versa.

Finding the right gender therapist can be challenging. Some are willing to Skype, which may be an option if you don't live near a large metropolitan area where many specialists are clustered. Noting whether or not a therapist you are considering has transgender dolls and books with gender fluid characters in their office is one helpful though not essential clue to their experience working with transgender and gender nonconforming children.[69]

Communicate and Connect

By breaking the silence and encouraging conversation and interaction about gender, we can help our children discover and disclose their gender identity. As we talk with them about how they feel about gender and how they see themselves, one of the questions we might ask ourselves is "Am I holding up an old reflection of her or him that's blocking my ability to see who they are today?" Moving ourselves toward objectivity is challenging but essential if we want our children to be open with us about who they are becoming.

Assuming a young child's gender nonconformity is indicative of their sexual orientation, conversations about gender may be overlooked until discussions about sexual orientation are age appropriate. Misinterpreting what a child is expressing can inadvertently delay a timely response. After all, you wouldn't ask a four-year-old about whom they feel attracted to. But since gender identity comes before sexual orientation, it could be critically supportive to talk with your three-year-old how they feel about their body and gender.

Without pushing or putting words in their mouth, create openings for them to tell you what they are experiencing despite fears you may have about knowing. Poignant accounts of adult transsexuals bear witness to the level of confusion and loneliness that marked their childhoods. You can break through the possible fear and isolation your child may feel by helping them share their thoughts, experiences, and concerns about gender. The reward for making that effort is an increase in trust, more open and honest communication, and a stronger emotional connection. Given how hard the road can be out in the world for our children, what parent would turn their back on these benefits?

Your Other Children

Stay close and connected to your other children as you learn more about gender development. Discuss gender with them and share what you're learning in age appropriate ways without overwhelming them. Observe ways in which their sibling's gender identity, expression, and behavior might impact them. This is especially important if your children are close in age, attend the same school, participate in the same outside activities, or share the same circle of friends since they may observe things that you don't. The weight of this knowledge can feel overwhelming so create opportunities for them to ask questions, talk about their observations, and express their feelings or concerns.

Self-Care

At the same time you are deciding what is best for your child, you probably have your own uncertainties, feelings, and fears about where your child is headed and what is in their best long-term interest. Taking the time you need to learn about the issues, research the right referrals, and talk to other parents on a similar path, while listening to your child and your own insights, can be difficult to balance. Keep listening, watching, and be open to clues that seem to come from unexpected places. Keep breathing. Take care to participate in activities that reduce your stress and lift your spirits. If you can, surround yourself with supportive friends who will listen without judgment. If that is not possible, find a parent support group in your area such as PFLAG, or online chat groups you can join.

Middle school

Ninth Grade

4

Acknowledging Feelings

I didn't mind when people used male pronouns toward me;
the problem was when people who knew "the truth"
were with me for one of these "mistakes."

I knew I wasn't "straight," but I wasn't "gay" either.
I just felt like I was in the wrong body.

I suppose a theory could be that since
my dad and I were both minorities,
I closely associated with him.

KENDRA, AGE 19

RECOLLECTIONS

Disappearing

As in fairytales, life sometimes forewarns us about challenging conditions in our future with people or messages that come along. When Kendra was eleven I took a trip with a group of eight women, and one shared with us that her husband was transitioning to become a woman. I remember thinking at the time what a difficult journey that must be for them, grateful for how ordinary my own life seemed by comparison.

Despite the closeness we once shared, Kendra, now fourteen, was not talking. The more I sought her out, the further she withdrew. When she wasn't on the family computer studying turtle species, she was in her room sleeping. Like a turtle herself, her shell was becoming hard and impenetrable. I knew I was losing her and became a silent vigilant witness to my daughter's descent into depression. She was a prolific writer, and like breadcrumbs to her heart, I found scribbles on scraps of paper at the desk, in her bed, and on the floor of her room. They helped me piece together what she was thinking and to feel less lost. I learned she was online as a boy named Jordan and in love with a girl. I was afraid of websites she was visiting and worried about her online world. I attributed her detachment to the recent traumatic separation from home.

With the single-minded focus of a first responder, I desperately sought to resuscitate the girl who left. I tried hauling her back to the world we had shared, in an effort to influence, perhaps overwhelm, the stormy inner world she was moving toward using walks in the woods, time outdoors, playing with pets, a change of scenery including a two-week vacation for just the two of us. I took Kendra on a trip to Costa Rica in March her freshman year to explore nature, another country and culture, and each other. I knew she'd revel in seeing tropical animals in the wild. I was ready to indulge my senses and hoped to relax, have fun, talk, walk, and swim. Since Kendra moves more slowly than I do, I prepared to synchronize my pace with hers. We rode horses around a volcano, drove through terraced coffee groves and mountain rainbows, hiked in the rain forest, sat in hot springs, crossed a canopy bridge over the continental divide, and saw the Big Dipper upside down. Kendra collected tiny hermit crabs and saw iguanas, geckos, lizards, turtles, toads, an owl, a fox, cotamundi, and spectacular birds.

Kendra became an experienced navigator as we drove on the most challenging roads I'd ever encountered and discovered that arrows to towns worked better than route numbers or road names for finding our way. Kendra's frequent phrase throughout the trip was "Mom, you're so embarrassing!" after every single human inter-action. It was true. I resorted to hand gestures and botched Spanish and once even said "ici" instead of "aqui." We came home refreshed and filled with wonderful fun memories that served to reconnect us. I hoped this feeling of happiness would ripple out in ever widening circles. Kendra too seemed different, lighter, more her old self in the beauty of natural surroundings and without the pressure of school and peers.

Away from everyday stress, glimmers of her former, vibrant, self shined through. I was encouraged to see the carefree child she had been instead of the brooding teen she'd become. But she couldn't stay for long anymore. Panic, despair, and rage could spill over from Kendra at any time, toward anyone, but never for the real unspoken and terrifying reason. It never occurred to me that Kendra, the daughter who left on that month-long school trip, would not eventually return after healing from what must have felt like my abandonment.

When tenth grade began Kendra asked to get her hair cut. She used to wear it proudly like a mane, wild and free, but the older she got the tighter back she pulled it and the more she disliked its wavy unruliness. I found a salon specializing in curly hair. Kendra frowned in the chair while the stylist suggested a layered, mid-length cut to complement her hair's texture. She showed Kendra how to straighten and style it after the cut. When she said, "You want to look feminine don't you—not like a boy?" I knew Kendra's look, and gave polite excuses as we made a speedy exit. Kendra held it together and then exploded in the car.

"Why is everyone against me cutting my hair?" she yelled. "It's no one else's business! Why don't you all just let me do what I want?"

I explained that with her curls she might not be happy with shorter hair since she wouldn't be able to tie it back. I couldn't imagine her spending hours straightening and styling it.

"Just take me to a barber shop then and not a beauty parlor," she insisted. "They'll know what to do."

So we went to a unisex salon. Despite Kendra's anger about how I was handling this, she refused to do the talking so I told the stylist to cut Kendra's hair as short as she wanted. Then I took a seat far away to not be implicated if she was still unhappy. The stylist cut Kendra's hair above the ears and then styled it straight—a totally new, chic look, but one that required work. It was questionable whether Kendra could or would do it herself. Before we left, I gathered up some of Kendra's long locks knowing it would be the last time I'd see them. Within weeks Kendra purchased a hair trimming kit and shaved her head herself.

Help From Friends

In November I got a call from the school. Kendra was not the type of student to ever be in trouble. In fact, quite the opposite—she was adept at staying under the radar. Two of Kendra's friends were concerned about her. Her emails and conversations felt hopeless and desperate so they told the nurse. After meeting with Kendra, the nurse called me. She suggested we consider antidepressants. I felt my face redden. Then she said Kendra felt relieved to have her sadness out in the open since she'd been feeling that way for a while but worried telling me would change my perception of her. It was alarming to consider that Kendra felt the need to put on a front for me. I'd worked in girls and women's health for most of my career and now here was my own daughter, hiding from me. Had I not been pursuing her in every way I knew how? What was this perception I had that she felt the need to maintain? I said I'd continue to talk to Kendra and figure out how to help her. I thanked her for calling and asked her to please thank the two friends but I couldn't help feeling like I'd just won the bad mother of the year award when I hung up. What would she want to hide from me?

When I picked up Kendra from school that afternoon, I reached out to hug her as she approached the car with her two friends. I wanted to reassure her that nothing she disclosed could change my love for her. As had become her habit that year, she avoided contact with me.

"This is so dumb," she snapped as soon as her friends left, before I even got a word out. "I don't know why everyone has to make such a big deal about things. Why don't they just mind their own business? I don't go around telling people about their conversations."

"Honey, I'm glad they did. They care about you and are trying to be good friends," I said. "There's nothing to be embarrassed about. Everyone goes through hard times at certain points in their lives. They were only trying to help."

"Yeah right. How would you know? Now the whole school will be talking about me. You don't know what it's like here," she said. Her voice cracked and she turned her head so I wouldn't see her eyes fill.

I had been searching for a family therapist. Fortunately our first session was scheduled for that very afternoon. While medication was something to consider, I wanted Kendra to have the opportunity to talk to the therapist alone if she would. Kendra was not interested and decided to stay in the car. I went in alone to pour out my concerns to the therapist. A few minutes later Kendra came into the office and to my relief, she joined me for the counseling session. She was tearful and tentative at first but recounted what had happened at school and how she'd been feeling. She seemed visibly more relaxed afterward. My plan was to continue with counseling. She was still resisting any questions from me so I was learning to read between the lines and moods. It was hard to know how best to help in so passive a role.

Three weeks later I got another call from the school. This time her friends had noticed scratches on her arms and worried she was cutting. Friends made her promise she would talk to me and told her they would call her in the evening to make sure she told me everything. Around 8:30 that night she asked if two friends from school could stop over. Since I'd been given advance notice that her friends were holding her accountable, I said yes. Both girls lived about thirty minutes away so I knew they were serious coming out on a school night. One was in her pajamas.

After listening to them giggle together in Kendra's room for a bit I came into the hall and asked if everything was all right. Kendra opened her door and her friends confronted her and said, "Go on." Kendra tried to dodge them saying she'd tell me later but then I persisted. We finally went into my room while her friends waited in hers.

"What's the matter honey?" I asked.

"I guess I've been feeling sort of sad lately—not all the time or anything but more than half the time maybe," she said. "I think it started last year when I went on that trip. I try not to think about that whole experience. I hated being with my class all that time. I had no friends there and I think I felt really lonely. I knew I wasn't ready and no one listened to me. And I had dreamed of coming home but when I finally got here, everything was different. Home was not what it had been."

My heart hurt hearing her say this. If only I had supported her instincts about it—that a month was too long to be away. She had been right. How had I betrayed her? And what could we do now to undo the damage? I was sad too—and guilty. I tried hard to continue to listen despite my self-recrimination.

"I know honey. I wish we had kept you home too. I remember all the phone conversations we had and how helpless I felt being so far away," I said. A lump was constricting my throat.

"I'm worried about SATs (Scholastic Aptitude Tests), what to focus on for college, what colleges to apply to, what if I don't get into any, how to pick a major. And what if I make a mistake and change my mind? You know how I always change my mind."

"These are big decisions honey but you don't need to make them all at once. You can make them one at a time and each step along the way the decisions will become easier. And it's no big deal to change your mind. Lots of people change their minds about what they study during college or what they do after college."

"No one else seems worried about this stuff. Everyone at school seems so sure about SATs and what colleges they'll apply to. I don't even like to hear them talk about it. It's all they think about now; like you're a nobody if you don't get into the best school," she said.

"That's a lot of pressure. I can't imagine what that's like. You're smart and you're a good student with a lot of varied talents. You're good in science and art; you're a good writer and actor. You'll get in somewhere just right. Does it make it worse being one of the few mixed kids in the school?" I asked.

"That's not as bad as feeling pressured to have a boyfriend. I have no interest in that but everyone else thinks I should. So many kids are getting paired up or trying to."

"It's best not to have a boyfriend at your age. It just adds to the list of things to worry about. And you'll figure out soon enough whom you're attracted to. Whether girls or boys, whether you're gay or straight, you're you, and Dad and I will always love you."

"I like dressing the way I do. I like that people can't tell whether I'm a boy or a girl," she said.

"Some people know right away what their sexual orientation is. Others take a while longer to figure it out," I replied. I still didn't understand that she was talking about gender not sexual orientation. She tried to discuss her discomfort with being female and I missed it. "Would you like to see the family therapist alone so you and she can talk about some of these things?" I asked.

"No, Mom. I don't really like her and I don't think she'll understand," she said.

"What if we look for a therapist that you do like? Someone who will understand?"

"If you want," she said. "But I'd rather just talk to you and not anyone else."

"I love talking to you and I'm glad you feel like that but we haven't been talking for a while now," I said. "There may be things you feel more comfortable talking about with someone else. I'm happy to be the main person you talk to but I want us to continue talking, especially when you feel sad. I also want you to promise that you'll tell me if you ever feel like hurting yourself."

"I will," she promised.

"I made an appointment for you with Allie, the nurse practitioner, next Monday to see what she thinks about antidepressants just to take the edge off of the sadness while you sort out your feelings," I said.

"I don't want to take pills. It's not that bad and not all the time."

"But think of all the coffee you need to drink just to get through the day," I said. "What if it's biochemical or something? I think it's worth checking out. It can't hurt."

She agreed and we hugged before she left my room to say goodbye to her friends. Those two girls helped us break the silence and I was grateful even though Kendra believed she had no friends.

I now knew we needed a therapist who specialized in sexual orientation, gender identity, and depression in teens. Kendra had just started a Myspace page and had been staying up late that summer instant messaging for hours. I found copies of printed messages or open windows on topics like depression and self-injury. Given how private and explosive Kendra had become I wasn't sure if or when to approach her about these obvious clues that something was terribly wrong. I needed some professional advice and fast. I didn't want to believe she was actually cutting but when I thought about it, I hadn't seen her upper arms or thighs in a very long time. She was always covered in several layers and I worried about an eating disorder even though there were no obvious signs of that.

Discovery

While picking up laundry in her room one day and straightening the sheets, I found a note under her pillow. Her words pierced my heart. I crumpled hard onto her bed and burst into tears. I saved the note but then lost it. It was only one or two sentences. Kendra longed to be a boy and always would. She wished no one ever knew or remembered her as a girl. There it was in black and white. No ambivalence, no questioning, no middle ground. Of all the issues I'd considered, I'd kept gender identity far out of reach though it had been right in front of me her whole life long.

I was expecting to deal with sexual orientation. That way she'd remain my daughter, keep her body, avoid the pain and disfigurement of surgery, stay herself, the person I knew and loved. I could live with her being a lesbian. I'd prepared myself for that while misinterpreting her gender nonconformity. I knew she was falling in love with girls and struggling to disclose that but I assumed the pain she was in was about coming out as gay—to herself, to us, and to others. But this was bigger. I hadn't allowed myself to consider, even for a minute, that my daughter was really my son.

This meant changing her body, her psyche. It meant taking a sharp turn off the parallel path of mother and daughter I expected we'd travel for life. It felt like mutilation: of her body, her beauty, her essence, her being. I walked around in shocked grief and horror for days. I didn't even tell Tony about what I'd found. It was unspeakable to me. Forming it into words only made it more real. With clues all along the way, it's hard now to understand how surprised and shocked I felt then. I was so attached to the little girl she had come to me as—it was hard to alter that long history, my knowledge of her that way. I was invested in holding onto her. There was part of me that *could* not see, and another part that *would* not see.

Just as childbirth had been long and arduous for us, this next birth was about to be as well. New birth pangs were just beginning. Kendra was working to birth herself in ways I had never expected and this birth was about to transform me every bit as much as the first birth had. As she moved toward authentic self-expression, I was forced ever deeper into my own resistance and rigidity until those places in me finally, painfully, gave way and opened for my own transformation. But before I accepted this child for who he had been all along I had to let go of some preconceived notions blocking my heart and my mind like giant granite boulders.

I hoped Kendra could live at some mystical crossroads between feminine and masculine; some androgynous place. The more I read of people who did, the more hopeful I became. Two spirit people in Native American tribes were esteemed, seen as gifted and chosen, bridging male and female, the spirit realm and this physical realm. I saw Kendra that way exactly, given her spiritual and intuitive connection to nature and animals. But that world was not where she resided. She was a teen living in America, not a shaman in a spirit-conscious culture. Still, I needed to hope that she could hold onto the girl in her while embracing the boy.

I loved her femininity, her tender heart, how she cared for living creatures, instinctively knowing how to nurse the sick back to health. She was gifted in creating beautiful living spaces whether habitats for reptiles or decorating our home. She once left bouquets at each of our bedsides in all our favorite colors. I grasped onto these stereotypes of femininity like a drowning person to a life ring, assuring myself these were not signs of a boy but a girl. My daughter would never in a million years so trample her girl side to become all boy. And if she did, I might be angry forever with the boy in her for overpowering the beloved girl. I felt protective of this tender, special girl and angry with the impulsive, inscrutable boy.

Maybe this was just some illusion she was under because she was attracted to girls and couldn't imagine being a lesbian. Surely she would come to her senses. After all, she was only fifteen, too young I believed to transition, take hormones, or have surgery and make irreversible decisions about her body, her future. So while girding myself with information and preparing for what might happen down the road, I was proactive about sexual orientation being the issue but resistant to the notion it was gender identity.

Since the very first time Kendra was handed to me I was totally, always in love with her—body and soul, one package, inseparable. It was too painful to consider losing my daughter even if it meant gaining a son. I was despairing of my own loss, exhausted by mothering this complicated child, sorrowful for her deep and frightening pain, saddened about the tension between us, grieving for earlier, easier days. After an argument one day, I sat on a rock overlooking a nearby lake. I dreamed of jumping in the water, releasing all of my sadness, swimming away to a cabin where the only thing I needed to do was to make myself some tea and read. I watched a horse on the opposite shore walk from green grass into yellow trees and disappear. I too longed to disappear. Just then Kendra joined me as I stepped off the rock to re-enter my world of worry. We sorted out our most recent fight staring into the water. A snapping turtle broke the surface delighting Kendra. My shelled heart cracked open once more. Every time we connected like that I rejoiced in my daughter and hoped she'd decide to stay.

Missing You

From you dear one
I have received the gift of sight and slowing down.
You have taught me to stop, stoop, and scoop.
You've shown me acorn top hats, small red berries, yayas
the texture of moss, how to wait to catch a turtle.

You have created beauty in my life, bouquets in every room
petals on a towel on the hillside of our yard
centerpieces on the dining room table.
Halloween decorations on the porch—hay bales and scarecrows
Christmas "yites" everywhere
animal settings and habitats in every room
a dollhouse to call home, murals on your wall.
Set design has always been your passion
make-believe realities the expression of your inner world.

You wept when Christmas magic wore off.
Now all the magic is gone.

How can I draw you back from your private sad edge?
Where are you now my dear, dear Kendra?
You wall me off, shut me out and I am in a cold dry desert.
I reach to you and you run from me.

I have taught you hot tea for a sad day
the love of pets
self-expression—being who you are no matter what.

I have taught you freedom from routine within limits
the beauty of the outdoors
the joy of risk
the importance of water and swimming
how to dig deep for courage
the magic of ritual
the safety of family and friends
the centrality of faith and hope.

But know that I know,
for whatever reason and for every reason
I let you down.
You begged me to protect you from going to Montreal and
I let you go
You wanted me to save you from that month away as well
but I did not.

You have changed in ways you do not like as a result, you said.
You are growing up,
separating from me.
You fear I will not be okay with that.
I fear I will not be okay with that.
I whine that you are shutting me out but
that is your job now
your right.

CANDACE, NOVEMBER 28, 2004

I'm a T

It was Tony who finally said it out loud even before Kendra did. One morning while dressing for work he said, "Kendra is dealing with gender. She's not happy in her body and it's only getting worse instead of better. Can't you see that? I can." He was right of course. My hope she would outgrow dressing in boys' clothes was not to be. But I still wanted to think she could make peace with her body.

By summer there was solid evidence Kendra was cutting. Despite the weather she was always covered in oversized clothes and swam in T-shirts and long shorts. I started finding bloody tissues in her wastebasket. Then I actually saw it. We were in a tent together on Cape Cod changing our clothes. There were a series of parallel scars on both upper arms and crisscrosses on both thighs. I tried to be brave as I touched them and asked her. She shrugged as though it was nothing but this time she did not rebuff me. I knew from my reading this wasn't an effort to kill herself but a release for pain too deep for words. It brought her some relief. It eased some internal pressure and was popular among girls her age. It also had an addictive quality to it.

At least now we could look each other in the eye and hold the truth. Her pain was deeper than she knew how to handle and she was exposing me to it. Before, whenever I asked I was greeted with explosive anger and deeper withdrawal, but here we were not talking, we were touching. My chest tightened and tears threatened to well but I blinked them back before they scared Kendra away. Why does my beautiful, graceful daughter so hate her body, herself? Am I as powerless before her self-hatred as I feel? Who could help me? Help us?

It was as if she'd been kidnapped and I was the first person in the search party to arrive. Time was running out and I felt terrified something worse was about to happen. If she could tear at her flesh when I knew her to be so frightened of pain, what else might she do? How I'd known and loved this child's smooth, brown, satin skin. Why couldn't she see what everyone else saw—a smart, creative, funny, talented, and inquisitive person who loved animals, plants, and nature. And where would this end? What would it take for her to stop? It was summer at the beach on the Cape. When I looked out at the serene blue horizon all I could see were the ragged scars in my daughter's flesh that raged at me to do something.

I searched therapists and books on sexual orientation and gender identity hoping that might help us broach the topic and asked Kendra to read, *Love Makes a Family: Portraits of Lesbian, Gay, Bisexual, and Transgender Parents and Their Families*, edited by Peggy Gillespie. That she read the book so quickly surprised me. It was a perfect August day when she brought it downstairs and said, "Mom, of all the stories in this book, I'm a T! I never knew there was a name for it but that's what I am." She was clear, bold, brave, and certain.

I swallowed hard and felt my heart race like a captured bird. "You are?" I said.

"Yes!" she exclaimed. "I never knew there were other people who feel like I do. I thought I was the only one."

"That must be a relief," I said. "How long have you felt this way?"

"For a while I guess."

"It must have felt scary to feel all alone," I said.

Even though I had instigated it and had seen the clues, it was still a blow to hear her say the words. She went away feeling lighter, happier. I, on the other hand, felt a crushing weight. Why did it make me want to cry I wondered? I had loved a little girl and I was afraid it meant she was leaving. I latched onto the fact that she had not said she was a boy so I still wasn't totally sure where her discovery would lead. Maybe there was a chance she could live in the middle; be both; androgynous. In 2005, there was little awareness about transgender children and teens, so I'd considered the chances of my child being transgender to be one in a million. In my heart I could not fathom Kendra as male. Always a shy, perceptive girl, I thought of her boy's attire as a cover; a way to protect her tender, sensitive spirit. But she'd disclosed to me her transgender identity and I finally needed to hear her.

It was a brilliant summer afternoon and I walked down the hill of our verdant backyard into the garden shed. Barricading myself against what I'd just heard, I closed the door behind me and stared at rakes, shovels, garden gloves, and bikes to get my bearings. I wanted to talk in private to the one person I knew would understand. I called my friend Char, a lesbian. I knew some lesbians wished they were boys when they were young and later became happy being women. It's a logical desire when a teen realizes she's attracted to girls. Maybe Kendra was in the process of coming out as a lesbian. I was looking for advice; grasping at hope. Other women eventually reconciled themselves to their bodies; even celebrated their bodies. I wanted to put Kendra in touch with them. Char offered to host Kendra at her house for a week to discuss her questions and explore her sexual orientation with Char and her lesbian friends. Kendra accepted the offer readily and went to Florida for March break of her junior year. Today we joke about how I sent her to lesbian camp.

I left work early the next day so Kendra and I could spend time together. We walked in the woods and talked about male/female issues and her feelings about gender. I reminded her that she'd been attracted to a girl in fourth grade and told me then that she was a lesbian. She had forgotten. Kendra said she didn't really identify with either gender. I told her about Native American two spirit people. One tribe held an initiation. A child was placed in a circle of brush with a bow symbolizing men's work and a basket, women's work. The brush was set on fire and whichever object the boy picked up as he ran away, identified his gender. Choosing the basket signified third gender or two spirit status.[70] This fascinated me when I read it because Kendra had a collection of bows and arrows of various sizes that she'd made over the years. Some wood was flexible for a bow; other wood was straight, strong, and light enough for arrows.

Kendra liked the idea of being two spirited and it didn't surprise me that she considered herself both boy and girl. After all, she was also both black and white. It offered me hope that she might be able to reconcile herself to her body if she held a spiritual and mental space for her masculine qualities. Could she balance both I wondered? If nothing else it offered a longer time frame if she decided to transition. I was used to her embracing masculine interests and activities but the thought of her rejecting and shedding her more feminine qualities is what felt the hardest. But at least the weight of her long-held secret was finally out wherever the path would eventually lead.

Even before having a name for how she felt, Kendra was already living part time as male. That summer she had an internship at a marine laboratory working Tuesdays and Saturdays. Her Tuesday coworker knew her to be a girl. Her Saturday coworker thought she was a boy—despite her name. This wouldn't be the first time her appearance so overrode her name that people went with what they saw instead of what they heard. Since she didn't correct her coworker in the beginning because she liked being seen as male, it was harder to do so later.

It was the first time she experienced boy talk about an attractive girl. Her coworker sexually objectified the girl, assuming Kendra would join in. Instead, it disgusted her and she found some project to busy herself with so she could extricate herself from the awkward conversation. At the end of the season, there was a goodbye party for their supervisor. Kendra wanted to attend but decided not to since both coworkers would be there and it could easily result in her being outed and everyone embarrassed, confused, or worse.

She shared how freeing and wonderful it felt when people saw her as a boy. It made her day better whenever she was recognized for how she felt inside and she hated it when friends or family took it upon themselves to correct strangers. Earlier that year we went to Trinidad and once again, a woman asked her gender and wouldn't believe she was a girl—which Kendra appreciated. One of her struggles going places with her class was whenever someone thought she was a boy her classmates intruded on what Kendra experienced as an affirmation, by correcting the person and making her feel invisible.

Before knowing how intentional Kendra was at being seen as a boy, it made me uncomfortable when people mistook her. I worried that it compounded her gender confusion. I wondered whether people seeing her as a boy made her think she wasn't pretty enough to be a girl. Could that be why she wanted to switch? But I was beginning to understand that she wasn't being misread at all. She was purposely presenting as masculine and people were responding to the cues she was giving by her dress, her gait, and her mannerisms. They were seeing his spirit, his person, his gender, rather than her birth sex.

Longing

Denial is one way to interpret my inability to truly see this child, but retrospective longing might be a more accurate description. Watching my daughter split into two, I desperately tried to keep both sides together. Every time I looked at the lonely, isolated, insecure teen, I saw the carefree wood nymph just beneath the surface. As her mother, I longed to mend the tear in the intricate and beautiful tapestry of her to make her whole again. I struggled to prevent her from abandoning the qualities I loved for those I feared. I wanted to grasp my little girl and pull her out of the sullen teen and show her to Kendra saying: "Look, this is who you are. This is who you've always been. Don't let this world crush you!" Then, "This is how I've always known you; who I want you to stay. Please don't leave me. I've come to love you so!" And even, "I don't like who you are becoming as much as I liked you then. Where have you gone?" Then finally: "I miss you so! Will I ever see you again?"

How can we open ourselves up to learning about the unique little beings that come into our lives as our children, without making assumptions and projecting our hopes, biases, and fears onto their futures? Much of my blindness to who Kendra was becoming was due to the movie screen between us that continuously featured our shared past, and the future I imagined based on what had gone before. I had taken aspects of who I knew her to be at three, five, eight, and ten years old, and woven them into a tapestry of her life based on that early, partial knowledge. Her past and future were so deeply embedded in my mind I considered the present a frightening interruption to be escaped and forgotten as quickly as possible.

The hardest work of my transition was just beginning. I needed to dig up and dislodge old beliefs and assumptions that interfered with my ability to support, and accompany Kendra on the next phase of her journey. Why was I so attached to her gender and body, even at the expense of her health and happiness? How had I explained away all the early clues? What was it about my perceptions and aspirations for her that got in the way of hearing her truth? Why all the tears?

She may become my son, I thought, but in my heart, when I reminisced about her, she would always and forever be my daughter no matter how she dressed today or in the future and what name or pronoun she chose to use. I had a baby girl and I loved, cherished, cuddled, rocked, and raised a baby girl and she was beautiful in every way. My heart would always be attached to the little daughter inside the grown son. Reconciling this duality was what my journey would require.

I needed to understand the sorrow I felt about Kendra wanting to be a boy. What was it that was breaking my heart? I worried it would forever keep her from fitting in and having friends and a normal life. In my heart of hearts I still saw it as a phase because everything I knew about her seemed so gentle and feminine. But now I needed to unpack what that even meant. Are boys unable to nurture animals, study nature, love flowers, and enjoy cuddling? I wanted to be supportive of her happiness but I also needed to be honest with myself. I tried to keep the depth of my sadness and feelings of loss hidden. I didn't want her to feel guilty for my grief. She had enough to manage. I even tried to make light of my adjustment when the opportunity arose. Once, when she came downstairs disappointed that a gecko she thought was female turned out to be male, I said, "Now you know how I feel!" We both laughed.

But every time I looked at Kendra I worried that she was going to mutilate her body, reign in her feminine spirit, and become a boy. It felt like pulling a spiral into a straight line. Was she going to these lengths to identify with her father; to gain his approval? Did she think he could love her more if she were just like him? Can she protect herself when living in the gap between two genders? Can we protect her? Neither of us had any experience with this. How could we best help her? While I was working through my many questions, feelings, and worries, Kendra was marching ahead more quickly than I realized.

Storm Clouds

Kendra felt marginalized, invisible at her school. She was a curious learner and a deep thinker and even though the school prided itself on helping kids find their voice, some voices, journeys, and worldviews were more valued than others. Like so many children of color in American schools, Kendra's detachment from academics was for self-preservation and survival, and not due to laziness, stupidity, irresponsibility, or recalcitrance as most of her teachers assumed, and some even said so. School was becoming a lonely place for a depressed teen of color, questioning gender. The longer she stayed, the worse she felt about her talents, abilities, intelligence, and worth. That spring Kendra asked to go back to the public school in the town where we lived. I encouraged her to visit the school before finalizing her decision but she was adamant. She wanted out of where she was and believed anything would be an improvement. This time we supported her decision.

At her sixteenth birthday party that May we were surprised when so many kids from her class came since she still believed she had no friends. But her class was close, even if only superficially, given how much time they spent together. Since sixth grade they'd shared classes, theater, music, drama rehearsals, soccer fields, annual fall camping trips, and other outings. So there she was, surrounded by at least twenty kids all singing happy birthday to her. Obviously some of these kids cared for her but she always pulled away rather than toward them. It was touching to watch Kendra say goodbye to everyone and I began to wonder if she was making a mistake to leave. Was she running away? Given how long it had taken her to trust and make friends, would she miss some of these kids? Were the feelings on their part real? Was Kendra in love with one of these girls and leaving because she couldn't be with her as a boy? Was she changing schools to be more anonymous so she could become who she really was—a boy? Was it just too hard to do that in this fishbowl? Was she putting distance between those who knew her so well as a girl?

As summer drew to a close Kendra finally visited the new school to finalize her schedule for junior year. Change was hard for her and as the actual day approached, her resolve was faltering. But she felt she'd lose face if she returned to her former school. There was something brave and boastful about just turning her back and walking away from that cocoon and she knew other students envied her courage. She didn't want to admit defeat. So it was a summer of waiting and worry. In the middle of August we rented a cottage on a crystal clear lake in Maine. Kendra and I drove up on a Friday. Tony was coming the next morning. A huge brown spider greeted us on the clean white wall of this charming country cottage when we opened the kitchen door. That and the cinnamon scented candle triggered a panic attack in Kendra the likes of which I'd never seen.

On this cold rainy night in the woods Kendra barricaded herself in the car with razor blades. I was in over my head and finally knew it. I stared at the embroidered "Welcome to Our Home " sign hanging hopefully on the refrigerator door while I thought "Hospitalization," that's what it had come to. But I didn't even know where the nearest hospital was or how to get her there since she had the only car key locked inside with her and she was in no state for reasoning.

My heart drummed in my ears while I struggled to think. How could cutting relieve anxiety? How bad was it and how could I get her to stop? Was she mentally ill? What if she seriously injured herself out here in the middle of nowhere? Why won't she talk? Is she suicidal? I'm the only adult here so whatever happens, it's my call, my responsibility. I need to get it right. Should I call an ambulance? My cell phone is out of range. Does the house phone work and what number should I call? Normally cool-headed and rational, this time felt different. Perhaps panic is contagious. In the pitch dark with only a tiny flashlight, I knocked on the window of the car. Kendra's angry response was muffled.

"Open the door!" I demanded.

"No!" she said. "I'm not going in there. I want to go home."

"We just got here," I said. "It's only a spider and it's gone now. You can come in. You'll be cold and cramped out here."

"What if there are others?" she asked. "Besides, I hate the candle smell. It's scary in there. I'm staying out here."

"You'll be cold out here"

"I'm fine."

"Promise me you'll be okay—that you won't hurt yourself," I said.

"Oh Mom," she groaned.

"What if you need something in the middle of the night? Or have to go to the bathroom?"

"I'll pee outside. I won't need anything. I'm not coming in there!" she shouted.

"Okay, but you'll feel differently in the morning. It's not scary inside. You'll see. You just got scared by the spider, that's all," I said.

"No. I hate it here. I want to go home."

"We can talk about it in the morning. Please come in now. I'll make you some tea," I pleaded.

"No. I am sleeping out here."

"Okay, but you need to promise me you'll be safe. And call or come get me if you need anything."

"Okay."

"I'm going inside now. Goodnight. I love you," I said.

"Night," she said.

How had we come to this abyss? Sleep escaped me so I got up to check on her several times to make sure she was okay. The moist, pine-scented night and the gentle lapping of the lake mocked my situation. I felt anything but serene and didn't even know what okay was anymore. Was it one cut or five? And how would I know if she cut too deeply? How on earth could a car feel safer than a warm bed on a cold rainy night? Was Kendra really on the brink? Was I?

When I awoke in the predawn and looked through the car windows, Kendra was still in there curled up in a ball. I was relieved to see she was still breathing. When had breathing become my standard for relief? What am I dealing with here I wondered, and how much worse can it get? If I could only see her arms and legs without invading her privacy it might lessen, or heighten, my fear. At least it would answer some questions.

Eventually that week she cried in my arms as we rocked on the porch swing. She was a knot of worry over school, friends, grades, gender, and more she wouldn't name. I shared some of my own fears—when she isolated and wouldn't talk; when I was left to guess; when she insisted on going it alone; when I worried she'd hurt herself. I knew the physical pain of cutting was a release for some of her pent up emotional pain but told her talking was a better way if only she would. She finally agreed to see her own counselor if I could find one experienced with gender identity. We also talked about her attending an LGBTQ youth group.

That week, as I watched her whittle wood, examine caterpillars, float in a tube, paddle the canoe, there was a veil of loneliness around her. When we nearly stepped on a baby green snake basking on a rock while we hiked up a mountain it seemed as if all her cares melted away like a morning mist. She could still be that light-hearted, happy child every now and then but those moments were fleeting and farther apart. I couldn't really believe she'd end it all when I saw her fooling around or concentrating on some project as she still did sometimes. But I knew she suffered, especially at night. I longed to know how to carve out a safer place in the world for my angry, depressed, transgender teen.

Some happy memories of that vacation were my birthday lunch on Jordan Pond; swimming in water so clear I could see the bottom even when my mind was opaque with worry; feeding the little red squirrel that visited our deck daily; sitting on an island rock to soak in silence; hearing the call of loons. But mostly, that cottage brings back memories of Kendra being broken. She was lonely, depressed, isolated from friends, uncomfortable in her own skin, in love with a girl in love with a boy. She was living on the line between black and white, boy and girl, and panicking about what awaited her at her new school.

She was joining the kids she was with in elementary school but so much about her had changed. Was she going there as the Kendra they had known? Was she escaping her current school friends to redefine herself as "he"? And while she was rapidly moving from she, was she really ready to become he, leaving behind all she had been? Was it possible to live somewhere in the middle for a while to let these answers emerge over time? If so, where in the world might be the safest place for that? And what about our mother/daughter bond? Could I, as her mom, her closest lifelong ally, really come on this journey with her or was I going to be left standing on some distant shore?

Kendra shared a dream she'd had:

> *Kendra and I are in the car. I am speeding over a drawbridge just as it is opening and we end up teetering on top of it high over the water unable to get out. Next, I am driving right off the edge of the quarry with a steep drop off to the water. I assure her this is no problem. We can just open the doors on the way down and we'll float right up to the surface. Then I tell her we are taking a ferryboat ride. As it turns out, we need to hold onto the back of the boat while we are dragged.*

At first it seems I am not a trustworthy and reliable ally to her. I make promises and don't keep them. I don't adequately consider the gravity of the situations we're facing. She and I had always moved at a different pace; mine fast and sometimes haphazard to her; hers slow, tardy, and sometimes immovable to me. But then I consider other aspects of her dream sequence. First, I am in the driver's seat accompanying her on each of our hair-raising journeys. At least I'm with her and have not abandoned her. And I'm reassuring her that everything will be all right—even if it turns out to be more treacherous than I'd known. Clearly I'm flying by the seat of my pants and the challenges and obstacles are coming more fast and furious than I'm prepared for. But I haven't left her to fend for herself and I attempt to find a way through each crisis as I instill confidence in each of us that we can handle whatever is thrown at us.

That summer after Maine I had this dream:

> *I was going into Kendra's school to make an appointment with her teacher. There was what appeared to be an old dog lying dead in the hallway outside her office. The dean was there looking on in horror about to tell someone, when the dog's owner walked by. The dog flopped over and got up, no problem, to follow her out. It was totally unexpected because he looked so lifeless.*
>
> *On the way to the school I walked down a narrow road and past a clinic when two men—doctors? paramedics?—were carrying out a naked baby boy on a tray saying how seriously ill the baby was and that they'd be right back. The mother was following behind them but I could not see her.*
>
> *When I got to the principal's office to schedule a meeting she asked what time Kendra got out to play? The question stopped me because first I could not remember what time she got out or even what school she was in but then I suddenly realized that she does not play—not anymore at least. Then I decided not to meet with anyone so Kendra would not be labeled but could just be.*

Dreams can be a way for our unconscious mind to reach out to us and inform us of something our conscious awareness is refusing to see. At the time, I was unaware of the depth of Kendra's suffering and the trouble she was in. In each incident of the dream there is someone in trouble and a concerned caregiver nearby. The lifeless dog is aroused when the owner comes in; the sick baby boy is accompanied by his mother; and I am coming to meet with staff about Kendra. The frightening images of the seemingly dead dog and near-dead baby, along with the sudden realization that Kendra no longer played, made me wake with a start. It was a foreshadowing of the crisis that was just around the corner.

RESEARCH

The Crisis of Puberty

Puberty ushers in the end of childhood and a child's relatively androgynous body. Preteens may resist puberty for any number of reasons: they aren't ready to give up childhood; they feel uncomfortable with their body's changes; they don't feel ready for new, emerging sex drives.[71] And while some gender nonconforming children may suddenly conform to gender norms at this age, others panic as their rapidly changing body begins to take them further away from the person they know themselves to be. They become alarmed by the hormonal and physical changes that arise and feel that something is terribly wrong.[72] For a transgender child, physical changes at this age can signal the bitter end of a childhood fantasy that by sheer will they can hold off the "wrong puberty." The dream that their body will magically conform to the gender they feel inside comes crashing down around them.

Puberty is the second common stage when gender identity emerges. A child who has kept their true feelings about gender a secret throughout childhood is now faced with disclosure or despair. For some, the physical changes alone create a crisis of clarity for feelings that were previously cloudy and confusing. Disclosing this secret seemingly out of the blue can cause parents to question their child's veracity. Not telling can intensify feelings of dysphoria with parents unaware of the cause for the symptoms they suddenly see. Puberty can be nothing short of traumatic for a teen certain of their affirmed gender yet forced to stand by while their body careens off the biological cliff. The child hidden inside an ill-fitting body can become an angry, withdrawn, hopeless, and despondent teen.

Whether your child has been gender nonconforming since childhood or has recently become so, the most urgent question parents ask at this age is, "Is this permanent and if so, now what?" When transgender children have been consistent and persistent in their cross-gender identity by this age, it becomes apparent that this is not a stage they will outgrow.[73] It's not uncommon for parents to first suspect that their child might be gay or lesbian as I did. Most parents do not as readily wonder if their child is transgender.

Even if a teen does not express their distress in words over the path their body is taking, they will likely show other signs of desperation. Depression, withdrawal, self-neglect, acting out, and self-destructive behaviors are common when a child experiences gender-related stress or an emerging and often frightening transgender identity. Some children this age realize on their own that they are transgender. Others need counseling to help determine the cause of their distress[74] and to prepare to disclose to others.

Disclosure

Young children may innocently state the facts as they see them: their heart, soul, and mind do not match their body. But the older the child and the more gradual the awareness, the more one has to lose. The longer the truth was hidden, the harder it is to tell.

Disclosing one's transgender identity can be terrifying when there are concerns about how others will respond and the long-term impact on relationships, so secrecy often feels like the best protection. But maintaining the secret takes a heavy toll and usually, eventually gives way. Some teens disclose in the car to avoid eye contact, others do it while away at school, some do it in writing, others wait until they are grown and gone. One of the most unfair but common accusations leveled against trans people after disclosure is that they purposely deceived others. Close associates may wonder if they ever really knew the person when something so fundamental has been hidden.

In many cases parents are the last to be told, not the first. A parent's inability to accept certain aspects of their child's experience can result in the child excluding those experiences from his or her own consciousness in an effort to prevent the caregiver from turning away or becoming unavailable.[75] A parent who cannot fathom the truth of their child's transgender identity can actually hinder or slow their child's own realization of it. The more society as a whole, and especially parents, are aware of gender dysphoria as they observe their child's development, the sooner and more easily a child will be able to disclose. A parent's responses to their transgender child's disclosure, and their support—have a greater impact on the child's future than any other variable.[76]

Disclosure is a vulnerable time for both of you and can create a crisis all its own. The child may wonder whether their revelation will part the sea and bring about some immediate relief for their confusion and suffering, or if the waters will simply close up again as they watch their parent let this new knowledge sink into oblivion. Gender may be something your teen has thought about and wrestled with for some time. They probably know more than you do about treatment and resources, having sought information online or from friends. Excited to have finally reached some clarity for themselves they may have high expectations that you'll get on board right away.

If their disclosure comes as a total shock, your immediate reaction may be confusion, questions, and an urge to apply brakes.

Words at this time may be difficult as you sort through a myriad of tangled feelings including the fear of saying the wrong thing. Even if you helped to initiate the breakthrough, you may need time to adjust and consider before moving immediately toward transition as your teen might have hoped. You may have to ask for some time while you gather information, sort out your reactions, and work to catch up. But stumbling assurances that you love them and will work with them to figure out the next steps can be crucial in helping your child hold onto hope.

Stages of Emergence

Every transgender person is different in how and when they come to awareness, and more research is needed on how young people disclose to parents since most of the clinical work has been done with adults. In her groundbreaking book, *Transgender Emergence*, psychologist Arlene Istar Lev identifies six stages of emergence for the transgender person:

1. Awareness
2. Seeking information/reaching out
3. Disclosure to significant others
4. Exploration: identity and self-labeling
5. Exploration of transition issues: presentation, possible body modification
6. Integration: acceptance and post-transition issues [77]

Lev also identifies four stages of emergence for family members:

1. Discovery and disclosure
2. Turmoil
3. Negotiation
4. Finding balance [78]

When you compare where you are in your own process of emergence with where your child or teen is in theirs it can shed light on some of the conflict. The turmoil stage is different for everyone but may be accompanied by withdrawal or isolation as you come to terms with your own feelings about the disclosure. This may hinder your ability to stay focused on your child at an especially vulnerable time. The very act of disclosure raises the child's hopes and expectations that help will come soon to alleviate their pain. If it does not, and if additional stress is added by other life circumstances shortly thereafter, the child's sense of despair and hopelessness can be heightened.

REFLECTIONS

Responding to Disclosure

Immediately following Kendra's disclosure, I was in the turmoil and negotiation stages, buried in my own difficult emotions and reframing what she was saying as sexual orientation instead of gender identity based on what I was able to consider and accept. By this time, Kendra was exploring self-labels and presentation in the world. Time was marching quickly for her and she wanted immediate answers and resolution before she got any older, while I was trying to slow down what felt like a speeding train.

While I never overtly urged Kendra to conform to gender norms, I am struck by how long my own biases, assumptions, and aspirations got in the way of my ability to see and hear Kendra's truth. Had we been exploring the feelings behind her gender nonconformity and talking about gender all along, she may have been spared the burden of secrecy. The idea of her being a boy may have come up naturally in conversation or play. If gender had been a topic woven easily into make-believe from the time she was young, perhaps it would not have been so emotionally charged during adolescence. If I had figured out an indirect approach or even come right out and asked if she ever dreamed of being a boy, it might have encouraged her to tell me. Even if she evaded the question at first, it would have given her permission to revisit the topic later, in her own time. It would have signaled to her that I was ready to hear and to help. But the truth is I wasn't ready so I couldn't ask. I was caught in my own unwillingness to see, afraid to "give her any ideas"; as if my avoidance could prevent her from pondering, wishing, and hoping.

You won't be alone if your world feels like it's crumbling when your child tells you they are transgender. We count on the gender of our child to be permanent, immutable, forever. Every parent's reaction is different depending on your child's age, your relationship to them, whether you guessed it first or were caught off guard, how attached you were to your child's assigned gender, your assumptions for your child's future, and your level of support from friends and family. It's not uncommon for fathers losing their sons and mothers losing their daughters to have a more difficult journey—as if the child, in moving away from the gender of a parent, is rejecting that parent.

We develop lasting bonds with the assigned gender of our child. Before a baby has any awareness of being a girl or a boy, we have held that knowledge like skin to skin and reflected it back to our baby with every gesture, gaze, word, and touch. And suddenly we're asked to take it all back and start over again. It can feel like returning to childbirth. A knot of emotions may surface, to be untangled, examined, and released. I wondered at times if it was any easier for parents of very young children. Does the length of time we've known our child in their assigned gender make it harder to welcome their affirmed gender?

Let Feelings Surface

Handling the feelings that surface while you focus on helping your child is daunting. Change is hard enough and change you didn't choose and can't control is harder still. Consider keeping a journal for this part of your journey. Over the next several weeks and months, try to identify and record the feelings that emerge. They may unexpectedly overwhelm you during these first weeks after disclosure or you may be able to keep them at bay until you are ready to call them up. An image from the past, a photograph, an object your child made are all potential triggers for powerful emotions. Feelings can run the gamut and can include disbelief, sadness, fear, shame, guilt, and loss. Resist the temptation to avoid or push away these intense sensations.

Keep your internal process separate from your child's. The clearer you are about your own process and the better your needs are met, the stronger advocate you will be for your child. Let the tears flow freely. See if you can travel deep into the emotion that causes pain or tears and gain some insight. What triggers these feelings? What are the thoughts behind them? What do you think will change now that you know this about your child? What is really at the heart of these painful emotions? Do you have a faith tradition or spiritual practice that helps sustain you during times of difficulty and how can you access that now?

Seek counseling for yourself. It will help you sort through your feelings and address your fears as well as keeping your internal process private and separate from your child's. If your partner and you are at odds as to how you interpret what is happening with your child and how to pursue the next steps, couples counseling can be helpful. A transgender child's disclosure can destabilize a family just at the time the child needs parental support the most. Each parent adjusts differently and in separate time frames. One parent can feel torn asunder when a child discloses; another can be accepting and ready to take the next step; and another may resist discussing the topic all together. Divergent viewpoints increase the stress level of families coming to terms with how best to respond. Many parents eventually find common ground with their child's best interests as their goal, even if it means reaching that destination via their own individual routes. Some parents may have to make the difficult decision to choose the child's well-being over staying with a partner who cannot move toward acceptance. Attending to the needs of your other children is also critical since they have their own mix of feelings and adjustments to make. Individual or family counseling for them may be warranted so their concerns are not overshadowed.

A period of mourning is often needed for parents of transgender children and teens. It is normal to grieve over lost dreams for your child; to experience a painful letting go of fantasies you once had and experiences you were going to share. You may need time to rework your dreams as your child takes a path different from the one you planned or hoped for. You may also feel grief over losing the child who goes away so the new one can come forth.[79] Our loss is complicated by the fact that the child we are grieving is still perceptibly alive in our memory at the same time that the new child is emerging.

This is unlike other types of loss because it is relatively uncommon and not socially recognized. You may feel isolated, alone, and embarrassed by your own sadness at the same time that your child feels reborn. You may even question your right to grieve since this is not a death; your child is still very much alive.[80] My child didn't have a terminal illness, so why all my tears? Part of me scolded the other part for being such a baby. But it's important to be gentle with yourself through this period. Many of these feelings are not rational so they cannot be reasoned away.

There may also be self-blame over prior parenting decisions and behaviors. You may feel guilty for not hearing sooner what your child was saying, if not in words, in behavior and dress; for missing signs along the way; for dismissing or avoiding conversations about gender; or urging your child to fit in and conform. Some parents have remorse for pushing their child to disclose too quickly to others rather than letting them take the lead.[81] Suffice it to say that parenting a transgender child comes with all the usual parenting missteps, doubts, and feelings of inadequacy but with fewer resources and social supports.

Your Child's Needs Come First

Do you ever feel shame or embarrassment for both yourself and your child when he or she doesn't conform to gender norms? Do you worry that your family will be singled out or that others will judge you for your parenting decisions even when they have no idea of your child's experience? This might be particularly distressing if you and your family are minorities in your community not wishing to stand out. Are there influential people in your community or faith congregation who believe LGBTQ people are sinful?

Attending to your internalized sense of shame or embarrassment is critical because these feelings can inadvertently lead to making rules or decisions that benefit and protect you instead of your child.[82] Remind yourself that this is not about you or how others perceive you. Helping your child have a healthy, happy, confident, and successful future is what matters. Your courage in the face of judgment will make you stronger and will model courage for your child. In fact, our gender nonconforming and transgender children are often our best teachers in courage! Speaking with those who judge you, your family, or your child with the goal of inspiring understanding and compassion is an act of courage. Letting go of people who cannot or will not be accepting and supportive is also an act of courage.

Stay particularly vigilant and connected to your child during the vulnerable time of disclosure. Their expectations are high that things will quickly improve at the same time that you are adjusting to their disclosure. You may need more time and they may need immediate relief. Negotiating how to meet both your needs will be critical as you move through this dangerous passage on your journey.

Your teen may feel angry and impatient, interpreting your need for time as rejection, negativity, or indifference. It is helpful to reassure them that you heard them, love them, and will support them as you plan the next steps together. Gender has probably been their main focus for some time. They may be elated to have a name for how they feel and their secret finally out. They may already have a solution in mind, such as hormones, and be anxious to get started. Remind them of the time they needed to understand their gender dissonance. Give them some idea of how much time you think you might need. Include them in your reading and research and find out what they are learning. Ask them to recommend resources: websites, blogs, online groups, books, and people to speak with. Research local counselors and health care providers that you can consult with to discuss treatment options and LGBTQ support groups for you and your child.

Waiting can be excruciating since time for children and teens is measured differently than for adults. Try to remember how you felt during adolescence to help you understand your child's feelings now. They are ready to get on with their lives and feel that too much time has already gone by in the wrong gender. You may have to do much of your inner work of acceptance at the same time that you are walking beside them toward their transition. Their happiness and uplifted spirits as they move toward living in their affirmed gender can be contagious, likely dispelling much of your fear and resistance. But if your child or teen becomes more agitated once transitioning begins, take note that something else is probably going on.[83]

Engage in routine and familiar activities or conversations. Remind yourself that these family routines are likely to continue and that only some things, not everything, will change. Imagine seeing the boy beneath the girl or the girl beneath the boy. Notice aspects of this person that have been there all along. Open your heart to your emerging son or daughter.

Dismantle Transphobia

Transphobia is negative feelings, attitudes, and behaviors toward transgender people. Your own transphobia may peek out from behind the curtain if you are honest with yourself. Your teen identifies with a community, a group you may have always considered "other," not you, not like you. You may have negative stereotypes and assumptions about transgender people and now your child is one. You may think being transgender or transsexual is a mental illness or a choice. You may worry what kind of life this will mean for your child since so many portrayals of trans people are negative, or sexually exploitive. It can be humiliating to confront your prejudices toward transgender and transsexual people yet that is often at the core of some of our visceral negative feelings when our child discloses. It's also one of the reasons it's so hard for transgender people to self-identify. When we learn our children are transgender we worry they will be bullied, harassed, or victimized in school. We wonder what it means for their education and career. Will they ever be accepted in mainstream society or be forced to live on the margins? Will their rights be respected—to be out, to transition? Who will they love and will they be loved back? Will they have a family and community? Will they face poverty, discrimination, unemployment, poor health, sexual exploitation, or violence?

Judgment, rejection, and abandonment are what can create the lifestyles we fear. The best way to avoid these negative outcomes is for us as parents and family members to accept and embrace our transgender children. Read memoirs, get educated, watch movies, attend meetings, and become friends with transgender, transsexual, and gender nonconforming people. When prejudice and barriers are lifted we meet together in our shared humanity with a mutual need for compassion and community.

Honor Your Process Toward Acceptance

It's important to honor your own process of decision-making and your journey toward acceptance while also supporting your child. You have a significant responsibility and you'll want to be sure you're doing what's best for your child. Since your child is not yet old enough to give consent, you may be making decisions—some irreversible—on their behalf that will greatly impact your child's life and future. Of all the feelings you confront, the one that trumps all others is love for your child. Our solemn, silent vow to a child the moment they are placed in our arms is to protect, nurture, support, stand by, and love them. Affirming that earliest promise with the knowledge that whatever pain you feel, your child's pain is greater, makes it easier to face the complex tangle of emotions that washes over you, unbidden and relentless, during these early steps along your journey.

Holding love aloft like a bright torch to light your way and burn through all that needs to change in you so you can unconditionally love and support your child is your truest guide. You will know the right course of action seeing the happiness and confidence in your child's eyes when they are living in their affirmed gender. Even so, parents for whom this is all new have every reason to want some time. Reaching full understanding and acceptance can be a slow process depending on where you started on the journey. Embracing gender diversity takes personal reflection, being open to hearing the experiences and stories of others, compassion for people who are different from you, and a willingness to unlearn old beliefs and learn new ones. Noticing what makes you similar to someone who differs from you is a good place to start to build common ground since our basic human desires for love, safety, security, and meaningful contribution in the world are often shared despite our differences in attaining these goals.

Your Other Children

Your other children are impacted every bit as much as you are when their sibling is gender nonconforming or transgender. Fair or not, others often form impressions of us based on our siblings. My older sister Sandy was a straight "A" student in school and every teacher who knew her seemed to expect the same from me. It was infuriating to walk in her shadow and not have the space to be my own person. Having a gender nonconforming sibling is far more dramatic. It can make a child the focus of unwanted attention concerning matters for which they have no control and about which others may have little understanding or compassion, at a time when they are trying to carve out their own identity and develop a circle of friends. Given all challenges there are for siblings of transgender children, parents have the responsibility to protect the privacy and support the individuality of their other children.

While siblings are spared the responsibility of decision-making that parents have, they often bear the burden of knowing more than parents do about their sibling's feelings and behaviors. Many transgender children and teens disclose to a sibling before disclosing to parents. Siblings may face challenges of their own about how to respond to the ignorance of peers or abuse directed at them or their nonconforming sibling. Encourage your children to talk about their experiences and feelings about having a gender nonconforming or transgender sibling. Take safety concerns seriously and get school personnel involved.

Even with their assurances they are fine and have no need to talk to you or anyone else, stay alert to ways their lives may be impacted. Are there changes in eating, sleeping, mood, interests, or academic performance? Are their friendships affected? Have they stopped playing with certain children or inviting friends over? Are there signs they are being teased at school or socially ostracized because of their sibling? Do they feel protective or resentful toward their brother or sister? If your nonconforming child has difficulty making friends, does he or she rely too heavily on a sibling for friendship? Are your other children holding back from making demands on the family because of the stress you are under meeting the needs of your nonconforming child? Are your other children withdrawn, anxious, or acting mature beyond their years? Is your nonconforming child manipulating, teasing, or targeting a sibling with their anger or frustration?

Give equal time to your other children in activities they enjoy where gender is not the central theme. Often, the best conversations with children can arise during an activity rather than on a set schedule for talking. Alone time with them can help keep you connected and attentive to their interests and concerns. They too have questions, feelings, and reactions to the behaviors and needs of their nonconforming sister or brother. While the special needs of gender nonconforming or transgender children can be overwhelming pay particular attention to balancing the amount of time and attention you spend with your other children. Take the time to show your love. Tell them you love them and that you are there for them.

Self-Care

Your child's gender identity is probably not the only concern you are facing. There may be other issues with this child, with your other children, or family members. You may have demanding jobs, economic worries, housing, legal, health, safety, or other concerns in the family. When disclosure that your child is transgender comes on top of everything else it can feel overwhelming. You may be going through a contentious divorce where care and treatment for your transgender child is at issue. If this is the case, you will want to add a lawyer experienced in transgender and parental rights to your treatment team. See some of the websites in the Appendix C for resources. Keep your friends aware of what you need to help you help your child.

Let go of thoughts that something you did caused your child to be transgender. Remind yourself that no one knows what causes this and that you are pivotal in the response and outcome. Continue whatever activities you have found that reduce your stress, protect your health, make you happy, and lift your spirits. Make time for friends, take breaks, and get away from time to time. Be open to laughter, fun, and joy. Make time to go out and get away with your partner to strengthen your relationship and enhance communication. What feeds your spirit or creativity? Connect with communities of faith, spiritual practices, or creative outlets that inspire you. Life is rich and beautiful. Your child is a unique blessing and you are his or her parent for reasons you may not understand. There are lessons for growth, awareness, and transformation in all of life's challenges, including this one.

Eleventh Grade

5

Accessing Help and
Aligning Goals

As of now, this very point in time, I feel love to be the most unpleasant feeling ever. I spend my whole time wanting something I can't have. I really want it to go away cuz it's unachievable, but at the same time, I really want it. I'm so annoyed by this I wish I could figure out a way to change into a guy without anyone remembering me as a girl or an easy way to kill myself. I'll brainstorm till I fall asleep:

> *Some type of poison or*
> *Natural venom/toxin*
> *But then I could always go hide*
> *in the woods and OD on somethin.*
> *I wonder if I can OD on pot or crack or coke.*
> *I'll ask someone. Or alcohol or go jump off something,*
> *   that would be good.*
> *Oh oh new plan, somehow get beer, wine, etc.—get*
> *   drunk, go kill myself by jumping off something/*
> *   running into highway. Fun-FUN, fun.*

KENDRA, AGE 16

RECOLLECTIONS

Phone Call

The August before Kendra started eleventh grade at the town
school, she finally agreed to see a therapist of her own. It was
with a woman I interviewed over the phone who came highly
recommended for her work with teens. My hope was that they would
connect instantly and Kendra could pour out all her concerns. I
decided not to ask Kendra about her first session on the way home
taking care to respect her privacy and space. What was still hard
to grasp was how good Kendra appeared on the outside—calm,
confident, articulate—and how sad and scared she was on the inside.

Where had she gotten the message that she needed to keep up
such a strong and impenetrable front when she was in crisis? Was it
time away on that trip that taught her to hold it all in? Had our high
expectations for her led her to split herself in two? Or was it her own
sense of pride and disdain for vulnerability; thinking her peers had
it more together than she did; needing to act the part? First a racial
minority, now a gender minority, she dared not become a mental
health minority. In so many ways she stood apart from her peers
learning to navigate the rough waters of adolescence, high school,
and prepare for her future when most of what the world reflected
back to her was that she was less than, invisible, other, not belonging.
I knew this on a rational level but I had never experienced it, so I
didn't fully understand just how alone she must have felt.

Kendra didn't connect with the first therapist. How was
a middle-aged, white, and heterosexual female going to help a
transgender teen of color struggling with racism, racial identity,
gender identity and expression, self-injury, depression, anxiety, and
thoughts of suicide? So we looked for someone else and met with
three more. Finally Kendra agreed to continue with the fourth
therapist. They had two sessions before the call came.

I was at an overnight meeting for work with executive directors from across the state on September 22 and my phone was on silent for the afternoon session. When I got to my room I noticed a voicemail and heard the fear in Tony's voice when he said to call him ASAP. My hands shook as I punched in the number.

"Kendra took an overdose. One hundred ibuprofen. We're in the emergency room," he said.

There was pounding in my ears as the room spun. My knees buckled and I heard myself scream, then sob. I hadn't unpacked so I grabbed my bag, my books. In the lobby I ran into a colleague and said I needed to leave. A family emergency. She walked me to the parking lot but I couldn't find my car. Panic swept clean my mind and all that had preceded that call was gone. I rushed from end to end of the lot like it was my first time there as my friend tried to calm me and help me envision where I'd parked just hours before. The image of Kendra in a hospital emergency room grew larger by the minute and all I wanted was to be by her side but I could barely put one foot in front of the other and I still had a long way to travel.

The week before, Kendra had changed her mind about schools and decided she wanted to return to her former school. She missed her friends, the familiar routine, the academic challenge, and the freedom to be outside as they walked between classes. To be re-admitted, the school required that she meet with the headmaster, dean, and some faculty members to discuss her reasons for returning. They were all impressed by her poise and persuasiveness and felt she had matured over the summer. They welcomed her back.

She sat at the computer the night before the overdose when I told her I had an out-of-town work meeting the next day and was planning to stay overnight. I was looking forward to the break— alone in a motel room for one night of respite. But her voice said it all. "You're not coming home?" She was hoping to get back into theater class to avoid the physical education option. She hoped to be in the upcoming play but had missed some rehearsals. I was playing phone tag with the drama teacher and said I'd call him during the day to ask if she could get back into theater. She worried it wouldn't get resolved with me out of town. I assured her I'd call her as soon as I heard back from her teacher.

I told her I didn't need to stay since the conference was only ninety minutes away and she could call me after school if she wanted me to come home for the night. I asked her if she would be okay. Coldly she said yes but her body said no. I trusted her words but they were her shield. I'd asked the therapist whether I should ask to check her arms and legs. She wasn't as frightened by the cutting as I was but then she wasn't finding bloody tissues in her daughter's bedroom.

The worry on Kendra's face and in her voice, along with the resigned way her shoulders slumped as she looked away, should've been enough to make me stay home. Part of me knew. But I'd grown so accustomed to the knife-edge of fear over what was ahead I'd learned to live with it. Signs were registering in my heart but dismissed by my head. I asked Tony to be gentle with her and patient when he picked her up from school that day. But instead he nearly left her there when she kept him waiting and then yelled at her on the way home. Everything that day had finally tipped the precarious balance inside her.

That morning, by the time I got to the meeting, my gas tank was on empty and I did something out of the ordinary. I proactively filled the tank as I told myself I may need to leave in a hurry and won't want to stop for gas. It's unsettling how we can know things and yet still be surprised when they happen. My denial, my trust in who Kendra had been—resilient and strong—clouded my ability to see her current, changed self—desperate and alone.

My whole body trembled as I absorbed the shock that Kendra had threatened her life. I would have been physically unable to pump gas in order to get to the emergency room. We were in treacherous, uncharted waters. Everything had changed and I was flooded with regret. Barely able to navigate the road I drove on autopilot. To help me focus and continue breathing, I made phone calls—first to

Joanna and Carol, who were traveling with me on this harrowing journey with my daughter; then Kendra's therapist. I heard the fear in her voice. I had asked her before how I could be sure Kendra was safe; that she would keep her word to not hurt herself. We both knew now that neither of us knew. I called Char in Florida and the Samaritans suicide hotline.

Tony was at home when the police came to the door. Then Kendra stumbled downstairs to tell him what she'd done. She'd called a friend at school who called the dean in the middle of a faculty meeting. The dean called the house but when Tony didn't pick up she called the police. Tony drove Kendra to the nearest emergency room but they transferred her by ambulance to another hospital. I arrived at the second hospital first since it was closer to me. I couldn't sit still long enough for the ambulance to arrive so I drove the fifteen minutes further only to find she had just left. I spent the night running, racing, and lost, barely able to catch up with where Kendra was. It was a metaphor for how I felt; as if Kendra's earlier dream had been true: we were teetering above a river, plunging into the quarry, and being dragged through the ocean too fast for either of us to control. She was the naked baby boy in my dream being carried out of school on a platter.

Survival

Kendra stayed in the hospital for two days under round-the-clock supervision to prevent another attempt. She assured us all she hadn't tried to kill herself—she just wanted the pain to stop. Tony and she had gotten into one of their usual arguments. He was impatient waiting for her when he picked her up from school and she said something disrespectful. When she got home she decided to open the bottle of ibuprofen that she'd purchased days or weeks before. Suicide was something she'd been thinking about for a while and she hid the bottle in a box in her room. In a rage at her father she simply shoved fistfuls of pills into her mouth and before she knew it, the whole bottle was empty.

Her torn and ravaged arm was finally exposed for the IV and against the white sheets of the bed it was an accusing witness to her lonely pain. I was grateful to finally have the help of others since this was obviously greater than anything I could handle alone. The attending physician and psychiatrist pressured us to have her committed to an inpatient psychiatric unit for a week or two to assess her risk and create a safety plan before discharging her to go home. Kendra panicked at the thought of psychiatric hospitalization and implored us not to let them admit her. Again I remembered her traumatic month away. She didn't feel she had a mental health problem but clearly she needed more help than I had found so far. After many phone calls—first to Joanna, a psychotherapist knowledgeable of local facilities, then to inpatient adolescent psych units, and finally partial hospitalization programs—we bucked the system and brought her home. From all I could glean, none of the places under consideration were equipped to deal with adolescent gender identity so we decided to keep her home for the weekend, and find the best partial hospitalization (day) program as soon as possible. Her school wasn't willing to let her come back until she received more intensive care for fear there could be another incident.

The entire weekend Kendra acted like nothing had happened while I lived minute to minute afraid to leave the house. If she didn't pick up her phone when I made a quick trip to the store or was late to meet me somewhere, my heart leapt to my throat and wouldn't settle until hearing her voice or laying hands and eyes on her. Once the call comes, the seed of fear is planted for life. For a week I lived in a trance, going through motions but feeling distant, detached. Every few hours, like a predictable geyser, my chest cracked open and tears came. My heart felt like crushed glass all broken and sharp. I was devastated that my daughter felt so hopeless. I felt sad, guilty, and ashamed to have failed her and not found more help sooner. Some days I just cried out the pain; unable to contain the deep ache in my soul for not being there when she needed me; grateful, so grateful to have a second chance.

Would I always wonder now, hover? Sometimes when walking alone in the woods I'd recall how Kendra used to love linking her arm through mine when we walked and it stopped me in my tracks, brought me to my knees—what we had so narrowly missed. Whenever I swam, tears flowed unbidden toward greater water. I felt my vulnerability acutely, and had a million regrets. If only I'd gone to my office instead of the meeting I would've seen the email from the theater teacher welcoming Kendra back to class. She could've stopped worrying. I would've picked her up that afternoon instead of Tony. The string of events cascading from just one might have turned out totally differently. What tiny threads weave our lives and a break in just one changes everything.

Monday morning Kendra had a psychiatric intake with a compassionate young woman at the local mental health center. She asked me to stay with her. The counselor's supportive, nonjudgmental manner felt like a warm embrace. She was not new to seeing the suffering of teenagers who longed to belong somewhere yet felt hopeless about there being a place for them in this world. Her kindness lessened my guilt and anxiety. She asked Kendra to sign a safety contract promising she'd get help if she felt like hurting herself again. This signed paper in my hand helped me feel a little less afraid of Kendra.

Next it was my job to find the right outpatient program since we had discharged her into our own care. We learned later that by saving the insurance company an inpatient stay, we were now responsible for two five-hundred-dollar copayments—one for the emergency room and one for the outpatient program. It was a huge relief when she was accepted into the adolescent day program at McLean Hospital and could start the very next day. For nine days I drove with Kendra the one hundred miles from home to McLean, then to work, then back to get her in the afternoon, and then home. I enjoyed this time with her despite the gravity of the mission. We talked about the program, the kids she met, school,

the disastrous month away from home, and everyday matters when
we needed to lighten the mood. We stopped to see the campus of
Tufts University on one of our trips home so Kendra could think
about her future.

The first thing she was asked to do at McLean was write a
symptom history. Her school trip played a central role in the start of
her depression. She had told us her truth and no one listened, or if we
did, we overruled her. By the time she got home she was practiced in
walling off her feelings after being inauthentic for a month. Instead
of being happy, she felt disappointed to be home. It was not the home
she left or the home she'd imagined. Everything had changed—her
innocence, her trust in us. And she had changed too. She sank into a
depression she could not speak of, and no one seemed to notice.

Kendra spent from 9 a.m. to 3 p.m. every day with teens whose
lives were torn apart by childhood trauma including neglect, physical
abuse, sexual abuse, domestic violence, substance abuse, homelessness, and foster care while they struggled to know themselves, their
gender identity, sexual orientation, and their hopes for the future.
Her eyes were dramatically opened to the suffering and strength of
others. She suddenly felt normal, even privileged in ways she had
never before considered. She also felt compassion and the desire to
help others with different journeys than hers.

*In the fall of junior year, I came face-to-face with death. It
had come as a surprise to nearly everyone, myself included. I
remember watching myself, seeing myself start the year before,
and I grabbed on to anything to stop myself. For several months,
it had been like attempting to back up a cliff with an 80%
incline, and I could feel myself starting to slip.*

*It wasn't of any avail. There was no point to breathing
anyway then. It was slowly becoming inevitable. Still, the fact
that I actually overdosed that Thursday afternoon and took 100
painkillers had been a sudden head-on collision. Before I even
knew it, I was in the hospital. . . .*

Going to the mental hospital was the worst part. Very few people are diagnosed as "crazy" in other people's eyes, and less are hospitalized because they simply can't deal with the life that "normal" people set out as playing rules.

I remember driving out to Belmont with my mother that morning. It was cold, but warmed up that afternoon. During our "free-times" and lunches, I talked more and more with the people there.

All of us were different; we all had our own gut-wrenching and sobering stories unique to only us. But at that very same time we were all the same. We all knew pain, perhaps too familiarly, and we were all unable to live in the world some "normal" person had constructed for everyone else and who had already marked out "our lives." We had all been diagnosed as "crazy" or "just incompetent teens" by almost the rest of the world. And so seeing the world telling us whom, what we should be, well, we naturally concluded we were the wrong ones. We never thought to question the world. To some extent I wish I had before taking 50 times the recommended dose, but quite often overdosing on something is the only way to see the truth. I never would have known it to be living a perfectly good life by being a multiracial queer kid that starts a Gay-Straight Alliance, loves science, theater, and the arts all at the same time. I do still question myself, and I'm not at all completely informed. I wonder if I'll go to hell for being who I am, but now at least I have the voice to whisper the other side.

The thing that saddens me is the fact that I see this struggle everywhere I go. I am friends with a transgender 14-year-old, who sees no point in living this life dealt out to him. I'm terrified that self-injury doesn't surprise me anymore. I'm terrified that what happened to me can so easily happen to my close friends, and they could be less fortunate than me. Had I not surprised myself that time, startled myself out of the circling thoughts, I would have died. And I can't express in words how

*glad I am that that didn't happen. So ask me if I'm glad it
happened? And to be honest, I am. I still have my life now, but
I'm still very much in the process of helping people struggling
with the same things find a different "overdose." Not one of
medication, but perhaps knowledge that who they are is who
they are, and nothing, no one can change that or take it away
from them.*

KENDRA, AGE 17

The partial program gave Kendra insight and support as well
as practical tools for naming and coping with anxiety, anger, mood
swings, panic, and depression using dialectical behavior therapy
(DBT). Yet despite having several patients for whom gender was
also an issue, the program staff did not provide gender counseling
or address treatment options for gender identity, just ways for
coping with the stress of living with the dysphoria. At first, Kendra
wanted to leave McLean after just one week and return to school
as soon as possible for fear she'd be too far behind in her classes
with junior year being so important for colleges. Then she wanted
to stay at McLean forever because she finally met kids like herself.
She dreaded going back to school because of the social isolation and
academic pressure.

Kendra was beginning to find her place in the world. Racially
mixed and transgender, she had been working out her identity in
settings where she always felt *other*. She never easily fit in and was
coming to terms with how to handle that. She had worried there was
something wrong with her; that compared to her peers at school she
was not enough—not smart enough, not popular, talented, white,
female, male; so she needed a whole new peer group where she was
enough; where she did belong. Family was no longer enough. It was
only when she found teens like herself—kids of color and LGBTQ
kids—who also knew what it was like to feel on the outside looking
in, that Kendra finally experienced a sense of belonging.

I wanted to hide behind dark glasses the next time I went to Kendra's school. I felt embarrassed, certain that faculty, administrators, students, and parents were discussing our child and family. It felt worse being one of only a few diverse families in the school. Kendra had been on the agenda of faculty meeting three weeks in a row: first to discuss her return; then to report the overdose; and later for assignments while at McLean. Because Kendra had impressed a formidable team of faculty and administrators at her old school to discuss re-entry in a meeting with them just days before the overdose, the school distrusted their ability to know her. She'd had a panic attack in the car before the meeting because of her ambivalence about returning and begged me to get her out of the meeting. But no one could have guessed she felt anxious by her self-assured presentation at that meeting.

Parents panicked when their daughters told them they'd seen Kendra's arm just after she cut. The school held a meeting about the overdose with Kendra's grade without so much as a phone call to us. Kendra found out when she received an email from a student to say she was thinking of her. This breach of privacy made it even harder for her to go back. Now no school felt safe. When Kendra finally did return to school in October she had changed and so had her friends. She was more isolated than ever and some former friends avoided her.

Her lifeline was weekly attendance at nAGLY, North Shore Alliance for Gay and Lesbian Youth, where she didn't feel so separate and alone. Developing friendships with teens that had similar questions and experiences opened a window that shined light in her life. For once she felt accepted. Since she was not yet driving and nAGLY was twenty miles from home, we had lots of time to talk in the car. I credit nAGLY with saving Kendra's life.

Attempting to regain some control when all else seemed out of control, I made a list of ways to help keep Kendra alive once the partial program was over.

- Helping her stay connected to what she loved; affirming her considerable talents and strengths and not letting her

lose sight of those no matter how discouraging her current
situation might feel

- Keeping her on track academically so she would have a
  history of success with solid life goals and career options
- Expanding her social relationships beyond school to include
  more LGBTQ teens as well as teens of color
- Finding knowledgeable professionals who understood gender
  identity, the symptoms that accompany it, and long-term
  treatment options
- Exposing her to employment to build self-esteem in the
  world outside of school and earning her own money
- Supporting her spirituality

Free Fall

Kendra's overdose was one day after the anniversary of my mother's
death seventeen years earlier. I often wondered how her life might
have been enriched by my mother's love and attention. I thought
myself a good mother but when your daughter attempts suicide the
fabric of that illusion unravels. When a stitch or two had dropped
with her cutting and despair—I was on it, figuring out what to do,
and working fast to fix it. But then the whole cloth ripped apart at
once, and I heard myself repeating, "Kendra, my daughter, tried to
kill herself!" It seemed incongruous, impossible. But I needed to
grasp that truth and hold onto it deep down lest I forget or deny
it—like when the body goes into shock after a critical injury to block
out the pain. I wanted and needed to feel the pain; to stay in the
knowledge of her deep and abiding despair because she was so good
at hiding it—from me and others.

It wasn't that I missed the intensity of her suffering. I'd seen
it and held her in it. I saw emails. I knew she was cutting; reading
websites about self-injury; writing poems of futility; considering ways
to die. But I thought I could stay ahead of her; spend time together;
find the right therapist; de-escalate her rage. But I couldn't carry it

all. It was too heavy a load and I needed back up. I'd been late to the scene and dared not forget that. A moment's delay to any rescue can be fatal. We'd been spared a tragedy; we were pulled from the brink. I wanted that to sink deep down so it would never happen again.

Lost

Like a broken winged bird
crushed glass
all jagged, cold and cutting
joy ground down to dust
trust blown to bits
lost footing and falling
sorrow forever etched on my face
I am a mother wandering.
Lost child lost time lost touch
when did the road turn
and I did not see you leave?
Finally stopped in my tracks
shaken awake by your one act
I see my love broken, bleeding, neglected
once offered and open.
I fight now
for your words
your story of our past.

CANDACE, OCTOBER 11, 2005

I asked myself a hundred times whether it would've made a difference if I'd stayed home that Thursday night. Kendra bought the pills two weeks earlier—walking home from the other school. What if she'd taken them one afternoon when she was home alone? How close had we come? No wonder my feet knew enough to walk me out of work early every day to get home for her. I couldn't go back and relive history but I had to listen harder to my inner knowing and honor that above what anyone else said. To do that best I needed to be centered, present, and alert.

Moving On

We wanted to move for a very long time—to a quieter street, more room, fireplace, yard, garage if possible, and the right price. We looked for years but I felt the urge to move now more than ever. Our tiny house on a busy road was filled with bittersweet memories— childhood, holidays, pets, writing fragments about suicide, and an overdose in the skylight room where Kendra used to reach out arms over her crib after a nap. I had to escape to save my own life.

We found a house in just the right area and put our old house on the market. "After all I've been through this year, why are you doing this now?" Kendra pleaded. But change can be good and that house was haunted with memories that I was ready to leave behind as we packed, cleaned, and prepared to sell. Running feet on hardwood floors, shrieks of laughter, standing guard over a sleeping baby, dreaming and tucked, hearing her breathe; the house at rest after hectic trying days of laundry, diapers, crying, and spills. Kendra used to love Christmas decorating whether a dollhouse, tree house, or our house. She strung lights on the tiny pine tree in her magic childhood garden and put blue lights on the pear tree out front. Her creative touch was magic and beautiful—a blessing to behold. It was precisely why I had to leave. It was the house where Kendra had been a girl. She no longer lived there and neither could I.

All my churned up feelings about Kendra's disclosure and her subsequent overdose were being acted out physically and I couldn't stay still. I packed, cleaned, sorted, tossed, scraped, painted, and moved. Instead of keeping my feelings at bay, repetitive, physical work took my thoughts into circling, spiraling interior space. As my body sweated, sanded, lifted, and carried, my mind moved through the wide arc of feelings that pulled at me. I steered the heavy electric sander over hardwood floors, got covered in sawdust that stuck to sweat on my face and arms, and filled my nose until I sneezed it out for days afterward. I hand-sanded floors coating them with polyurethane, sanding between four coats until they shined like glass. I painted walls, ceilings, moved furniture and packed dishes. The empty new house became my retreat and sanctuary. I created order out of chaos; brought beauty and hope to my outside world while each tangled feeling had its time in the spotlight to make its case, rage, and recede.

The fall after my mother died, my dad came for long visits at our old house while he and Tony renovated the kitchen. He hammered nails alone during the day while we were at work. One rainy, blustery night we found him on the back porch nailing up a huge sheet of plywood with no one to hold it. He needed the challenge, a project, and to be out in the elements. When our kitchen was finished he pounded nails with Habitat for Humanity any place in the world they needed him. Now I was my dad, running thoughts through my mind like paint off a brush; letting grief pour out through my hands. I don't know how else I could've recovered. The constant motion of my body and the rhythmic lapping of my thoughts helped me move on to safer ground when writing kept me circling back. I would've climbed the walls with recrimination, grief, anger, sadness, and worry had I not been active with tangible, positive, forward momentum.

We closed on the new house in January, renovated through February, March, and April, and moved in on Mother's Day weekend during a monsoon. A week later we surprised Kendra with a birthday party at our new house on the last day of eleventh grade. Many of her classmates had just started driving after dark and some got lost. Several gathered out front and came up the walk to the front door together to surprise her. Once again, she was happy and amazed so many came.

Boy Girl

Kendra was slowly transitioning to be a boy. Since puberty she'd been wearing boxers and swimming in T-shirts and rounding her shoulders to hide her breasts from outing her. Since she was nine, she'd been praying to wake up a boy, she told me. On one of our rides to nAGLY she asked if our health insurance covered breast removal and whether testosterone built muscle mass. Just for fun one day she drew on a moustache and sideburns with mascara.

Her lightness and enthusiasm about the topic was in direct proportion to the heavy weight I felt pressing down on my chest every time she brought it up. It still felt to me as though someone was dying, but who? It sure didn't seem like her. She'd finally come out of her shell. The cutting had stopped, she was talking about the future, and was bold and defiant instead of sullen and withdrawn. Was it me that was dying? Was it us; some fantasy future for the two of us that I'd conjured up over the years? Now that her fearful secret was out I was the one feeling afraid. Had she been protecting me all this time?

Kendra knew she was loved, respected, and a member of our family always and forever but we struggled to find our footing together as she carved out her new authentic identity. We cried, yelled, talked, walked, hugged, and went to therapy. We stormed out on one another; came back to one another; gave up and gave in; wondered how we got here and where we were going; but through it all we held onto love, communication, and connection.

Kendra's class and their parents were responsible for organizing and staffing an auction for their senior class trip. The class was center stage hosting the evening, entertaining guests with singing, a video, and comedy routines. It was a formal affair for parents and students alike. All of the girls wore dresses and heels; boys, jackets and ties. Kendra wore a tux, tie, and sneakers. She'd put off deciding what to wear until the last minute due to dread and denial, wishing she could avoid the whole event.

That morning we ran to the local vintage clothing store to see what they had. We were in luck. We bought tuxedo pants and a formal jacket that not only fit but were reasonably priced. But the shirt was a problem. It was bulky and long and even when cut shorter it looked awkward and uncomfortable. The collar gathered in little pleats around Kendra's feminine neck when a tie was added so we tried hiding the folds toward the back. Then there was the haircut. Kendra made the setting too low on her electric razor so shaved off all her hair instead of giving herself a trim. It was too short even for her standards. Helping her dress for this compulsory school event was just one more painful reminder of how Kendra didn't fit in there—or anywhere, in fact. How little she fit in her own skin and how alone she felt. What was expressed as lethargy, shouting, and storming out, was fueled by loneliness, fear, and estrangement from her body and appearance. She knew the soul within, however, and that gave her the strength, courage, and confidence to buck the tide. I always admired this child's brave resolve.

In June Kendra's class went on another trip. Before they left, Kendra insisted on planting a vegetable garden in our new backyard. With everything else needing work and the yard not in shape for a garden, it was quite an undertaking. She wanted to transplant some of the fruit trees she planted in the old yard but they were too big to dig out. A vegetable garden was her way of connecting to the new house and yard since she'd been very attached to the old one. She reasoned that if she got homesick this time, and then remembered home was no longer as she'd known it now that we moved, at least she could look forward to her garden. The plan made sense and we'd learned to listen. By the time she left, her vegetable garden was orderly and gorgeous with carrots, beans, lettuce, broccoli, watermelon, tomatoes, zucchini, pumpkins, and herbs. On this trip the class stayed together instead of with host families. She visited interesting places, took great pictures, had a good time, and wasn't homesick. The trip was good for her.

Dating

As if making up for lost time, Kendra's focus during senior year was on friendships outside of school, and dating. For seven years she'd been with the same twenty-five kids in her class and was now spreading her wings with kids that more closely resembled her racially, and in their gender identity and expression. She went to meetings, parties, and dances with new groups of friends. It is affirming and exciting for both teens and parents when our LGBTQ children start dating since we hope they will love and be loved. As parents, we cannot take for granted that our LGBTQ teens have the information they need for safe sex. After visiting the local family planning agency for brochures, I was dismayed to find they were ill-equipped to discuss safe sex with gay, lesbian, and bisexual teens and even less so for educating transgender teens. Our children fare best when connected to LGBTQ-specific health care providers or health centers for their overall health care since few family practice or mainstream providers are trained in the unique health education and medical needs of our children.

Next Steps

The focus at school was on the competitive college application process, which heightened Kendra's anxiety about the future. High school was stressful enough. College felt worse. Her essay was about bridging her opposing sides—black/white; male/female; romantic/warrior. It was insightful, revealing, and authentic. But as the time approached, it was obvious that college was feeling just like that freshman class trip. Kendra didn't feel ready. There was considerable social and academic pressure to step up to the challenge and go with the flow of what everyone else was excited about. But I saw in Kendra a palpable sense of ambivalence and dread. Kendra needed time to sort out gender before embarking on this next new phase.

So what was our position as parents before this next big launch? I knew it was time to stop, listen, observe, and reflect. I wanted to get the college call right since the stakes were so high. I didn't want to let go too soon or hold on too long. I had forgiven myself for the freshman class trip. We hadn't known. We'd done our best. I knew more now. I was going to read her better, listen harder, and see into her silence. I wanted to wrap all of who this person was—the tender ya-ya girl and the tough rapper boy—in a cloak of love and protection so we'd do what was best for her. Between her headphones, cell phone, and the Internet, there was little opportunity to talk. In the car it was her music and when we were alone she seemed to hide behind a silent, simmering anger that kept me at a distance. Every so often there was a spark from that former bond and a meaningful conversation ensued. I didn't want to miss those moments so I made myself unobtrusively available to watch and listen to better understand this enigmatic adolescent who kept me in a perpetual state of anxiety.

Anger is healthier than depression. It moves the pain outward; away from self-blame and loathing to root causes. I could only imagine how enraged she felt being born in the wrong body. It pained me to think about it. But it also hurt when she turned that rage against me since I felt like I was doing everything I could to help her. Even my love had its limits and I was reaching them during this tumultuous period.

All year I couldn't wait for graduation to come and when it finally did, I felt out of time, out of sorts, and sad. It had been a very hard year and I was a churning sea of mixed emotions. The ocean that morning was steely gray and shrouded in heavy fog but the birds were busily chirping as they went about their morning tasks. As I walked the coastal path I marveled at the work Kendra had done that year, not just academically but in personal growth. She'd gone against the tide and carved out her own clear transgender identity amidst a group unlike herself. She started a Gay-Straight Alliance at her school, developed a whole new circle of friends and negotiated

her way through her first dating experiences. She'd also gotten and
kept her first paying job and saw firsthand from her supervisor that
life gets better for LGBTQ people after high school. And despite
her reservations, she'd kept an open mind, visiting colleges and
completing applications.

Seniors who wanted to were invited to give graduation speeches.
Kendra, who had entered school like a turtle in a shell, now had a
few things to say to everyone:

> *My mom always used to call her mother my guardian angel. I
> never really believed her, but went along with it. Angels didn't
> exist, and even if they did, why would they spend their time
> taking care of us? Why would we matter in the least to them?
> They were too far away. Somewhere off in the stars I'd look up
> at, at night.*
>
> *My grandmother died when my mother was pregnant with
> me, and I never "met" her, so my young mind came up with the
> question of my meaning to her wherever far away she was, and
> my answer was insignificant.*
>
> *One day, I remember getting stuck under the lap lane
> divider in a pool, and I couldn't get air. No matter how much
> I kicked, or tried to go under, I got more stuck. It didn't help
> that I was terrified of the long painted lines at the bottom of
> the pool, and now was forced to make an awkward eye contact
> with them. That was the first time I remember thinking about
> a guardian angel.*
>
> *I've stumbled a lot in the past, and I plan to do so in the
> future. It's not as though I want to, but more like something
> that happens to us, no matter who we are. Waking up in a
> hospital bed, from myself, looking out at the sun, over pines
> through the window; that was one of my close experiences. But
> I'm still here, talking to you.*
>
> *At the same time, another feeling is thinking about all the
> chances I've been given, and didn't chase. "I can't end here,"*

I remember thinking in the hospital, reflecting on the words I heard from someone in that blackout.

So all of you, don't let your own fears hold you back, because you will always have a guardian angel to save you if you fall. As one of my favorite quotes goes: "Play your cards. Go against all odds. Shoot for the moon. If you miss, you are still amongst those stars." And once all of it's done, if you take that jump into the unknown with the slightest taste of succeeding, then you'll win a hundred more battles had you not; if you only laid down and watched the stars instead.

So, shoot the moon. Who cares if you don't hit it. There wouldn't be any constellations for others to admire if people always got the moon on their first try . . . Missing is also a good thing. You find yourself in the stars, on your journey there. Orion becomes yourself outlined in burning suns, your tracing map.

I've come to find out that people are angels. Maybe not the ones with wings and silver and gold halos, but we all have potential to change someone's life, to save them. It doesn't happen in divine miracles, but rather through . . . everyone doing what they naturally do. So all of you, thank you for being those angels, for not only shooting the moon, but missing. Give what you have to give, and light your part. We each have our place across the night sky.

The college decision loomed large and immediate. Kendra was considering the University of Massachusetts–Amherst, so it made sense to attend an orientation to see what it was like before just packing up and attending or declining outright. There was a parent orientation at the same time so after checking dates with her, I reserved a spot for us in June and booked a room for myself at the campus hotel. As the date approached, Kendra wanted to reschedule but by then all other dates were taken. It conflicted with a camp that her girlfriend wanted her to attend in Maine. Kendra hadn't wanted to go to camp but as with most things that summer, pressure from her girlfriend mounted and she found it difficult to stick with her decision. I negotiated dropping her off at the ferry for Maine once the orientation was over.

It was a stressful trip to Amherst. In addition to her usual resistance, there were last-minute items she needed for camp and I was frustrated by her change of plans and additional errands. As we packed up the car she asked if I'd be devastated if she started hormone therapy. I said no, I'd been expecting it at some point. But then I corrected my reply and said it was true, I had been expecting it but I had also been dreading it. She said she knew that.

As we walked toward registration at UMass orientation, the organizers sorted students by gender. When Kendra approached, the greeter said, "Gentlemen go over there," pointing to the men's dorm. Kendra broke out of line and started to lose it, heading straight toward the car. She was not yet using male pronouns or men's bathrooms so this did not feel right yet, but then neither did a women's dorm.

"I hate you for bringing me here!" she shouted, starting to cry. "You don't understand. You never listen. I want to defer college. I always have."

"I'm sorry," I said. "You can defer if you want to. We're not making any commitments here. It just seemed like a good idea to see what it's like before you decide one way or the other."

"I want to get out of here and go to Maine. I don't want to be here. I'm tired of taking care of everyone else. For once I want to take care of myself," she shouted.

"UMass is supposed to be one of the best universities for LGBTQ students so I'm sure they'll make accommodations for you if we speak with them."

"They don't get it Mom. Can't you tell? I can't do this dorm thing—not for tonight and not for the next four years," she insisted.

"I understand honey," I said. "Dorm life is tough for transgender students but more and more colleges understand that and are creating LGBTQ dorms or offering private rooms," I said.

"I want a smaller college. This place is too big."

"Deferring might be exactly what you'll decide after this visit but since we're already here, we might as well get as much information about the place as possible," I said. "Why not find out how good it really is for trans students? Maybe they just overlooked it for orientation and if we ask, they'll make arrangements. I'm sure it won't be the first time they've been asked."

To my surprise and relief, Kendra agreed to stay. The organizers gave her a private room in the women's dorm. They asked about her comfort using the women's bathroom—and suggested she might want to get up early to shower while everyone was still in bed or use the bathroom in the basement.

Of course Kendra was right—I had no idea how she felt or what she was going through. I could only imagine the discomfort and stress of wondering how you were being perceived, the urge to withdraw and be left alone, the loneliness of never quite fitting in, and the anger at having to ask to be included. It made complete sense why she was so enraged all the time. I knew it was time to stop pushing so hard and to let her take the lead. I also knew it was time to back off if college was not meant to be—now or later. I was open to leaving this place as soon as she said the word and taking her to the ferry for Maine. It would probably be very healing for her to get into the woods and away from all the pressure.

But I was also worried. What would she do if she didn't go to college? Would she live at home, do nothing, and get more isolated and depressed? We barely survived the past year and summer was going to be hard enough. Were we looking at another twelve long months? Was she planning to go on hormones to become a boy? That made me sad to think about, but then who was I to say? This was not about me; it was about this soul, this being who was lost right now. It was about my love and how far my love could go with her. I thought I could go to the end of the world, but not if I was to become the punching bag for her rage. I wouldn't be able to hang in there under those circumstances. I would need some kindness and connection as well. I remembered her withdrawal and irritability preceding that first school trip. Was she getting ready to feel betrayed again by going along with something everyone else thought was right for her when she knew it wasn't? I was going to pay attention and vigilantly guard against that this time.

Around 10 p.m., Kendra called me. I was in the campus hotel—which could not have been more inhospitable. The concrete walls made the room feel as cozy as a parking garage. Kendra reported being stared down during the welcoming meeting at the dorm because all the girls thought she was a guy. It was excruciating. The idea of studying in that environment seemed ridiculous, impossible. I invited her to stay in my room but there was a curfew and she was locked in.

In the morning she told me how she had to stumble over trashcans in the dark to use the bathroom in the basement so as not to freak out the girls by using their bathroom. She wasn't interested in anything else on the program that day or the next and just wanted to get out of there. I suggested we at least go meet with a lesbian friend of mine who was director of the Everywoman's Center and then see if we could meet with the director of the LGBTQ center. As it turned out the director of the LGBTQ center was out that day but we did meet with the director of the women's center who was sad to hear about Kendra's experience. It seemed as though orientation was not as well thought out as the actual school experience might be. But first impressions matter and Kendra was not impressed.

We left that morning feeling like we were playing hooky. College was officially off the table—at least that year. Kendra was relieved. We laughed all the way to Maine feeling light and carefree without the pressure of trying to make something work before its time. Kendra shared how she'd lied to a guy the previous night about what high school sports she played. One guy saw her "Kendra" nametag and asked what her parents were smoking when they gave her a girl's name. Gender is often determined by visual cues making everything else follow. Most people become incredibly uncomfortable with any gender dissonance. It was crazy how many situations like this Kendra and other trans people face every day. How awkward and stressful it must be to have to lie about your past, yourself, in order to fit in. But tears came when she said these were the same kind of guys that, if they found out they'd been fooled, would beat her up. It went fast from funny to frightening. The trip from Amherst to Maine felt like a jailbreak. It was a bookend to that trip freshman year. We talked, laughed until tears came, and had fun again after so many terrifying confrontations that spring. Our body language said it all. Finally, we'd made the right decision! Kendra was staying home this time.

It was easy saying no to college. It was much harder knowing what to say yes to. I slept soundly that night after releasing Kendra into the wilds of Maine certain we'd made the right decision. But I awoke the next morning with a stab of pain as I rolled over—like waking from a nightmare I couldn't quite recall. Then it hit me: Kendra was working on a plan for how to transition before going to college. I had been lulled into believing she might be able to live in an androgynous middle ground for a while before being sure. But based on what she told me during our drive the day before, there were too many ways she had to hide and lie to live on the gender line long-term. The threat of being caught, made out, and read, was dangerous, highly anxiety-ridden, even life-threatening. While gender was critical, it also felt important to support her efforts to stay on track for work, life, and educational goals so that once gender was resolved, she'd be successful in other ways too. Once again I made a list for how we could live together for another year since the past one had been hell:

- Find a therapist experienced working with LGBTQ adolescents and teens of color
- Explore gap-year experiences that might interest Kendra— maybe some time in La Paz, Bolivia, with my sister Debbie or something with endangered reptiles
- Help Kendra get her driver's license
- Encourage her to expand her work hours for less unstructured time

- Consider getting her a life reading from a reputable astrologer
- Keep her connected to family by contributing to household jobs and being respectful
- Get into family counseling as needed

Attachment

I worked on myself that year as well. I needed to move from ambivalent consideration that my daughter might become my son someday to the realization that this person had always been my son deep down and was finally demanding his right to emerge and become fully authentic and visible to others. But as this seedling tried to put down roots in ground already fully planted, the soil of my mind needed pruning and weeding. I'd been putting off this work because I loved the old garden but it was time to uproot all that was old and sow seeds for new life to emerge.

I sought solace where I always did when life's challenges became overwhelming—my journal. Writing helps me digest life. It makes me stop, focuses my attention, and puts things in black and white that I might otherwise overlook. Writing, walking in the woods and along the ocean, and recording dreams whenever I recalled them, composed my therapy. Gardeners seldom talk while tending their plot of land and so it was for me while I tended the chaos in my soul. I unearthed some heavy and irrational boulders as I cleared the way for a new perspective. I had already begun to acknowledge and face some of my painful, confusing, even embarrassing feelings surrounding Kendra's transgender identity but it was time to drop down deeper into them. I saw a new urgency in Kendra and could no longer kid myself. Time was running out.

I knew I needed to prepare myself to bid goodbye to this precious daughter of history so I would be ready to let go when the time came. Kendra had survived the full-term grief of my pregnancy and I had welcomed her as a joyful miracle. Now it was my turn to grieve, so that the boy who she was could finally, joyfully emerge. I hadn't known how short-lived my time with Kendra would be. But then life itself is a shape shifter and mothering a metamorphosis. Just like the shrieks of delight when we come home from work, the book reading and rocking, each greeting and goodbye, each stage and age of our children disappears before we know they're gone for good. But this departure felt more permanent. While Kendra was only changing form not totally leaving, I didn't know what, if any part of her would remain. Will a new gender, new name, pronoun, hormones, and surgery disappear her completely or will her spirit still peek through?

I cherished the connection that our shared history and memories had built and didn't want to lose that. I was attached to the baby girl placed in my arms, nursing at my breast, picking flowers in the yard, galloping, or growling as a cat of every kind. Kendra was an affectionate and cuddly child and I hadn't had enough of that in my own childhood. It came naturally for her and cracked open my own shell. She'd climb into bed to snuggle, latch onto my neck in water, and tuck her arm into mine every time we walked together. I loved her easy, wordless closeness. While those physical attachments had already left, they were replaced by conversation, shared experiences, inside jokes, and laughter. I'd looked forward to this mother-daughter bond lasting my lifetime.

I felt angry to have been misled, as though an imposter had been placed in my arms and loved by me until poof, the gods decided to take her away and replace her with another. It felt like a kidnapping; an abduction. Unlike the disappearance of Persephone from Demeter, my mirage daughter was never coming back. In that ancient Greek story Demeter, mother earth herself, is so grieved by her daughter's absence that the land is overcome with the stark barrenness of winter. It is only with the return of Persephone to her mother six months later that the land rejoices and life erupts anew every spring. The Persephone myth reminds us that "the fertility of the earth is in some mysterious way tied to the continuation of the mother-daughter relationship."[84]

Yet my daughter was repudiating that passionate, enduring bond between a mother and daughter that can make life bloom for some. I had known that joy with my daughter whether because of how she came to me, or what her little spirit awakened in me, it hardly mattered. All I knew is that I too was about to enter that barren cold landscape of an interior winter whenever I thought of her leaving. She was about to disappear forever before my very eyes and in order to save her soul I had to be complicit. It felt like betrayal—of her, of me, of our love—to stand by while she was taken apart bit by bit. Had my love been a fraud? I no longer seemed to know who she was. I couldn't make any sense of it. What did gender really matter anyway and why was I so wrapped up in it? We were dealing with Kendra's life not mine and if this was what she needed to be happy and healthy, I would have to trust that. I would let go of her so he could emerge.

We lose our children anyway, every step of the way. The death of my mother made me aware of each fleeting moment with Kendra. At first I tried holding onto time by keeping a journal of each day's activities so nothing was lost and I could revisit it. Life was so perfect; a baby in springtime after a long, lonely winter. But capturing minutes was a tyranny. Time flies visibly and rapidly with young children because they grow and change before our eyes. We can put them to bed as infants and they wake up toddlers.

I was going to miss Kendra but I was going to miss my little girl whether she remained a girl or became a boy. I missed rocking, nursing, reading to her; crawling around on all fours playing make-believe; singing to her and tucking her in. My baby was an adult now and the baby/child/teen was gone forever. I was lucky to have had those years with her as my daughter. Had she been born a boy we might not have shared the closeness we did. I might have been pressured by the culture to make her grow up sooner; give up her blanket; sleep alone when afraid; explore outside on her own and not at my side. She may have been wounded by that and closed her sensitive heart. But now I was sending out into the world a boy who was raised a girl to become a man—hopefully a conscious, responsible, loving, and sensitive man.

Many mothers and fathers fall hopelessly and shamelessly in love with the amazing and adorable bodies of our babies. We wait and delight in their first smile meant only and always just for us. We watch their curious eyes track us with every move and nuance of facial expression when they are tiny infants. What parent has not snuck into their child's bedroom to gaze at them as they sleep so peaceful and innocent, despite the tantrums and trials we may have endured during the day and how relieved we are for the respite of their sleep?

Our children come to us in these irresistible bodies and we are all about the physical. We caress their soft skin, smell their aromatic heads as they nestle against us, feel their tiny perfect fingers around our own, and kiss their pudgy toes. The first indicators of how well we are doing as new parents are measured in physical ways. We keep our babies safe, warm, fed, and dry. We come to them when they cry to soothe their fears and discomforts. They grow, gain weight, stay healthy, get stronger, and explore the world. Everything we do for our babies and children revolves around tending and caring for their little bodies that we memorize over the years as we change, bathe, dress, and cuddle them. We learn what comforts and distresses them; what they like and what they'll spit out. We are even able to recall when a freckle first appeared or how a scar occurred. We come to know their bodies like we know our own and we become attached to these precious beings. Parenting is physical and this attachment is as physical as it is emotional.

Our mothering bodies were their first homes, their first food. They toddle to us for safety and love and we lift them up into the protection of our arms. Even in the dark we know their cry, their smell, their hug. Whatever else we face in life, providing safety to a child with a simple touch, reassuring smile, or affectionate embrace creates a bond and seals a contract. Parents and children are tied together for life in the knowledge that slowly but perceptibly we are turning their bodies, like their lives, over to them as they grow more competent and confident. We may divorce a partner, shun a sibling, or leave a friend, but we carry our children forever—first in our hugs and then in our hearts.

But it was sad and frightening knowing my daughter felt like a stranger to herself in her own body. I felt sorrowful and helpless for the tragedy and unfairness to her. The fact that she could not love her female body seemed the worst sort of tragedy. How I wish I had given birth to her in the body she longed for. There were senseless feelings of guilt that somehow I had let her down; been responsible for this mismatch. And even though there are more remedies now than ever before they are painful and can be scarring and disfiguring. The health side effects of lifelong hormone therapy are virtually unknown and conceivably dangerous. And there is the expense of the treatment, making some unattainable and others unsatisfactory.

I felt grief and physical revulsion that she wanted to alter her body, mutilating and destroying her beauty. I found myself feeling protective of my daughter's lithe, sensual female body that I was so fond and proud of. I loved her smooth, brown skin; wild, wavy hair; long, shapely legs; scrutinizing brown eyes; slender skillful fingers. It physically pained me that she scarred her perfect body with self-inflicted wounds of rejection. I took pride in my daughter's beauty. Though my politics and Kendra's temperament would never have allowed it, I was pleased when people suggested she could be a model as if I was partly responsible for her looks. If her attractiveness reflected well of me, did I consider her an extension of me? Do beautiful daughters evoke narcissism in mothers? Was Kendra's desire to transition also her need to claim autonomy from me? I shuddered as I peeled back my own deeply buried attachments.

Instinctively I felt like battling with her to protect this body that I had so tenderly nourished and nurtured. How could such a good body be unsuitable or wrong? It felt like a shameful waste, a cruel twist of nature. How dare she be so ungrateful and uncaring toward her perfect, holy vessel? Yet I knew it was a war I would lose and that if I went full tilt, I'd lose her too. My only hope was that if Kendra couldn't reconcile with her body, at least she'd be totally certain she'd never miss it.

I was never the type of mother who bought matching mother-daughter dresses, imagined planning the perfect lavish wedding, or shopping together (Kendra loathed it), living down the street from her, or even holding her baby. These were not the types of losses I felt. So how had my expectations about having a daughter differed from having a son? My bias, based on my very limited experience, was that a daughter is closer to their mother than a son. I never expected a daughter to mirror me or live her life like I live mine. I did expect my daughter to remain my daughter, however—and for me that implied remaining close, in touch, and connected. When I thought about the future, I liked the idea of meeting for lunch or dinner from time to time for a good long talk, walking together in the woods or on the beach, traveling places for new sights and experiences, spending time together for celebrations and holidays.

Surely the infant, toddler, elementary school girl, and preteen had all been lost to me for years already. What then was the source of the grief that suddenly brought me to tears over the loss of four-year-old or eight-year-old Kendra? I was surprised to finally realize that those little girls had bonded with my own inner child. Deep down, I wondered if the little girl in my psyche might get lost to me again once Kendra departed. Since I had only recently been reacquainted with her I wanted her to stay. Was my struggle over Kendra's transition really more about the integration of my own psyche? Why, with the knowledge that she was on a path to becoming my son, did she suddenly seem so far away? Was it me, her, or both of us creating this distance?

Getting Help

In addition to writing and walking to digest my reactions, I found a therapist for myself as well as one for Kendra. Kendra's counselor had experience working with adolescents, brought an eclectic spirituality to her work, studied herbal medicine and flower essences, and was a lesbian. Kendra connected with her easily and she worked with Kendra's strengths and insights rather than seeing her through the more traditional mental health lens clouded by a diagnosis of gender identity disorder. This approach made all the difference in Kendra's willing participation in therapy, personal growth, and well-being. Kendra continued to attend nAGLY, the LGBTQ youth group, and became a youth mentor, supporting younger teens, participating in mentor meetings, and getting paid a stipend. She was beginning to feel more comfortable in her own identity and as a leader among other LGBTQ youth.

A gender nonconforming or transgender child can shake the foundation of a marriage or parenting partnership. Each parent has their own way of coping with raising such a unique child with biases rooted in their own gender, culture, upbringing, and personality. Couples counseling can be helpful in improving communication, naming and negotiating differences, and creating tangible plans for helping your child and yourselves get through the journey.

Tony's and my differences were considerable but not insurmountable. We both wanted the best for Kendra. Tony was more accepting of Kendra's transgender identity and open to the idea that she might one day proceed with hormones and surgery. What worried him most was her disinterest in school and his concern for her future. He wanted her to excel academically for professional and financial success. Another challenge for him was her disorganization. Tony valued neatness and order while Kendra was wired for creativity amidst chaos. He saw her habit of borrowing items without asking and not cleaning up after projects as disrespectful. I considered it a minor form of attention deficit. My mother was similarly content in clutter so I knew how to stay ahead of it. What sent Tony over the edge seemed trivial to me. The feelings of loss that brought me to tears seemed extreme to him. This was her life. What right did we have to impose gender? Tony and I sought the help of couples counseling to improve our communication, understand each other's viewpoints, and discuss how best to parent.

Public Accommodations

By now bathrooms in school, public places, and college dorms were a major source of anxiety. Once, as Kendra came out of a stall in the restroom at school after a play, a shocked grandmother scolded, "This is the ladies' room!" Without saying a word Kendra hurried out and tried to disappear into the crowd of students and parents. After that she feared other public humiliations so we went to great lengths to find unisex bathrooms or avoid restrooms all together. This piled stress onto every public outing. When I shared this experience with my Aunt Roz, she sent Kendra a note suggesting she pass out a card with the following so she wouldn't need to say a word in case anyone ever harassed her again:

> *My name is Kendra. I am a girl.*
> *Although I feel more comfortable in male clothing,*
> *I do not feel comfortable in male restrooms.*
> *I mean no harm to anyone.*
> *Thank you for understanding.*

Kendra never acted on this suggestion because she didn't feel she owed anyone an explanation. She also didn't feel like a girl and was working up to being comfortable in male restrooms. Nevertheless we were grateful Roz took an interest in helping us consider ways to handle these stressful situations.

The worst came at Fenway Park. A colleague had extra tickets and amazingly we were free that night so we headed to our first Red Sox game ever. It drizzled on and off all day threatening to rain out or postpone the game but just as we came over the bridge into Boston the sun broke through. As we approached Fenway

Park, Kendra said she had to use the bathroom. I offered to go on the hunt with her for a unisex restroom and meet Tony in the stadium. Tony, not fully appreciating Kendra's level of discomfort with public restrooms, even more so in a sports stadium, insisted there were bathrooms inside and that we all stay together. In panic and anger, Kendra bolted. Tony protested as I started to go with her saying it was her choice to leave, she'd find her way back, to stop giving in to her outbursts. As soon as we got to our seats, my cell phone rang.

Never having been at Fenway Park before, Kendra entered one gate and then exited thinking she was in the wrong section. She was refused entry at the second gate. Tony convinced the guard to let her back in but by then Kendra had stormed off to walk the two miles to North Station for a train home. At the train station she discovered it was a two-hour wait for the next train so she made her way back. We picked her up just outside of Fenway Park as we left for home. The Red Sox beat the Tampa Bay Rays that night but no one was celebrating in our car. Kendra missed the game and we missed out on what had started as a fun family outing because of a bathroom and the conflict over how to parent our explosive adolescent. At times like this I felt stuck in the middle, torn between my husband and my volatile transgender teen.

RESEARCH

Health Risk Indicators

Hopefully other families won't have the devastating experience of a suicide attempt such as we had. The prevalence of suicidality for transgender teens is high, so it's important to be aware of the warning signs that your child is feeling desperate and alone despite how confident you might be that it would never happen. Living between genders, with no gender, or with a different gender, in a culture whose social foundation rests upon two distinct and opposite pillars of masculine and feminine traits, dress, and behaviors is harrowing. Every human encounter and interaction requires that one be labeled and placed at one end of the gender spectrum or the other. People who fall outside the boundaries of rigid categories are feared, discounted, ridiculed, and pressured to conform lest the entire gender system itself come tumbling down leaving us all adrift.

Transgender and nonconforming children and teens are at risk for isolation, anxiety, poor self-image, and misdiagnosis.[85] These risks increase or decrease depending on how satisfied they are with their physical appearance and whether they feel accepted or rejected by others. Preoccupation with cross-gender wishes can impact daily activities and the achievement of developmental milestones. Children may refuse to attend school or have poor concentration due to bullying and teasing by other children. Jealousy of gender conforming siblings and peers can create anger, resentment, withdrawal, or acting out. Relationship difficulties with peers can increase after puberty as others begin to date, leading to anxiety, depression, substance abuse, negative self-concept, self-injury, thoughts of suicide, or actual attempts.[86]

Well-meaning but uninformed referrals to school personnel, religious leaders, family practitioners, or mental health providers lacking knowledge about gender identity or harboring biases toward transgender people can negatively impact transgender youth, and misdirect parents.[87] Medical and mental health providers inexperienced in treating transgender children may mistake the symptoms of gender dysphoria for the core problem and provide treatment or prescribe medication for substance abuse, anxiety, insomnia, mood swings, impulsivity, anger, and depression. By missing the root cause, precious time and resources are wasted chasing remedies that may exacerbate the symptoms and stigmatize the child as having a mental illness, while the real issue goes undetected and untreated.

The impact of social isolation, ostracism, and feeling one does not belong, at a time when belonging is central to self-worth, cannot be over-estimated. Even with family support, parents of transgender teens need to be vigilant for signs of substance abuse, self-injury, depression, and thoughts of suicide. With studies indicating 50 to 88 percent of transgender youth contemplating or attempting suicide, transwoman and gender specialist Gianna E. Israel and psychiatrist Donald E. Tarver II, note the following warning signs to watch for in their book, *Transgender Care*:

- Marked changes in sleeping or eating, personal hygiene, mood, and attitude
- Decrease in social interaction and previous activities
- Decline in attendance and academic achievement
- Sudden changes in friendships[88]

Standards of Care and Treatment

The *Standards of Care for the Health of Transsexual, Transgender, and Gender Nonconforming People* (SOC) by the World Professional Association for Transgender Health (WPATH) provide minimum guidelines and time frames for patients seeking hormone treatment or sex reassignment surgery. Most gender therapists, physicians, and surgeons follow these standards, which are periodically updated to stay current with research, changes in clinical experience, and emerging needs of transgender children, teens, and adults.

The following treatment components are included in the Standards of Care (SOC):

- Gender expression and role changes (living part time or full time in the gender role consistent with one's gender identity)
- Hormone therapy to feminize or masculinize the body
- Surgery to change primary and/or secondary sex characteristics (e.g., breasts/chest, external and/or internal genitalia, facial features, body contouring)

- Psychotherapy (individual, couple, family, or group) to explore gender identity, role, and expression; address the negative impact of gender dysphoria on mental health; alleviate internalized transphobia; enhance social and peer support; improve body image; promote resilience

The SOC recommends three months of psychotherapy with a mental health professional who meets the minimum standards of competency and who utilizes standard psychological assessments for gender dysphoria prior to the start of hormone therapy (see Chapter Three). Many health professionals wait six months before prescribing testosterone because of the irreversible changes it creates whereas estrogen's effects are usually reversible.[89] There is a recommended twelve-month wait prior to surgery, whereby the patient lives continuously full time in the gender congruent with their gender identity. A letter from the psychotherapist is required for hormone treatment, and two letters, from both the physician prescribing the hormones and the psychotherapist, are required for proceeding with surgery. Some revise these guidelines for adolescents in crisis at the onset of puberty for whom these wait times can cause life-threatening reactions including thoughts or attempts of suicide.[90] The most recent SOC version addresses reversible interventions for children and adolescents that include puberty suppressing hormones and working with parents and caregivers in their roles as decision makers.[91]

If you catch yourself wishing there was some sort of counseling or therapeutic method that could align your child's mind and heart with their body, which you probably consider fine, you are not alone. There has been considerable historical debate in medical circles whether gender dysphoria is primarily a physical or mental condition.

To date, however, there is no evidence that psychological counseling can bring body and mind together. The conversion or reparative counseling methods that have been recommended in the past create deprivation and sadness in the lives of children since everything that brings them joy is removed and replaced with clothing, toys, and even playmates, that are gender conforming. These methods are not effective in achieving their intended long-term objectives and actually harm children by instilling and reinforcing shame and the need for secrecy. Few parents today can tolerate the severity of these approaches and experts in the field no longer consider them ethical.

Altering one's outward appearance and gender expression to match the inner experience of self and affirmed gender is a more promising and effective treatment. Parents often notice this just by watching the light come back into their child's eyes when he or she is allowed to dress and play in their affirmed gender. Treatment options vary depending on the child's age. A counselor experienced in working with gender nonconforming children can help parents and their children explore whether there is gender dysphoria and plan the next steps. In addition to any medical treatment, fostering an environment of support within the family is critical. Home life and social settings that allow a child to dress and live in their affirmed gender will reduce the child's distress. Participating in activities and groups with other gender nonconforming children can lessen feelings of isolation.

Fully reversible interventions

The first treatment option may be social transitioning so that a child can live full time in their affirmed gender. Social transitioning can be partial—such as clothing and a hairstyle of the affirmed gender; or complete—choosing a new name, altering pronouns, and disclosing to others the change. The benefit of social transitioning is that it offers immediate relief for gender dysphoria. Over time, if the child wants to change back to their assigned gender they can, since nothing permanent has been done. This is often the choice made by parents of young children. Because of the low persistence rates of childhood gender dysphoria, some health professionals raise concerns about social transitions in early childhood since transitioning back to their assigned gender may cause further distress. Parents are encouraged to present this option to a child more as an exploration rather than being permanent, and explicitly remind them they can switch back if they choose.[92]

As adolescence approaches, puberty suppressing hormones are the next reversible treatment option. The criteria for receiving puberty suppressing hormones are: persistent and insistent gender nonconformity or dysphoria (overt or covert); gender dysphoria that surfaced or worsened with puberty; functional ability to begin treatment without any underlying medical, mental health, or social issues interfering with adherence; informed consent of the adolescent or, if under age, consent and support of parents or guardians.[93] A knowledgeable endocrinologist can prescribe pre-adolescent children with hormone suppressors (GnRH analogues) or progestins to decrease the effects of testicular androgens, and oral contraceptives to suppress menses for teens not taking GnRH analogues.[94] These hormones hold off the wrong puberty and delay the development of unwanted secondary sex characteristics such as breasts and widened hips in females, and a lowered voice, Adam's apple, chest and facial hair in males. This limits the number of surgeries required later if your child decides to transition. If the child decides not to transition, biological puberty will resume once suppressing hormones are stopped.

Many physicians will provide cross-sex hormones to minors with parental consent. WPATH takes the position that delaying treatment is not a neutral option for some teens.[95] Withholding timely medical intervention for adolescents can prolong gender dysphoria and contribute to a physical appearance that provokes abuse and stigmatization throughout their life. Transitioning as early as one is certain of their gender identity can be beneficial in that it allows for more socialization time and life experiences in one's affirmed gender and may create an easier adjustment for family members.[96]

The long-term impact of going through puberty, especially for biological males, should not be underestimated. Because of the powerful and permanent physical effects of testosterone on height, hair growth, voice, bone structure, and musculature, it is not as easily counteracted with estrogen later in life. A national survey found that transgender people who do not visually conform to their affirmed gender are more likely to experience harassment and discrimination.[97]

Partially reversible interventions

Cross-sex hormones can be prescribed upon the completion of puberty and at age sixteen with parental consent, or at age eighteen, to feminize an anatomical male or masculinize an anatomical female. Some hormone-induced changes may need surgery to be reversed such as enlarged breasts in males taking estrogen, while other changes are irreversible such as deepening of the voice caused by taking testosterone in females.[98]

Irreversible interventions

Sex reassignment surgery including penectomy and vaginoplasty in a natal male and mastectomy or phalloplasty in a natal female are additional steps in altering the body to conform to one's affirmed gender. Many transgender people opt not to undergo every available surgery for a number of reasons, including cost, less than ideal outcomes for some procedures, and the ability to live and love without them. Moving gradually through these interventions is recommended to give patients and their families time to assimilate and adjust.

Timing Treatment

Gender dysphoria over time can lead to impaired function, with a child refusing to attend school, becoming depressed, anxious, withdrawn, using substances or engaging in self-injury, all signs that intervention is needed even if your child does not explicitly say what they are feeling. The two most common periods when your child will indicate to you that something needs to be done to help alleviate the gender dysphoria they feel are when they are very young (early onset) and when they reach puberty (late onset).

Every child is different. Some are clear and persistent early that they are the other gender. Others move across or blend gender. Since gender can be fluid during childhood, a parent's greatest worry is making the wrong decision. But doing nothing when a child experiences marked distress that interferes with development such as attending school, relating to peers, and engaging in activities also has negative consequences. Waiting can seem prudent with an eye to the future but may cause considerable harm in the present.

A parent's role is critical in finding resources and making decisions on behalf of a minor child. Young children are often very vocal about their gender incongruence because they have not yet internalized the notion that there is something wrong with them. In their innocence and clarity, they believe the world is wrong and they say so! Once children become aware of how emotionally charged gender is, they may suppress their feelings of dissonance, believing instead that the problem is theirs. By the time a child reaches adolescence, you may only be given clues to their inner pain such as changes in mood, body language, increased withdrawal and silence, acting out behaviors and risk taking. When a child has demonstrated long-lasting gender nonconformity and subsequent gender dysphoria—whether suppressed or expressed—that has emerged or worsened with the onset of puberty it is time to consider both social and medical interventions.

REFLECTIONS

Identify Resources

It's normal to feel confused and anxious about all you need to consider before being certain about what's best for your child. If you haven't already done so, it's time to seek help! The more you know, the sooner you'll be able to understand what's going on with your child, find appropriate resources, and plan the next steps. Getting answers to your questions and locating local resources and allies is critical while you work through your decisions. Websites and online resources for parents of transgender children and teens are helpful in locating local, regional, and national resources, and support groups. If you don't live near a large metropolitan area, you may find more resources for yourself and your family online than in your own community. It's likely your teen has already found many resources so you may want to ask. The following suggestions may be helpful:[99]

- Explore where and when your child or teen feels most comfortable and accepted. Expand those times and visit those places as much as possible.
- Connect with PFLAG (Parents, Families, and Friends of LGBTQ People) online to find a local chapter and attend a meeting in your area to meet other families with gender nonconforming children. Today there are specific groups for parents of transgender youth sponsored by many PFLAG chapters.
- Connect with LGBTQ health centers, or hospitals and mental health centers that serve LGBTQ people, to find support groups, therapists, and medical providers knowledgeable of gender identity.
- Attend LGBTQ youth conferences or camps with your family to meet other families, as well as medical and mental health professionals, and learn the latest research and resources.

- Attend a Pride event or Transgender Day of Remembrance held annually on November 20 when you are ready. Many colleges hold events and lectures and have LBGTQ centers.

Your Treatment Team

To guide you in caring for your child, look for compassionate, knowledgeable, and experienced professionals in at least these three disciplines:
- Primary care physician or pediatrician
- Psychologist/mental health provider trained as a gender specialist working with children and teens
- Pediatric endocrinologist

Each member of your interdisciplinary team needs to be willing to work together on treating your child. The therapist also needs to be willing to contact teachers and other school personnel to advocate for your child as needed.[100]

Depending on your needs, your team may be larger. Finding the right medical and mental health team to help you understand options and guide your decision-making will greatly ease your mind. Professionals experienced working with transgender children and teens may see aspects of your child that you may miss, and know how to address their needs. Sometimes we're just too close to see the forest for the trees, or too tied to our history with our child to clearly see the present or prepare for the future. For example, without me even knowing what to call it, Kendra was already partially transitioning socially between ages nine and fifteen. She was wearing boy cloths full time before finally demanding to wear a boy's hairstyle too.

What help does your child or teen need right now to address her/his current situation (medical, psychological, social, academic)? What help do you or your family need now? If you aren't sure yet, make a list of your questions and concerns and see what comes up.

Then begin to seek resources and helping professionals based on the most pressing and/or most frequent concerns. It's not unusual for the whole family to benefit from counseling since everyone is transitioning, not just your transgender child.

It's important to work through your own feelings away from your child's hearing. They have their own concerns to attend to. Watching you struggle through yours may lead them to question their feelings, delay their emergence, or isolate from you out of guilt, disappointment, or anger. You may want someone you can speak with alone so you are better able to assist your child. If you have a partner, it may be helpful for both of you to talk through your feelings with a trained gender counselor about what lies ahead so you can assist your transgender child in tandem. Sharing reading material, resources, conversations with other parents will help you stay in touch with where each of you are, away from your child's hearing. It can also help you identify and work through areas where you and your coparent may be in disagreement.

Dating and Safe Sex

Knowing whom to trust and when to disclose are two questions that arise when dating begins. Peer support from the transgender community online, at trans youth conferences, camps, or support groups, as well as conversations with a gender counselor can be important resources for addressing these concerns. If your teen is dating peers from school or the community who already know their gender identity, disclosure will not be an issue. Fortunately each successive generation seems to be more accepting of gender nonconforming peers as more youth identify as gender queer or transgender. But if your teen is meeting new people at parties, dances, events, and at college, they will need to be prepared to disclose if they become sexually involved since it's best not to surprise intimate partners. Discussing this with your teen may feel awkward because of your inexperience disclosing a transgender identity but it's our role as parents to protect our children from danger. The use of alcohol, marijuana, and other drugs can impair their decision-making abilities and elevate their risk when they are in unfamiliar locations with people they don't know, which is an important topic to raise with them. Planning who they can call, including yourself, if they need a ride from a dangerous situation is crucial in ensuring their safety.

All teens are at risk for dating abuse, be it emotional, physical, or sexual, and LGBTQ teens are at higher risk, so helping them work through relationship challenges is critical. If your child has a history of not feeling accepted, he or she may be vulnerable to settling for dating partners that are disrespectful or controlling and relationship dynamics that are unhealthy. If you think your child is being bullied or controlled in a dating relationship it can be difficult to know what to say or do. Forbidding the relationship may have the opposite effect, making your teen defend their partner and become secretive about the relationship. Keeping the lines of communication open, building your child's trust, and offering feedback about what you observe, can help them negotiate safety and respect during this vulnerable next step in their development.

If they are with an abusive, controlling or manipulative partner, it's important to let them know you are there for them even if they break up and then get back together since it often takes several tries to leave an unhealthy relationship. If they think they'll be judged by you or if they feel embarrassed or ashamed that they didn't see the signs or stayed as long as they did, they may not tell you what's really happening. The more you know, the better you can protect them, so staying connected is critical. Contacting your local domestic violence agency can help you learn the subtle dynamics of abuse, what the local resources are, and how to establish a safety plan.

Your Other Children

Consider counseling for your other children, with your family or alone. They may need a place of their own apart from your family to talk openly. Depending on their age they may not even have words for how they feel about their sibling. Expressive arts or play therapy may help them uncover and discover their feelings. Gender identity may not even be their central concern. They may have difficulty coping with family reactions or their sibling's negative, acting-out behaviors rather than with gender identity per se. Getting counseling early is especially important if they have witnessed disturbing or traumatic incidents.

Navigating the conflicting feelings of protectiveness toward their sibling as well as resentment for being singled out or targeted because of them can cause feelings of anger and guilt. They may worry about the survival of your family and whether or not it can sustain the pressure it's under. They may try to protect you by hiding their own needs so not to burden you, only to have them erupt later. Siblings may withdraw, exhibiting signs of depression, substance abuse, or acting out in response to the stress in the family, especially if they feel they are unable to get the attention they used to get.

Your Allies

We all want to be good parents and to have our parenting choices respected by others in our community. Supporting and advocating for our unique children can be difficult when others know so little about transgender children and their needs. When our gender nonconforming or transgender children are their most expressive, those around us can be their most judgmental, leading us to become our least confident. Be prepared to face opposition and hostility for supporting your gender nonconforming or transgender child and consider what you will need to protect yourself, your children, and family.

Allies build our courage and help us remember it's our child who matters most, not the comfort of others or our own approval ratings. Create an accepting community for your child or teen and your family by attending LGBTQ conferences, meeting and socializing with LGBTQ people, finding role models for your child, and sharing resources. Surround yourself with supportive friends and family members. Look for them everywhere—your child's school, online, groups you belong to, other parents, family, and community.

Self-Care

Consider ways to nurture yourself at this critical time. Make a commitment to do something that lifts your spirits every day. Your child needs you now just as you need him or her. Do what you need to be your best self, and don't burden your child with your internal process. Take special note of any guilt, self-blame, or judgment. Is there a voice in your head scolding you for not knowing sooner; for prior harsh statements or unhelpful actions? Recall any incidents you feel guilty about and decide whether you want to apologize to your child. Then forgive yourself, release the negative feelings, and gratefully embrace the present.

The guilt and shame I felt about Kendra's overdose and the impact it had on her, her sister, our family, and Kendra's relationships at school was paralyzing. In addition to figuring out how to keep her alive and help us all recover from the trauma of the overdose, I was the executive director of the local domestic violence agency with responsibility for three community-based offices, an emergency shelter, twenty-five staff, and a Board of sixteen. Between trips to the partial hospitalization program, meetings at work, and time with our family, I'd well up with tears and berate myself for attending that fateful out-of-town meeting. If ever there was a time when I longed for a redo, this was it. But of course that was not possible. The only option was moving forward but guilt weighed me down. I apologized to Kendra, who didn't blame me. In her mind it was an incident destined to happen and it freed her to let go of the allure of death. Forgiving myself was harder and took longer but slowly the accusing voices subsided.

Surround yourself with supportive friends who will listen without judgment. Take the time you need to come to peace with your child's transgender identity yourself before disclosing to family, friends, and community. There will be questions, concerns, and possibly difficult conversations so wait until you are ready to share. I couldn't speak without crying about my child's transgender identity for months but I made sure he never knew that. You may have a totally different response but it's okay to tell only your closest confidants at first, until you get stronger in your ability to speak from a place of pride and understanding.

6

Acceptance and Action Steps

I remember the day of my first shot of testosterone clearly.
I was walking toward the Park Street T stop,
across the Boston Common.

The wind was blowing, and the April sun was shining through
the flowering cherry trees on the corner of Tremont and Boylston.
For once I felt that everything would be okay.

KAI, AGE 23

RECOLLECTIONS

Taking the Driver's Seat

The first step I took that summer to help Kendra officially get in the driver's seat of her life was to trade in my standard shift car and buy an automatic. This made it much easier for her to learn how to drive. By fall, she'd obtained a driver's license and found that rather than being afraid to drive, she loved it. It was the start of a new sense of freedom and mastery. Kendra also pursued a growing interest in geckos, slowly building an Internet reputation based on extensive research and experience. Before long, people began to request information and advice on how to breed and care for various gecko species. Along with expanded hours at the pet store, Kendra began selling geckos, custom-made cages and vivariums, as well as plants and materials online and at local reptile shows. Thus began Kendra's thriving online business as well as an extensive array of contacts and colleagues.

The phone rang one Sunday in January when Kendra was out. It was the long-term substitute teacher that Kendra had in kindergarten when the permanent teacher got sick. She was a Tufts alumna and had been asked to interview Kendra for admission after another interviewer had to cancel. Because of the tight timeline, she was hoping to meet with Kendra the next day, Martin Luther King Day, at a coffee shop downtown. When Kendra got home I gave her the message and the interview took place as planned. Kendra had decided to reapply to Tufts Early Decision this time, because they'd review applications in winter rather than spring. She took the process more seriously now, responding to optional essays and submitting artwork.

Tufts was the only university on her list the previous year that had a third box for "transgender" as an option. It was a rare, welcome relief when all the others forced an impossible, inauthentic choice. For that reason Kendra chose no other schools the second time around. It was Tufts or nothing based on that third gender box and the disappointing UMass Amherst orientation. An astrologer had said winter was a fortuitous time for Kendra and so far, the interview seemed like a promising sign. After all, how many college applicants are interviewed by their former kindergarten teacher? As I walked to my car one cold, dark afternoon in early February I heard Kendra's voicemail. She'd been accepted at Tufts and was elated!! I saved that message for many weeks. It was the happiest I'd heard her in years.

The year between high school and college felt like an intermission between acts. Some call it the gap year. A gap is defined as "an opening . . . a pass through mountains; a suspension of continuity; hiatus; a conspicuous difference;" and in computer science, "an absence of information on a recording medium."[101] For Kendra and me it was all of these. It was a respite from watching Kendra struggle with balancing the academic pressures of high school while feeling increasingly estranged and isolated from her gender conforming classmates. The more attached she became to her new circle of friends, the wider the social gap at school. This new opening of time and space felt like a heavy lid was lifted off a confining box. Suddenly there were new possibilities and a sense of freedom. Kendra could make herself into whomever she chose. It was the juncture from which she could walk entirely away from her past if she wanted.

I knew Kendra was trying on transitioning but I was grateful for every month she waited. She was living in a state of androgyny, balancing both her masculine and feminine aspects. It made sense that in order to move from girl to boy she had to traverse the midpoint, a place of equilibrium. I'd grown to appreciate the ways Kendra transcended gender all her life; how she was both female and male. But the limitations of our Western minds seem unable to hold onto life as a circle gravitating instead to the hierarchy of a pyramid, so that one aspect takes precedence over another. Living in this perfect middle is difficult and definitely not for everyone since the world strives to gender us with every encounter just as it strives to place us on the color continuum. Kendra's ability to reside in this space between genders was made possible in part because her engagements in the world were mostly online or within a small community who knew her. Traversing that gender line full time forever was a big decision and I knew Kendra was weighing the gravity of her longing along with the losses.

I threaded my own way through the pass before me: between past and future, daughter and son. I went about preparing myself for what I had long dreaded: watching Kendra disappear right before my eyes. I feared living with her while she transitioned. I didn't want to witness her slipping away so close up. I couldn't imagine hearing her voice deepen, seeing her face change, losing this precious, soulful daughter in stages. I hoped she would go off to college, move away from home for this stage of her journey because in my heart it still felt like a death. It was hard work to prepare to say goodbye to the child to whom I felt so connected. The spirit of that little girl was still within her, just below the surface, in her face, her laugh, her voice, her touch. I didn't yet know this emerging son—who wasn't going to come to me as a darling little boy but as an angry teen, almost a man. I had no idea how to get ready for this shift so I started by looking for the boy inside the girl.

We all begin life deeply attached to those who care for us when we're young. We couldn't survive otherwise. Boys are encouraged and rewarded for moving away from these bonds of connection thereby proving their strength, independence, and masculinity as they grow, while girls are allowed, even encouraged to remain close. Mothers have long been blamed for sons that are too feminine, emotionally expressive, too attached. Boys are humiliated and punished for not repudiating or repressing feelings of vulnerability and the need for others. I was thrilled to have avoided this push to detach having had a daughter yet here we were, at the threshold of his adulthood and I'd done it all wrong for him. We'd missed all the early, critical steps for how a mother is expected to launch a son into the world of men. Could we catch up? Instead of letting go slowly over the course of his childhood so the space between us felt natural by the end, were we to sever completely in one sudden blow?

It had already begun. There was almost no physical affection between us by then and I felt the loss. But I couldn't tell if the increasing distance between us was typical mother-daughter leave-taking or the separation my new son was creating. It didn't really matter except I wanted to foresee the future. If it was mother-daughter space I felt confident the closeness would return, perhaps in a new form but not be gone forever. In mother-son space I worried it would grow larger and last forever. At times it felt as if my mere presence annoyed Kendra, then other times she wanted my help or advice. I was disposable it seemed.

And she annoyed me as well. It bothered me how boy-like she was becoming. She was weightlifting and taking protein supplements to build muscle and wanted binding material to hide her breasts. As crazy as it sounds, it felt personal for me that she was so rejecting of her female body. I wondered whether she felt similarly repulsed by mine. One gesture she did accept from me was when I offered to help her find a bra that compressed her breasts. She thanked me for that because she wasn't comfortable shopping for bras and going into fitting rooms. I pondered the ways our relationship might change; how gender defines and confines us. Could I still hug and kiss her? Would I still call her honey? Her body language already indicated these forms of endearment now felt uncomfortable.

Like handing over the car keys, it was time to hand over her life. While part of me still hoped to avoid the inevitable I knew that simply postponing it was not the answer either. Moving slowly helped reassure me she'd be mature enough before taking so permanent a step she'd hopefully never regret. While I was not completely ready to be her primary support through a process I hadn't fully made peace with, I decided to walk beside her and trust her to guide me. What she was celebrating I was still grieving. Not wanting to mar those first steps as she tried on living full time as male, it was my turn for hiding. I was relieved she'd be leaving for college soon. She was ready—happier, more successful, independent, and confident than ever and we both needed the space. As I prepared for a son part of me felt relieved to release the broken, sad daughter.

Blessing

That August, right before Kendra started Tufts, we took another family trip to Trinidad. Kendra said she wanted to talk to her Grandma Iyine alone at some point. That was hard to do with so many family members and friends wanting to see Tony. Evenings were often spent sitting on the front porch reminiscing together with cousins dropping by unannounced. Finally, on our last night there, I told Tony that Kendra still had not had a chance to speak alone to his mother.

"Oh Mom, Kendra wants to talk to you about something," he said as he and his brother went inside. I motioned to Kendra it was now or never so she came over and sat in the chair on the front porch next to Iyine.

"Yes, darlin', go ahead and tell me," Iyine said.

"Well, I've been feeling for a while that I wish I had been born a boy. I don't feel like a girl. I don't want to live my whole life like this," Kendra said. "I know it seems strange and not everyone understands but I wanted you to know."

"Well, the way you feel is something no one can change for you honey," Iyine said. "God made you the way you are. Today this type of thing is more out in the open. It used to be more secret and hidden but now there are ways of dealing with it."

"That's one of the reasons I want to study science in college," Kendra said. "I might want to go into medicine and help people who feel like I do someday."

"What do your mommy and daddy say about how you feel?" Iyine asked. "Have you told them?"

"Yeah, they know. They don't really say that much about it," she said.

"I will always love you. You'll always be my grand whether you're a girl or a boy. It makes no difference to me. You have a right to go about your business and do what makes you feel happy in this life," Iyine assured her.

Kendra smiled and they hugged each other.

"Thanks Grandma," she said as she kissed her goodnight and hopped down the porch steps lighter than before.

I sat with Iyine to see how she was doing. As she told me Kendra had spoken with her she turned her head and put her face against my shoulder and wept. I knew the feeling immediately. She had said all the right, loving, brave, and encouraging things to Kendra—to her credit—while in her heart she grieved for the lost and missing granddaughter she had known and loved. And who could have prepared her for what she was about to hear from Kendra. Kendra had made herself an enigma to Iyine up until now but was coming into her own and out of her shell.

"Oh child," Iyine said. "I wasn't expectin' that. You must pray for her and never let her feel discouraged. Make sure to always keep her spirits up. She has a heavy load to carry."

"She was so glad she had a chance to tell you Iyine," I said. "She's been saying she wanted to tell you ever since we made plans to visit. I was worried she'd let the time pass and not take the opportunity. We've been trying to support her in this for a while and it can be pretty hard so it's better when other people know and understand. Still, it's hard to take in and I cry about it a lot," I said as we both sat there in tears.

"This can't stop her from doing what she has to do in life," Iyine said. "But you and she need to take care who she chooses for friends because there are all kinda people out there and she could get taken advantage of," Iyine said. "She may just decide to have the surgery someday too so you need to be ready for that."

"I'm hoping she'll change her mind and not go that route," I said.

"She's not going to change her mind at this point in her life," Iyine said. "She's too old for that. She would have changed her mind by now. You just need to be ready to stand by her whatever road she takes."

"I still miss my little daughter Iyine," I cried. "Sometimes I feel so sad."

"But you cannot change that. It is who she is," she reminded me. "I told her I'll always love her like I love all my grands. As long as I hear my grands are behavin' and gettin' along in life as they should, then I will live a longer life."

"Thank you for saying all the right things to Kendra, Iyine. It made her day I can tell," I said.

"What else is there to say?" she asked. "She has been given this path by God and God and we should support her."

We hugged goodnight. She thanked me for coming and said she enjoyed my company.

Through Iyine, I felt the support of sages reaching across
countries, cultures, and generations to support the spirit who was
Kendra—or whatever name he would eventually choose. This
woman, so different from me in her ways of old, knew and said
exactly what any wise, loving grandmother would say. I was grateful
that Kendra had the commitment and courage to be open with her
Grandma. She received the blessing she had longed for and felt elated
afterward—cheerful, light, and unable to sleep—talking about how
it would be to someday have chest hair. On most nights that would
have repulsed me but on that night I just laughed. Maybe it wouldn't
be so bad after all.

Changing Pronouns

As Kendra got ready to leave for college we began getting used to
male pronouns at home. It was the obvious next step and a critical
affirmation for Kendra. He felt male inside and presented as male
outside. Strangers used the right pronouns so it was odd that those
of us closest to him were the last holdouts. But pronouns evoke
pictures in our minds and pictures stir feelings, making this one
of the hardest parts of the journey for me. I believe it's one of the
reasons people are so attached to masculine pronouns for God.
Feminine pronouns evoke new and different images from those one
is accustomed to which totally alter one's perception of the person or
spirit being referred to.

My heart and mind had a visceral attachment to the gender
of my child. Audibly altering the pronoun felt like talking about
someone different, certainly not someone as close to me as my own
child. It took longer than expected to stop saying "she" and "her."
"She/her" evoked a person, an image I knew well, my child, the
essence of someone I'd known since birth, whereas "he/him" felt
distant, impersonal, conjuring up a stranger I was just now meeting.
Of course all of this was unconscious and irrational since I knew

this was one and the same person but my mind played tricks on me for those first few months making my heart rebel over the change. The new pronoun solidified the fact that Kendra was fast becoming a person from my past and it was time I got used to the new person. I was fortunate that Kendra was patient with me as I gradually adapted to the shift.

Still using the name Kendra or signing only "K" with the pronoun "he" put him in a new, somewhat confusing and androgynous place, especially with new acquaintances. It took Kendra two more years to settle on a new name so he lived in this middle space with both genders for a while as he tried on his new identity. Were our culture more gender fluid, transgender children and teens might have the option of living between genders, with both, or alternating genders. But that is likely reserved for some future time.

It was confounding to introduce Kendra to new people during this time. He sometimes stopped in at my work and one day out of habit I said, "This is my daughter Kendra," to the parking attendant. The person looked confused because Kendra's gender expression was all male now. I felt Kendra bristle. But I was not yet ready to say, "This is my son," and since Kendra had not yet selected a new name we were both being patient with the other I guess. There was no gender-neutral name for our parent connection that I could come up with, "This is my teen, child, offspring?" "Child" felt demeaning at his age and the other options were stilted. "Kid" might have worked but eventually it just became easiest to avoid introductions all together despite being rude because it avoided awkward exchanges since "Kendra" and "K" were both feminine and he presented as masculine.

The more I glimpsed this new son, the more I began to like him. When my mother's twin sister, Aunt Rayetta, died in her sleep that year Kendra offered to come with me to New York for the funeral. Tony couldn't make it on such short notice. It was wonderful having Kendra's support and I was glad he could be surrounded by the love and memories of family. He had strength and sensitivity and I hoped he could keep both. When he walked with me to the graveside, he took my arm as he always had as a child and for the first time I sensed the son in him. There was a protectiveness that felt male for some reason. As these experiences multiplied, the new pronoun no longer felt quite so strange. Slowly it began to feel normal, natural.

I attended the Matriculation Ceremony on the quad as Tufts gave the freshman class a heartwarming welcome. In addition to noting the many languages, varied backgrounds, unique hobbies, and considerable accomplishments of this incoming class, three transgender students were included in the welcome. A gecko breeder was one of the innovative businesses noted so Kendra was actually included twice. It was clearly a promising new day after a long, painful journey. Kendra had a single room in a freshman dorm and while officially registered as Kendra he was quick to rip off the welcome sign on the door of his room and replace it with only the K. He signed his name as K as well and was using male pronouns in new settings.

While it was a relief for me that Kendra didn't transition during the gap year I wish I had found a gender counselor for him to see then. I had encouraged him to call Fenway Community Health Center but given his aversion to phone calls, the tendency to procrastinate, and the gravity of this step, it never happened. I wonder if Kendra marked time that year waiting for me to catch up. College would've been easier if gender had been settled beforehand.

Time's Up

Kendra was home for winter break after his first semester of college. I was driving home in a rapidly worsening blizzard when my cell phone rang. It was Kendra. He asked where I was. I could tell by his voice that something was wrong. I was about five miles from home but well over the usual ten-minute drive as heavy, wet snow quickly mounted up on roads and car windows.

"I did something stupid," he said. We'd had an argument that morning before I went out as I tried to hold him responsible for something I considered serious. His voice sounded urgent. I felt the old panic rise. He'd taken pills again. This time it was thirty extra-strength Tylenol; even more dangerous since permanent liver damage or blindness can result. He knew that from the last time.

I was shocked, angry, numb. Just like that, he tried to kill himself again? I thought that was behind us. What was really going on? I called Tony. He was grocery shopping and farther from home than me. I steeled myself, clenching my jaw and the wheel, and inched home as fast as I dared. Kendra was standing in the driveway ashen and lost.

Fighting the urge to scream at him and at how frighteningly slow we had to travel thanks to the rapidly escalating snowstorm, I continued my panicked methodical course to the hospital. I knew that if I spun out or skidded into something we might never make it. I considered calling an ambulance but they were further away and would take even longer. Plus I couldn't imagine waiting. At least this way I could do something; make forward motion. Kendra kept saying he was sorry; that his allergies were bothering him, and when one Tylenol didn't stop the congestion and he just kept taking more; one after another, after another and before he knew it, he'd emptied the bottle.

The first semester of college was difficult. Getting back into the rigors of academia after a year off was hard. The issue of gender was looming larger by the day and adjusting to dorm life, the distraction of a new, nonstudent girlfriend and maintaining his gecko business, was too much to juggle. Kendra also struggled with the internalized belief that he was a bad student based on the last few years of high school and getting lower grades than he'd expected affirmed this self-image.

How had I gotten so lax to have so full a bottle around I wondered? It'd only been three years since the last attempt when I cleaned out the medicine cabinet of everything dangerous. I'd managed to let the same false impression of Kendra's stability lull me again into complacency, negligence. But this time, my panic and fear was mixed with anger at being manipulated, and exasperation over such impulsivity. This kid had the ability to turn all of our lives upside down in a split second and did not hesitate to do so. That's what seemed so chilling this seemingly normal Sunday right before Christmas.

Tony had the good sense to call Mike, Joanna's husband and one of our best friends. He was also a minister and former executive director of a residential program for troubled adolescents. He joined us both as we sat stunned in the family room of the hospital while Kendra drank charcoal to detoxify his system. We tried to take stock of where we stood and where we were headed. Despite the last overdose, we'd fooled ourselves into thinking that with the pain of high school behind and a new life at college ahead, there'd be time to sort out our next steps about gender. When so many externals had the potential to go right, we were devastated, angry, hopeless, and confused. Though not saying the words, Kendra was obviously still very unhappy.

Mike was not new to this journey with us and said out loud what we were beginning to realize. It was time to help Kendra transition to the life he wanted. We were face-to-face with the fact that yes, he'd not done as well at school as he wanted. Yes, he didn't make friends easily and was feeling lonely. Yes, he was devastated that we were disappointed in him for several other issues as well. But none of these were the main cause of this second overdose. He was disconnected, detached, and in dissonance with his body and unhappy with how he was perceived in the world as a result. He needed our help to change that or his future felt hopeless. Living in the middle was not viable anymore. The stress and distress was piling up and we needed to work with him on a plan for transitioning. We'd been telling him we loved him and accepted him no matter what he decided and were taking his lead about transitioning. Since he wasn't pressing we weren't pushing. Maybe he needed permission and direction and didn't know how to ask. Maybe it was too painful being in the middle, struggling to decide.

This overdose was much more ominous. He was older, less impulsive. He knew Tylenol was more damaging long-term than Ibuprofen. The nurses told him last time they were relieved he hadn't taken Tylenol since it can cause permanent liver damage. This could end his chances of taking testosterone not to mention a lifetime of dialysis. It took two days to run the liver tests while Kendra stayed at the hospital.

I didn't sleep there this time. In fact I hardly slept at all. We wanted him to feel the gravity of this second more dangerous overdose. There was an ice storm that first night and I lay in bed thinking of Kendra in a cold, sterile hospital room. We faced the unnerving prospect of additional suicide attempts when least expected, or a successful attempt since research shows that prior attempts increase that likelihood. Second chances at life are a precious gift. Did I dare ask for a third? With all that was starting to go right in Kendra's life, how could this have happened?

Christmas never felt so bleak as we awaited news of the test results. I called my Dad that night to thank him for his gift check. He was a man of few words so I planned to limit myself to small talk. I was pretty sure that his conservative faith would make it hard for him to accept his transgender grandchild. He had a very traditional understanding of God's order when it came to gender roles and would struggle with human attempts to disrupt that. When my dad asked how Kendra was, my wall of silence crumbled. I choked through tears as I told him she (we hadn't yet changed pronouns with my dad) was in the hospital for a second overdose and that we were waiting to see if she would need kidney dialysis.

"She wants to be a boy, Dad. She says she's never felt like a girl," I said.

He listened quietly. This was the grandchild he anxiously awaited after my mother died. I remember the joy in his face as he awkwardly held her tightly swaddled bundle against his chest on a whale watch boat that July 4. Kendra loved to climb all over him between hammering and sawing while he helped us renovate the kitchen in our old house. He tickled, wrestled, and played with her just as he did with my sisters and me. Her delight in being naked made him uneasy and she scowled and fumed whenever he told her to put clothes on. By the time she was a teen he asked me once if she ever wore dresses or had a boyfriend. He hadn't seen Kendra in years and wouldn't recognize him now.

"Give her lots of love," he said quietly. "I'll pray for her. That's all we can do right now."

He hoped for her happiness. He was the one person I thought would have the most difficulty with this disclosure but now he knew and the sky hadn't fallen. He called me every few days throughout that winter to see how we were all doing. It was a much-appreciated comfort I hadn't expected. It was a relief to not feel judged even though I suspected the churchgoer in him struggled to reconcile his granddaughter's life-threatening pain with his understanding of God's design. Yet the older my father becomes the more he chooses God's love over laws.

The lab tests finally came back fine and Kendra was able to leave the hospital just in time for Christmas. I never felt more blessed and grateful to have been granted yet another chance to clear a path for this child that would keep him alive. I felt sad and sorry that it had taken so drastic a measure as a second overdose for us to understand how difficult life between two genders had been for Kendra. Because the possibility of his transitioning had been out there for a while, it was worrisome that it was still too difficult for him to verbalize directly that the time had come. It was as if a part of Kendra thought he could wait while another unconscious part was living in too much pain. Tony and I knew that we needed to hear and heed his pain if we were to keep Kendra alive.

Gender Counseling

To kick off the New Year and as part of the hospital discharge, we had a plan in place. We were ready to wrap our minds and hearts around seeing Kendra as fully male. Over the next two years, from the end of freshman year into the middle of junior year at college, Kendra transitioned from female to male. The steps included gender counseling and starting testosterone (T) while living full time as male by changing his name, telling family, friends, school and work, and having chest surgery.

Kendra began gender counseling at the Sidney Borum Junior Health Center, affiliated with Fenway Community Health Center in Boston. Up to this point, in addition to her primary care provider, Kendra had met with four therapists she chose not to see, two therapists she saw for a short time, and attended the partial hospitalization program at McLean Hospital for nine days. Over the years she had been prescribed Adderal, Citalopram, Clonazepam, Concerta, Depakote, Lexapro, Provigal, Prozac, Ritalin, and Zoloft. These were prescribed to address anxiety, depression, mood swings, and attention issues. Some of these drugs helped for a time; some made the symptoms worse; and some had such frightening side effects I never filled the prescription. No provider mentioned or addressed gender identity. Even when I began suggesting it as the main issue, the treatment goal was focused solely on managing the symptoms and never treating the cause. No provider thought to refer us to a gender specialist so when we finally found one it changed everything fast.

The Borum specializes in working with LGBTQ youth while Fenway works with adults. Kendra immediately connected with Marissa, his therapist. In March, after several sessions, Tony and I were invited to meet with them to review the gender timeline they had worked on. The room was lined with newsprint depicting various periods in his life when he felt he was a boy instead of a girl. We were surrounded by visual evidence that our daughter had always thought of herself as our son.

The first memory was very early, when Kendra was about two and told Sue, her daycare provider, that he had a penis and could pee standing up. He asked whether Sue had ever told me that. I did recall a conversation with her now that Kendra mentioned it. At the time I chalked it up to a universal fascination for little girls—especially when the other kids—all boys—were standing. After all, it looked like fun. I remembered the time my sister Sandy showed me how she could pee standing. It seemed pretty common and nothing to be concerned about. But as we talked about it in that session, I thought more about what Sue said and how she said it the afternoon I picked Kendra up from daycare. It went something like:

"Kendra seems very confused about her private parts," Sue said.

"What do you mean?" I asked. "We've talked about body parts and looked at pictures of boys and girls." I remembered bristling a little at the implication that I had not told Kendra the words for her body.

"Well she insists she has a penis and can pee standing up," said Sue. "I told her it wasn't a penis and that only boys have penises but she seemed pretty insistent."

I remember feeling a little afraid because Sue seemed so worried. But then she blew things out of proportion sometimes. And since Kendra never told me she had a penis and Sue never mentioned it again, I forgot about it. It wasn't even something I recorded in my journal. Too bad I didn't ask Kendra about it directly. But maybe I didn't want to know. Maybe she'd already picked up on my resistance. Maybe she told Sue because she was a more neutral adult to tell this truth of hers.

During that family session we discussed each incident posted on newsprint. There were about eight spanning every age. It was a difficult session for me but a critical, enlightening step. Kendra was surprised when I cried. I'd done a pretty good job protecting him from my tears up until then. I'd put on a brave front and prepared myself for what we would hear. We weren't surprised. It was the next logical step in Kendra's journey to finally feel at home in himself. He was our child whether female or male and we loved him. We were going to be there for him whatever it took.

I was relieved we finally found someone Kendra could talk to, trained in this area and knowledgeable of the process. I still wondered if we were moving too fast toward irreversible treatment but the weight of the evidence of Kendra's long-standing pain was undeniable. Furthermore, he did not want to go through his young adulthood in a body that was incongruent with his identity. He had already lost enough time. And I had been given plenty of time to prepare for what was next. He was already eighteen and did not need our permission, but he wanted our understanding and support. Tony was more objective and articulate than I was.

"This is your life, K. We have our lives already so this is not our decision to make. It's yours. Whatever you decide, we'll support you and love you no matter what," he said during that session.

Testosterone

In addition to counseling, physicians at the Borum could prescribe hormones for transitioning. The first hurdle was lab work to be sure Kendra's liver could tolerate testosterone. We held our breath. How tragic it would have been if the last overdose had compromised his liver, permanently preventing his ability to take "T." Once again we were fortunate. Kendra began intramuscular injections of testosterone just before turning twenty.

After three months of talking to a counselor, she diagnosed me with Gender Identity Disorder, and I was scheduled for a medical exam in order to start taking testosterone. Walking away with the letter she wrote me for my diagnosis, I didn't care that I was apparently diagnostically crazy, because I knew that in my heart I wasn't, and that this was the happiest I'd felt since hearing that I was accepted to Tufts. My mom was scared

that it would change me; I know I had disappointed her by
coming out as trans those years ago, but I knew she'd be okay
in time.

KAI, AGE 23

After his first few shots, Kendra reported feeling more embodied almost immediately as a mental fog seemed to lift. He felt present, grounded, focused, and aware. He also became more outgoing and self-confident.

The first harbinger of my daughter's physical disappearance was when Kendra's voice began to crack. I spiraled back into grief over the loss of her. I had loved her voice. As a child Kendra loved to sing. Her favorite singer was Raffi. She knew many of his songs by heart. We listened to music whenever we were in the car—which was often—and she frequently sang along. She also sat at the piano with songbooks and pretended to play while singing. But as she grew, the singing stopped. He hated the sound of his girl's voice I later learned. I reasoned with myself that the girl I was missing was already grown and gone anyway. But replacing her felt different than losing her.

For a time I avoided speaking with him. He sounded like a stranger; a man I never knew rather than the daughter I'd known for two decades. That daughter had a smooth, soothing voice. His was raspy and scratchy, all the music in it gone. First it deepened as if he smoked. Then it sounded croaky like a frog. It was months before his voice settled into its new timbre. He'd laugh about it with us as a family. I cried about it alone. I was glad he was away at college, creating a life of his own. I wanted to lose this daughter from a distance. Tufts is only an hour away so he frequently came home on weekends to tend to his gecko business. But conversation was intermittent and we could spends hours in the same house busy with our own projects and hardly communicate.

Testosterone triggered male puberty and after several months menstruation stopped. Always a traumatic intrusion this was a welcome relief. His shoulders, arms, and legs began to have more muscle definition and his neck enlarged. Veins popped out where there had been none and hair sprouted. None of these changes could happen fast enough as far as he was concerned. The adolescent turmoil of hormonal fluctuations is hard so watching your teen go through it twice, first as a girl then as a boy is not for the faint of heart. I was grateful and relieved he had emerged from his previous life-threatening feelings of despair and anxiety. But soon it was obvious that testosterone created changes of its own in behavior and demeanor.

What had previously manifested as panic was now explosive anger, and learning how to respond and control these powerful emotions would take time. He became more self-absorbed; hard to converse with; physically stronger; more distant and detached. It was not as though these tendencies were new they just became the norm. After a few months on T, he reported he'd lost all language for feelings—he still had them but could no longer put them into words. At times I felt I'd lost more than I'd gained; as if my daughter had disappeared but a son had failed to appear in her absence.

Had I raised a boy from the start I would've known to encourage empathy, compassion, and connection. Those qualities had already been there in the prepubescent girl but somewhere along this arduous journey toward male puberty it seemed like they'd been dropped like a cumbersome burden. I felt my heart retreat for its own protection from the stranger this young man was becoming. I began to feel like the mother who gets killed off in fairytales so the son can come of age, leaving behind his past and the warmth and tenderness of childhood.

Tony was having his own issues with an adolescent son in the house. What had begun as a father's tender love for his daughter turned into combat with a son. I wondered whether it might've been easier if Tony had time to bond with a boy first before living with a teen who seemed driven to defy him. There were times I wondered if I even wanted a connection with this son—he could be so arrogant and self-centered; not the child I'd raised; the sensitive daughter I'd known. Whether it was testosterone, individuation, trying on what he thought masculinity required of him, or the considerable stress of transitioning, I felt estranged, sad, and alone. It was easier when Kendra wasn't around. We were awkward together those first few months. I had no role models for mothers and sons, let alone mothers with trans sons, so I mostly stayed out of his way and let him seek me out. I let go of any expectations of what our relationship would ultimately become.

He felt better in his body and for that I was glad, relieved. But along the way testosterone exiled the daughter I'd known, and more than his body was changing. She was a boy now, almost a man. I tried not to blame him for the fact that I missed my little girl, since I would've missed her anyway if Kendra were a woman. So why was it so painful and final? She was never going to run to me as her four-year-old self and hug me tight saying, "Mom, look!" She was never going crawl into bed with me in the middle of the night. But she was never going to do that again anyway, girl or boy.

What did I really miss? The way she wanted to be with me always? No, I was glad he had friends now and a life of his own. I worried when his life was small, sad, and lonely. I missed that prepubescent girl, ten to fourteen: soulful, studious, sensitive, nurturing, close, before the wall of puberty came down. I missed her long, tousled hair; her beautiful body so languid and limber, her young-at-heart spirit so wild and carefree. Her face was there for a time despite the clothes—she still smiled and laughed, still took walks in the woods or gave me a small gift of her love—a flower or bouquet, a rock or shell. Then she was entirely gone and nothing was left of her—only anger and panic and all the taking away. From that very first glimpse of the ultrasound and in my dreams he was a boy. I'd prayed for a girl but prepared for a boy. So now he had come.

I caused it
Praying so hard for a girl
After my mother died

And you
Wanting to cheer me
Showed up that way

You used to pray to become a cat
We'd paint your face
Pin on a tail
You'd stalk and growl and lick

Then you started to cut
Like a snake you'd outgrown your skin
And when God didn't answer your prayers

You birthed yourself
A boy!

CANDACE, JANUARY 2010

Name Change

Next came the search for a new name. If only we'd chosen a gender-neutral name to begin with. He wanted one that started with "K" and meant something he could relate to. Kendra meant "knowledgeable" and suited his entry into the world—face first and wide-eyed. It was not too girly, unlike Ariana, which even then I somehow knew was crucial. For months we shared ideas for new names. I never expected to be pouring through baby name books again and remembered how much harder it was to choose boys' names than girls'. This time it was going to be his choice.

As with many big decisions, Kendra faced this one with ambivalence and vacillation, so finalizing the right name took awhile. Without a new name it was difficult to fully embrace the new pronoun so we found ourselves moving between Kendra and he, taking care to be consistent when talking to people unaware of our journey. He liked Kaiden, Kai for short. It has Celtic and Arabic origins with meanings that include friend, companion, and warrior. The nickname, Kai, means sea in Hawaiian. But more than that, he liked the sound of it. By the start of sophomore year he decided to keep it and notified Tufts to make the change.

I began telling my sisters Kai was transitioning. None were surprised. The older he got, the less girl-like he became. He had traveled through an animal phase, an androgynous phase, and then become decidedly more male with each passing year. Donna and Sandy visited that summer with their children, Kai's cousins, ranging in age from ten to twenty-eight. Each cousin had their own questions about how they were going to feel seeing Kendra as Kai for the first time. They wondered about how they should act; what they should say. No one wanted to do something unintentional that would offend him. At first they all worried it would feel like meeting him for the first time but once we were all together they realized Kai was pretty much the same old cousin they'd known apart from some physical changes. We tripped over names and pronouns while Kai answered to both, sometimes not even recognizing the new name himself. His transition seemed as gradual a process for him as for us. His patience and understanding put everyone at ease.

We witnessed him slowly becoming more comfortable, authentic, open, himself. I hoped to do a naming ritual to mark his transition and to welcome Kai, our son, nephew, and cousin. I imagined him surrounded by family along with photos and mementos linking his past with his present and future, as we named, blessed, and welcomed his new self. He seemed receptive. But when the time got closer, he still wasn't sure he'd settled on the name so the ritual didn't occur.

The summer before college Kendra began a four-year internship at the life sciences company where Tony works. Everyone met Kendra as Tony's daughter. The following spring, Kendra notified his supervisor and the Human Resources department that his name was now Kai and his gender was male. The company was fine about Kai's transition and made the change promptly, which helped him feel welcome and relieved when he returned to work that summer.

One day as Tony and Kai were getting into the elevator and leaving for work, a colleague passing by said, "Hi Tony. Is this your son? He looks just like you."

Tony said, "Yes, this is my son, Kai."

When the elevator door closed, Kai said, "Thanks Dad."

"For what?" Tony asked.

"For introducing me as your son," Kai said.

But there were times when Tony found himself answering questions and correcting pronouns as colleagues continued to refer to his daughter, Kendra, despite Kai's decidedly male presentation. Some found it harder than others to understand and adjust.

As I witnessed Kai's obvious relief and happiness, his transition gradually became easier and less anguished for me. His long-term happiness had been the goal all along so the tug of war over who knew best and when to act had ended. I finally let go of my secret longing that I could keep even a glimpse of my daughter. The memory of her would forever remain hidden in my heart as this new son took up residence in our home.

Just days before Kai's twenty-first birthday, we went to Probate Court and filed papers for a legal name change. On the way to court he talked about his women's studies class and I was impressed by his analysis of feminism. I asked how he could be such a committed feminist yet want to transition his gender.

"I just never felt like a girl," he said. "Ever. And not because I don't like to do girl things." In fact, he still did "girl" things—like keeping his middle name Leilani, which means "heavenly flower," in Hawaiian. He always loved plants and flowers but then so do many men in our family including his father, grandfather, and two of his great-grandfathers—and my mother.

A few weeks later we received notification it was time to return to court with his original birth certificate. For the first time in years I opened his baby book. There was a photo of the pink balloons we hung on the porch, a copy of the "It's a Girl" birth announcement, and all the cards from family and friends congratulating us on our baby girl. When I handed over the birth certificate in court I asked if I would get it back and was told I needed to file a separate motion for that. I considered forgoing it but something loud and persistent inside told me I'd be sorry. I wanted that original certificate back in the baby book where it belonged. So I filed the motion. With no questions asked the court officially and legally changed Kendra's name to Kaiden. The name I had so carefully chosen was tossed.

The certificate announcing Kendra came back to me in the mail. It served as a relic: testament of a mistaken identity rather than documentation of Kai's actual birth. That had been taking place over the last two years. Still, it was important to me since it had once been so defining.

Surgery

Kai wanted to look in the mirror and see the "he" he had always known himself to be. In the fall of sophomore year he signed up for the men's dorm and had been using men's restrooms in public places for several years. That was a sea change from when every public outing was a crisis due to gender-specific bathrooms. One day after Kai had been on testosterone for nearly a year and was looking, sounding, and behaving more masculine than ever, Tony hugged him goodbye as he left for campus and said, "It's probably about time to have your breasts removed don't you think? I mean after all, you're a man now." Kendra gave his dad a huge smile. Tony's encouragement gave him permission to start exploring surgeons.

During Christmas break Tony and I found a note from Kai on our bed. It was a challenge for him and a request from us.

> *Dear Mom and Dad,*
> *I know my having transitioned has been easier on me than it has on you. I can't thank you enough for the support you've given me. As I grow, I'm realizing all you've given me in fact. My morals, my strengths, and love from and for you has motivated me throughout my life—to better myself, love others, critique the world, and harass both of you. I'll save that for another, much longer letter.*
>
> *I'd like to make a selfish proposal, namely for my own much needed motivation and to provide an ease of heart, mind, and energy, so that I may focus more on my studies and less on transitioning.*
>
> *I know that finances are tight for you, and I want to thank you for having given me so much financial support. My proposal is this: I get all B's or higher this semester, and for that, I was wondering if you wouldn't mind helping me with a loan for top surgery.*
>
> *I realize that this is a lot to ask and I would be extremely happy to talk further over any specifics of this with you.*
>
> *I love you both so much. Hope to see you soon and I hope all is well,*
> *LOVE*
> *Kai*

There was a time when I shuddered at the thought of my child undergoing sex reassignment surgery. But during his transition, I too was transitioning. I saw how happy Kai was, finally in a body that matched his heart and soul. It suited him in ways his prior form never did. Our main objective concerning gender confirmation surgery—and the entire medical transitioning process—was making sure it was the right decision before proceeding. There was no evidence whatsoever that he would change his mind but then many of us make bad decisions in our teens and early twenties. I certainly did. Some of them can be reversed but this one could not. Based on the gender timeline we saw with Kai's therapist and what we knew of him through his life so far, gender transition finally felt right to us. It was obviously not a phase he'd outgrow and we could see how much happier he was as a man. Of course we would support him in getting top surgery. We not only agreed to loan him the money, we agreed to pay for half the cost. Needless to say, he got a 3.0 GPA and was on the Dean's list for the first time. It seemed like he was reborn.

That spring Kai began to actively search for surgeons for chest surgery. He researched the best surgeons and techniques with the least scarring. One day in March I cleared my work schedule to go with Kai to Pennsylvania for a surgical consult. Finally there were no tears. I was strong, confident, and ready to support him on the continuation of his journey toward gender congruity. I was honored he wanted me to join him on this six-hour excursion.

Kai was interested in having the keyhole procedure but we learned that this surgeon would only perform double incision chest surgery. The keyhole procedure is possible on small breasts and is performed with an incision around the areola through which breast tissue is removed. Sutures around the areola disappear, resulting in less scarring. The double incision procedure involves cutting under each breast to remove breast tissue and repositioning the nipples. The surgeon's post-operative photos showed a wide "U" shaped scar under each breast. Kai's biracial background put him at risk for keloidal scarring and there was usually little or no sensation in the nipples or chest from the waist to the neck after this type of surgery. Kai was disappointed this surgeon did not do the keyhole procedure and decided to consult with other surgeons.

When I closed my eyes to sleep that night all I could see were red, raw, screaming scars. I felt heartbroken that Kai and others have to face this drastic procedure to finally feel at home in their bodies. I began to comprehend the depth of Kai's pain. That the same person who, as a child, was terrified over the slightest cut or scrape was willing go to these lengths to bring his body into alignment with his soul said it all. Puberty blocking hormones were not even available at the time Kai approached puberty, but had they been I was more certain now than ever that that treatment method would have been the right decision. He was so clear and direct in his questions at that appointment—brave, articulate, informed. He had done his research, talked to other transmen, viewed photos online of surgical procedures, and weighed his options. He knew what he wanted. We were both on the same page. Gradually, at critical times like this, we could once again connect. I was starting to feel at home with him—refinding my same soulful child, now an adult.

I tried calling him to see how he was doing with this new information because I felt such overwhelming sadness. But this time was different. I was sad more for him than for me. I had crossed a threshold of empathy that I hadn't noticed this strongly since the disclosure he was trans. I certainly felt it when Kendra was depressed, cutting, and lost and I was desperate to know how to reach her. But once I understood that Kendra's future and happiness would result in my loss of her, it was as if I got lost in my own tangled wilderness. I finally found a pathway out and was emerging into the light of compassionate understanding for Kai's pain rather than my own.

All day I'd needed a good cry for what Kai was facing and how unfair it felt. I couldn't imagine what he was feeling after so disappointing a visit. One of his dreams since adolescence was the freedom to go shirtless again yet those defining scars would always out him as trans whether he wanted that or not. I was proud of him, his growth, our growth; his insight, focus, research, and courage; his love and talent for science; his growing desire to help others on a similar path. But I also felt a heavy weight for the uphill journey he still faced. I was grieved I'd birthed him into the wrong body. I wondered if he ever blamed me like I had blamed him for wanting to change that. This journey was teaching us about the depths and elasticity of love. When we finally did speak days later he too was traumatized by that first consultation but his commitment to having his breasts removed was unwavering—just not with that procedure or surgeon.

Later that spring Kai and I drove to New York for a second surgical consult. This visit stood in stark contrast to the first one. The second surgeon said Kai was a good candidate for the keyhole procedure. We were elated when we left his office. We had found the right surgeon—just before Kai's twenty-first birthday. We talked about a lot on the way home from New York, including his memory of telling Sue he had a penis. He knew very young something wasn't right and tried to tell someone. I wished he had told Tony or me or said it more than once.

Surgery was scheduled for December 17. The calm I experienced the whole week before was surprising. Surgery was once the looming specter on this journey that caused me the greatest pain and fear. Waiting for him to outgrow his gender dysphoria and hoping happiness was achievable without body morphing were rooted in avoiding this. I'd spent a lot of time and plenty of ink wishing to not be where we were now. There were numerous practical matters to distract me leading up to our trip like where we would stay and how to pay for everything since health insurance didn't cover this surgery. There were also last minute preparations including lab work and buying a compression vest. Both arrived just in time for our trip.

This was the culmination of a dream for Kai. He had asked about top surgery at seventeen. Waiting four years at his age was a long time. Yes, there were risks that the outcome would not be perfect and there would certainly be physical pain. But Kai couldn't wait to be rid of his female chest. It was the one physical marker he struggled with most. Since thirteen he'd refused to wear a bathing suit. I wish I'd known it was his chest he was hiding when he began wearing large baggy T-shirts to swim. His clothes were so big I feared the weight would drown him. I knew he'd never wear a skimpy bikini but thought a one-piece Speedo might do. It was maddening because everyone else saw a perfectly good body for an adolescent female. Even with all my experience in women's health it never occurred to me than this was exactly the problem. He couldn't wait to go topless again and feel the sun, wind, and water on his bare skin.

One crisp clear December morning I picked Kai up at Tufts for our drive to Manhattan. Kai talked nonstop the whole way. The two of us used to do that when no one else was around. Surprisingly, it was happening again. He seemed tentative about the next day; scared. Tears welled up when he considered what he was about to undergo. I worried we should turn back; cancel this operation. But he had lashed out at me the week before when I brought up postponing. So rather than focus on my own fear of regret I focused on his feelings about the procedure itself.

"I like my feminine qualities," he said. "I'm even proud I was a cute baby. It doesn't bother me that you still have old pictures of me around." He knew how hard—impossible—it was for me to get rid of them. "I sometimes wish I didn't have to commit to one gender or another," he said. "I'd be all right living in between if I could." He wondered whether he felt he had to be male to have more power and stature being biracial in a white community or whether growing up with more women of color he might have been more at home as female. "I sometimes identify as white because of how I grew up but I seldom pass as white," he said.

"I want this surgery so I can go to the beach again, swim during the day, and have the freedom of not hiding," he said. Ever since puberty he had rounded his shoulders to hide his chest rather than standing up tall. As a child, he loved the freedom of being topless. It was a shaming confinement, a betrayal of self, to have to cover up.

He wasn't worried about the irreversibility of the surgery, he was worried about the pain. "I am looking forward to having a male chest," he assured me. "I can't wait!"

A weight lifted to hear these were not second thoughts and to know he was realistic about the gravity of surgery. I felt so sad for all he had to go through just to have a body that matched his heart and mind. So many of us take that birth right for granted. It was unfair.

"Thanks Mom, for all your support," he said. "I have the best family. So many others I know don't. They wouldn't have the support I have. Do you reminder when you told me you'd never help pay for surgery?"

I didn't recall saying that but I did recall feeling it.

"You said, 'Why would I pay to have my child's body mutilated?'" he said.

I felt ashamed. Then I marveled at how far I'd come. I remembered when he asked me if our health insurance paid for it when I was driving him to nAGLY. I had focused my thoughts like lasers on my hands as I tightened my grip on the wheel trying to close my mind and my ears to what I was hearing. At the time, I couldn't fathom how my daughter could be so disdainful of nature's gifts to her. It felt tragic to me.

He read the letter that diagnosed him with gender identity disorder (GID), granting approval for surgery. "I don't feel like I am 'disordered,'" he said. "I hate having to have a diagnosis to do what's right for me. It's like they're telling me I'm crazy or something. It makes me feel labeled." Again his eyes welled up indignant.

"That's unfair," I said. "And with time that'll change. More people will understand how many transgender people there are in the world. Everyone has the right to be at home in their own body." I told him about how women used to need a diagnosis for permission to have an abortion.

He felt so happy to be taking this step toward gender affirmation. We talked about my evolution in accepting this step. He shared his surprise at how hard it had been for me. We also talked about the ways he can become just another arrogant male. "I took women's studies this semester so I could stay connected to you; so we'd have something to talk about. I didn't want you to think you'd lose me entirely," he said.

It was touching to hear him say that. I figured he took the class to meet women. I was surprised he even thought about how I might feel since he'd been so detached. I didn't want him to do things for my sake. I was reminded of how hard I once worked to please my dad by excelling in school. But I also felt honored that our relationship mattered to him.

"Thanks Kai. I'm glad you want a connection. And I'm glad you took women's studies because it will make you a better man," I said. "I lost the five- and ten-year-old you to time and the twenty-one year-old man is so much happier than the sixteen-year-old girl was, that I'm okay now. I was afraid of watching you totally change your personality, so maintaining some of who you were has helped."

"I think I willed away puberty until I was fourteen. I was in such denial when it started to happen I really thought something was wrong—like I had a tumor in both breasts or something," he said. "I'm looking forward to my new body. I like being transgender because I have something to look forward to."

I imagined him worrying about a tumor and not telling anyone. I remembered how irritable he was during that period. How frightened and lonely he must have been.

"Many adolescents look forward to the changes their bodies go through during puberty—developing breasts or getting chest and facial hair. Since you didn't have that experience then, it's your time now, at twenty-one, to finally look forward to what others looked forward to earlier," I said.

Just as the funds appeared, so did a place to stay. At dinner with friends in November I was given the name of a woman in Manhattan who rented her apartment from time to time. I called Joan and learned she was walking distance to the surgeon's office. The apartment building was decked out for Christmas with huge wreaths, white lights, and a red velvet bow on every wall sconce. It felt like entering an abbey with its white stucco walls, dark oak trim, and heavy, ornate doors. Surgery was scheduled for Friday and since the sutures and drains needed to be checked before we left, we expected to stay until Saturday at least, possibly Sunday. Joan could not have been kinder. Her home was warm and welcoming. She stayed with her friend upstairs.

Kai jumped up out of bed and hugged me long and hard the morning of his surgery. He couldn't be happier with this Christmas present. He hadn't slept well and was tired and hungry but excited. He was scheduled for 10 a.m. but the office called shortly before we left to say the anesthesiologist was running late so we didn't need to arrive until 11 a.m. We walked the several blocks to the doctor's office on Central Park South stopping at a street vendor to buy Kai a gray, black, red, and white striped scarf. He looked very New York in it. It would help him stay warm so he wouldn't have to stiffen his shoulders against the winter chill after surgery. We would both remember this day—and this scarf I thought.

During the preliminary exam, the surgeon reviewed Kai's medical history and lab work and discussed surgery and post-op instructions, chest contouring, and areola size. He explained where he would cut, how he'd remove the tissue, and said he'd avoid at all costs cutting under the breast or making a vertical incision under the nipple.

"Given your body's overall tone and musculature, I couldn't even tell you were transitioning. The first time I met you I thought I had the wrong patient," he said. "Someone put breasts there by mistake. You're a man and you want a man's chest so we'll take care of that. We have all day if we need it." He also mentioned that sometimes revision surgery is needed after the first procedure to fine-tune the outcome.

The anesthesiologist finally arrived so at 1 p.m. it was time for Kai to be prepped. He was halfway across the waiting room when I called to him. I needed to hug and kiss him before he left. He was only slightly embarrassed. The office manager asked if I was all right.

"Yes," I said. And I was. I had cried that morning in the shower. Water had a way of bringing out the tears. "It's a strange experience to have your daughter become your son. Do you have a lot of surgeries like this?"

"Yes," she said, "although not usually this young. But most who have surgery wish they'd had it sooner. Do you feel all right about the procedure or have any questions?"

I realized she was asking about medical issues, not emotional ones.

"I'm very confident with the doctor's manner and competence. I'm sure everything will go smoothly," I said.

After getting suggestions for a good place to eat I left the office and wandered down Fifth Avenue at the height of Christmas shopping. Sidewalks were three and four people deep. Shoppers in fur coats with designer bags on their arms walked briskly past me. Cars and taxis honked; buses pulled away from the curb; carriages and bikers pulled carts; police directed traffic. It was cold but not bitter. I walked in a daze, witness to the hustle and bustle but not a participant. My heart and mind were elsewhere.

The driver of a horse-drawn carriage asked if I wanted a ride through Central Park. I smiled and politely declined. I had to be frugal on this trip trusting I wouldn't run out of cash or credit before getting home. I had no interest in shopping even if I had the money. Friends and family called to wish us well—Sandy, Donna, Char, and others. I decided to walk.

I was alone in Manhattan with nowhere to be and nothing to do while my daughter became my son. He had really already done that so many years before. I felt closer to him on this trip than I had in several years. I felt connected, happy—like some spiritual part of him was back during this ordeal. Or maybe it was a spiritual part of me that was finally open and accessible to him rather than sad and scared. I was grateful to have had him as a daughter when he was young. We might not have been so close had he been a son from birth. I asked him that morning if he was going to miss his breasts. He looked at me sideways as if I was crazy. "No," he said without a moment's hesitation.

I never did find the food place that was recommended. I probably walked right past it. Eventually I ordered pasta at a café and then found my way back to the apartment. I made myself a cup of coffee, ate a cookie, and wrote. At 3:30 p.m. I got a voicemail, though my phone never rang. The only place in the apartment where I had reception was at the kitchen window. I listened to the voicemail while walking in a rush thinking it was the doctor's office but it was only my office. For once I wanted a break from work. When I arrived at the doctor's office at 4 p.m. Zoe said to plan on another two hours. I started to worry.

"Everything's fine," she said. "They're finished with one side and are working on the other. We'll call you when Kai is out."

I wandered aimlessly through stores but the crowds were intense. Everyone but me was heading somewhere with purpose. I felt like the oblivious slow driver in the fast lane holding everyone up. I simply couldn't keep up. It was too much work winding my way through the dense crowd of driven holiday shoppers. I needed to find a place to sit and stop so I returned to Joan's place. It was a comforting refuge. It wasn't until the next day that I wished I'd thought to visit St. Patrick's Cathedral. It was an odd day of aimless wandering while my mind paced and prayed. Maybe it was walking meditation in one of the most nonmeditative places on earth.

I finally decided to make my way to the office even before hearing from them. It was a good choice because it took a long time to get back. First the garage couldn't find my car. Then the traffic to Central Park on Friday evening was brutal and I caught every light—sometimes twice. Then I noticed my phone was nearly dead. Why hadn't I charged it at Joan's! Just as I found a place to tuck my car—in an illegal space—my phone rang. Kai was out of surgery and they needed the compression vest. Why hadn't I given it to Kai?

All day I was losing things. I went to get my ATM card to pay for parking and it was not in my wallet. I ran back to Joan's but it wasn't there either. It turned up in my car. Good thing I hadn't needed it. Next, I got out of the car and heard something fall. When I looked back, my wallet was in the street. Then my car wouldn't lock. The key fob was lost inside somewhere, but where? The office was waiting for me. I found it in the cup holder. Obviously it was a stressful day.

I ran the three long blocks past families getting into carriages, couples hailing cabs for a night on the town, and cars splashing pedestrians. Kai was just waking up so they ushered me into the recovery room. I didn't realize how much I'd worried until my eyes filled as soon as I saw him. He was groggy but conscious. He needed to take a full IV before leaving and a nurse was cleaning him up. They showed me the sutures hidden around the areola and the drains that were attached and flowing. They helped him into the compression vest while I settled the final fee.

While the IV finished dripping into Kai, I went to move the car closer. I double-parked right outside the office but when I got to the door it was locked for the night. I knocked but no one came. I was now using Kai's phone because mine was dead but his did not have the office number programmed in it so I went back to the car to look for it. When I got back in the office we put Kai's coat on him and the nurse walked him to the car. Finally, we were on our way back to Joan's. What a relief. It had been a very long day.

When Kai fell asleep I went out at midnight to check on the car. I'd forgotten to read the sign and wanted to know what time I had to move it. It could stay there all night. Gratitude welled up in me as I re-entered the sanctuary of Joan's building. How far we had come since Kai's hospital stay two years ago after his Christmas overdose. I considered the suffering we might have avoided if we'd known in 2005 or 2008 what we now knew in 2010. We work with what we have at the time so I forgave myself for how long it took me to get here.

At 6 a.m. I heard Kai moan. He was in pain so took another pill. The drains hurt, the compression vest to prevent swelling and facilitate draining was tight, and the mattress was harder than he was used to. I liked sleeping next to him to rub his back and shoulders, check his forehead for fever, and get his pain pills. We were seeing the surgeon at noon. We stayed in bed and talked until Kai fell back to sleep. Joan came in around 10:30 Saturday morning. I'd told her the day before why we were here. She noted this was major surgery and how painful and difficult recovery might be. We'd hoped to leave Saturday but given how late Kai got out of surgery, we were prepared to stay one more day. Joan offered to let us stay another night at no charge. She wanted to sleep there too, on the living room couch since she wasn't sleeping well upstairs. Her friend had a territorial rabbit that didn't like her there! We were fine with her return and grateful for her gift.

Kai got up around 11 a.m. He barely ate breakfast because of pain in this mouth from the anesthesia despite taking painkillers every four hours. He moved gingerly and winced. The right side of his chest was more painful and swollen than the left and he needed help dressing because he couldn't lift his arms high enough for his sleeves. He wasn't able to shower because of the drains and the pouch was nearly full. I worried it would open and spill all over Joan's white sheets.

We were due back at the doctor's office so he could check the drains and hopefully remove them. I offered to bring the car closer but Kai wanted to walk. When we got to Central Park South it was as crowded as the night before so parking was difficult. I suggested I drop Kai off in front of the office and then park but he wanted to walk. We parked pretty far only this time we couldn't run. I called the office to say we were running late. We both noticed the funny animal hats with attached mittens on a cart in Central Park. There was a time when Kendra would have begged for one. I felt the hint of a lump in my throat. Babies in strollers were bundled up against the cold and I thought of how many times I'd pushed Kendra up and down Main Street, nestled on a sheepskin in her pink or lavender snowsuit. That stroller was long gone—as were so many other reminders of her childhood after moving out of our first house.

The doctor asked if I was all right before letting me join them in the exam room. I assured him I wouldn't pass out. Kai very slowly removed the compression vest. Guys are not accustomed to hooks and eyes as closures so he struggled with them. The surgeon removed the gauze bandages to check the stitches and drains. He disconnected the pouch and measured the volume of fluid. Then he washed out the tubing to get it flowing and asked if we could return on the next day.

Saturday was the worst day for pain. Kai had looked forward to getting the drains out. They itched and pulled and added pressure to the bruised tissue. The pouch hung just below his shirt and could be seen. It jostled with every step and he feared someone might bump into him as we wound through the throng of people and got back into the car. Pedestrians, now five and six deep, stampeded in front of cars so we made little headway. When we got back to Joan's we decided to watch movies in bed so Kai could relax. After two movies we both had cabin fever. Kai wanted to drive to Long Island but it was already dark so we decided to drive around the city. We went to Ground Zero to see the building going up, then Soho and Chinatown. Before long, every bump and pothole exacerbated the pain and swelling in Kai's chest. It hurt so bad it brought tears to his eyes. By the time we returned to Joan's he felt worse instead of better.

I could tell he felt trapped by that vest as it squeezed the last vestiges of girl out of him. There was a time when Kendra was conflicted about not ever having children. I could never see him as a mother but maybe a father. It was excruciating to see how painful it was for his body to be rid of breasts that never belonged there in the first place. Does a breast feel phantom pain like a limb I wondered? They didn't look totally gone yet, just deflated and bruised; shadows of themselves. I felt sure the skin would tighten, the color improve, once the vest came off and Kai could breathe strength into his masculine chest.

We picked up some food for dinner and climbed into bed for another movie before falling asleep. Kai slept better that night— until almost 11 the next morning. There was much less fluid from the drains so that was a promising sign they were ready to come out. Kai was wearing his new scarf and looking very handsome as he walked stiffly from the car to the doctor's office.

The doctor removed the stitch holding each drain and then pulled out the tubes. It looked painful given how high up on Kai's chest they were. He used a syringe to pull additional fluid out of the right side, which was still more swollen, then placed a band-aid and gauze where each drain had been. Kai put the vest back on and we were instructed to return in a week to have the stitches removed. As we left, the doctor gave Kai a big hug. He said that if he could, he'd only do this type of surgery because it is so rewarding; it makes a real difference in people's lives. I shook his hand and thanked him for everything. We were finally off for home.

There was a haze over the full moon as it rose over Central Park. It looked like snow was on the way. The drive back home was as quiet and pensive as the drive there had been talkative and anticipatory. It had been a very long day and we were physically and emotionally exhausted. Kai was in considerable pain on the long ride home. Every bump in the road made him wince from the pain in his chest. His back hurt, and the compression vest felt suffocating. Everything ached despite the painkillers.

The Christmas carols reminded me of earlier years with my daughter, Kendra. Now I was driving home with my son, Kai. He read me well and changed the CD when Celine Dion sang a lullaby. He knew I was with her, my little girl. It was a weird split. He knew my melancholy and it was a counterforce to his relief; an odd dance between us to be sure. I dodged every pothole and willed us home quickly as we drove the four long hours.

Christmas Gifts

The next day I couldn't stop crying. Everything inside came to the surface; the entire seven-year journey from the crisis of puberty and disclosure to top surgery: fear, denial, guilt, confusion, sorrow, longing. I spiraled back into the center of it again but this time I felt comforted knowing Kai was home, upstairs in bed, safely healing, happy, and on his way. We were finally emerging from a long tunnel of darkness. I wrapped myself in a cloak of melancholy, sadness, and inertia. I waded through pages in journals filled with denial, disbelief, then gradual awakening, and acceptance. I needed to revisit that tunnel to see where we'd been. How unprepared I was and how much I would have done differently. But these tears were a mix of relief, gratitude, even joy. I was proud of myself for being with Kai since surgery had once been the symbol of my greatest resistance and fear.

It was around this time that I received a note from my Dad who had remarried when Kai was six. He was diagnosed with Parkinson's disease several years later and was no longer able to write so his wife wrote on his behalf. The note said my Dad was concerned about Kai having surgery; that surgery wouldn't make him happy, only a miracle would, and Kai needed to accept Jesus into his life. I interpreted this note as my Dad's expression of love and concern for Kai. It was something he felt compelled to share out of love, so I accepted it in that spirit. I knew I probably couldn't make my Dad and his wife understand Kai's need to transition. In subsequent conversations with him however, I was able to help him understand the choices we faced between transitioning and a lifetime of suffering. When faced with either a child's gender transition or their possible death, there is one obvious path.

Christmas that year was auspicious, with the full moon, winter solstice, and a lunar eclipse converging. Kai was instructed to take it easy after surgery but his first act in his new male chest was to drive to Maine and cut down a Christmas tree. It was a real Charlie Brown tree—spindly and sparse but we loved it. He also got the snow he wanted for Christmas—a nor'easter in fact. When the electricity went out, Kai and I sat by the wood stove while I rubbed his back and shoulders which were stiff from the vest and the tension he held from the pain. It was strange to see Kai with his shirt off but he seemed perfectly at ease with it. We'd all get used to it with time. At the end of the week we headed back to New York for a checkup and to have the stitches removed.

In mid-January we took a trip to St. Barth's. It was the first family vacation in eight years. Since Kai's name and gender on the plane ticket did not match *her* passport, we worried he might have trouble getting through security. Changing his gender with social security and getting a new passport were now possible since he'd legally changed his name and had surgery, but not feasible time-wise. To be safe, he brought court documents with his name change and when asked by a TSA officer, he simply said he'd changed his name. She was fine with that. And for the first time in years, Kai walked on the beach without a shirt. He felt free and looked great.

RESEARCH

Horizontal Identities

One of the challenges for families of transgender youth is watching them form identities that diverge from their family's identity. In *Far From the Tree*, Andrew Solomon speaks of the vertical identities that parents pass on to children through culture and across generations such as ethnicity, race, language, and religion. Horizontal identities are traits in children that differ from their parents such as being multiracial, having different physical or mental abilities, a chronic illness, or criminal behavior. Gay, lesbian, and transgender youth develop horizontal identities that diverge from their parents unless their parents are also LGBTQ.[102] Young adults who change religion from the one they were raised in, marry outside of their race, religion, or culture, or move to another country also have horizontal identities apart from their parents. While vertical identities are often celebrated as a symbol of belonging in a family, horizontal identities may be seen as divisive or a threat to family unity. Participating in subcultures with others who share one's identity can strengthen and solidify one's sense of self, while also posing a threat to family unity. Consider for a moment Solomon's insightful observation, "Though many of us take pride in how different we are from our parents, we are endlessly sad at how different our children are from us."[103]

Horizontal identities are born from shared experiences and mutual support often in the face of pervasive oppression and marginalization in mainstream society. Transgender and gender nonconforming people face barriers and challenges in daily living that those outside the community might find shocking. The 2013 report on the *National Transgender Discrimination Survey* (*NTDS*) of more than 6,450 transgender and gender nonconforming people from all fifty states ranging in age from 18 to 89 years old (19 percent of whom were 18 to 24 years old), found that more than half (53 percent) of respondents reported being harassed in places of public accommodation such as a retail store, police department, hospital or doctor's office, hotel or restaurant, government agency or while using transportation, with 64 percent of those who identified as "visually nonconforming" experiencing harassment.[104] Survey respondents had double the rate of unemployment as the general population and 90 percent reported experiencing harassment, mistreatment, or discrimination in the workplace and took efforts to hide their identity to protect themselves.[105] Sixty-three percent of respondents experienced a serious act of discrimination impacting their quality of life and their ability to survive emotionally and financially. These events included: job or housing loss due to bias, school bullying so severe they dropped out, teacher bullying, denial of medical service due to bias, physical or sexual assault due to bias, and incarceration due to identity or gender expression.[106]

According to the National Institute for Mental Health, any one of these experiences of extreme distress can increase one's risk for attempted suicide. Respondents to this survey reported serious losses in nearly every major area of life, including education, employment, housing, health care, and family life.[107] When family supports are strained, intermittent, or nonexistent, the LGBTQ community can become an essential lifeline for survival. When family supports are strong, compassionate, and consistent, the LGBTQ community can become part of one's extended family.

Family Acceptance

Gender nonconforming and transgender children do better when surrounded by adults who are informed, open, compassionate, and accepting. Research shows that family acceptance of gender nonconforming and transgender children and teens is one of the most effective ways of ensuring that they will have healthy, productive futures. Acceptance by family supports their self-esteem, protects them against discrimination and bias experienced in the world, embraces them as important members of the family, contributes to their ability to love and care for themselves, prevents them from engaging in behaviors that put their health at risk such as substance abuse, self-injury, HIV exposure, and suicide, and helps them plan and work toward a positive future.[108]

With so little knowledge and compassion in society, love, understanding, and acceptance by parents and families is often the only lifeline for transgender children and teens. Many parents do the internal work required to support their transgender child's search for well-being and authentic self-expression. But some teens face total family rejection and abandonment when they disclose their true gender identity. A 2010 report by the Center for American Progress cited the following alarming statistics on the health and well-being of gay and transgender youth:[109]

- Twenty to forty percent of homeless youth are gay or transgender but compose only 5–10 percent of the total youth population.
- Sixty-two percent of homeless gay and transgender youth experience discrimination from their families compared to 30 percent of non-LGBTQ youth.
- The attempted suicide rate is 8.4 times higher for LGBTQ youth when rejected by their families in adolescence, compared to those who are accepted. They are also 5.9 times as likely to have experienced depression and 3.4 times as likely to have used illegal drugs.

- LGBTQ youth are 2 times less likely to finish high school or pursue a college education compared to the national average.

The *NTDS* found that 40 percent of respondents reported that their parents or other family members "chose not to speak or spend time with me" as a result of their gender identity or expression.[110] Sixty percent of survey participants did not experience this type of family rejection. Family rejection rates—49 percent—were higher for multiracial respondents. Without family support, most adolescent transgender and gender nonconforming youth face insurmountable barriers navigating higher education, access to health care, identification documents congruent with their affirmed gender, employment, housing, and a living wage.

This groundbreaking *NTDS* asked survey respondents to report their experiences with family life, education, employment, housing, health care, public accommodations, and law enforcement. In summarizing its findings, the report noted the damaging impact of "institutional structures weighted against transgender and gender nonconforming people and from blatant acts of personal prejudice perpetrated against them just because they are different."[111] It also found that family acceptance had a protective effect on the lives of transgender and gender nonconforming people in the face of "pervasive mistreatment and discrimination outside of the home."[112] Family support lowered numerous health risks including suicide, HIV infection, use of drugs and alcohol, homelessness, and incarceration.[113]

Protecting your child from family members, friends, and acquaintances who hold intolerant, transphobic, or homophobic attitudes is critical to ensuring their mental, emotional, and physical safety. Listening to your child's feelings of distrust or observing their resistance to being with someone, even if it's a person you consider trustworthy, is crucial. Learning more about the LGBTQ community through reading, attending events, and getting to know LGBTQ youth and adults, will create a diverse and supportive community for your family and your child. Embracing your child's difference and celebrating the ways it broadens, enlightens, and strengthens your family, and welcoming those they care for are all part of fully accepting your child.

Acceptance takes time. Most parents need time to re-establish their equilibrium after a child or teen discloses they are transgender since few of us are prepared for a change this fundamental in our child and our families. Many factors contribute to how quickly or slowly you will reach acceptance. But as nearly all parents of transgender children can attest, equilibrium does return if parents and children are committed to loving, learning, adapting, and growing. Parents, just like their children, change during the process. Consider taking the following vow developed by Stephanie Brill and Rachel Pepper from their book, *The Transgender Child*:

A Vow of Parental Acceptance [114]

I start here, and from wherever I am, and from this day forward, I will:

- Speak positively about my child to them and to others about them
- Take an active stand against discrimination
- Make positive comments about gender diversity
- Work with schools and other institutions to make these places safer for gender-variant, transgender, and all children
- Find gender-variant and transgender friends and create our own community
- Express admiration for my child's identity and expression, whatever direction that may take
- Volunteer for gender organizations to learn more and to further the understanding of others
- Believe my child can have a happy future

REFLECTIONS

Deciding for Our Children

Making decisions about irreversible medical interventions on behalf of our minor children is a daunting responsibility. Having the right treatment team to consult with and guide you makes all the difference. Our delay in getting Kai the help he needed was due in part to how long it took to find providers knowledgeable and experienced in treating transgender teens. Time and energy were wasted treating only the symptoms instead of the cause. Fortunately you do not have to consider irreversible medical interventions for young children but you will want to have knowledgeable providers you can work with if there are emotional issues to address since the tendency may be to write a prescription without delving deeper.

Socially transitioning your child is a reversible option to consider when your child shows marked signs of discomfort or sadness (gender dysphoria) with their assigned gender and physical body. The biggest challenge with young children is knowing whether their gender nonconformity is playful and fluid or symptomatic of emotional dissonance and discomfort with their gender and anatomy. Observing their play, how they speak about their gender and body, and whether their nonconformity or discomfort increases over time, will help guide you in deciding whether and when to consider social transitioning. Working with a gender specialist and involving key school personnel if you pursue social transitioning can help ease the process for your child and her or his siblings.

Medical treatment decisions arise as puberty approaches. The looming question for parents of preadolescent children is whether or not to have them take puberty suppressing hormones to temporarily stall their biological maturation and avoid the development of secondary sex characteristics. While this intervention is reversible, it means having conversations with your teen about their gender identity before the early stages of puberty, which can be anywhere between eleven and sixteen years old. Some children are ready and waiting for this discussion and intervention. Others may feel surprised, unprepared, or frightened by what this step suggests about their gender identity. They may not yet know what their gender nonconformity means. Suggesting your child meet with a gender specialist to explore their feelings about gender might help them gain more insight as they decide if they are ready for treatment. Be careful that your need for guidance and answers does not make them feel pressured or rushed. Working with a knowledgeable pediatrician and pediatric endocrinologist to consider appropriate timing based on your child's development is critical. They can assist you as you work with your child to make the best decision, explaining risks, benefits, and side effects, and answering your questions and concerns about puberty suppressing hormones.

By puberty, if your teen is hinting or telling you in every way except in words they need medical intervention, don't wait for her or him to communicate their needs in some drastic and life-threatening way as we did. Ask your teen questions so you can move thoughtfully, consciously forward. Walk beside your child on this path and resist the temptation to take the lead or lag behind. Bring up the topic of medical transitioning yourself if necessary. Your teen may be subtly testing the waters, and if you miss or ignore the clue, you may be communicating that you're not ready to hear them and help. Waiting for Kai to take the lead kept him in a holding pattern for longer than was needed or helpful to him. It did, however, give me time to come around, which is probably why Kai tolerated it. He needed and wanted me fully on board. It's a difficult balance to find—not pushing sooner than they're ready but avoiding too passive a role, especially if they're used to you organizing their lives.

Although your teen may choose to medically transition to be fully authentic, never underestimate how daunting the journey is and the strength of character required. Weighing the gains and losses may take time and thoughtful consideration. Our restrictive gender binary system forces only two options, requiring the suppression of "feminine" traits to become a man and "masculine" traits to become a woman. Many transgender people find this limiting since they have lived with and appreciate both sets of traits. Even with certainty about the transition, there can be a sense of loss when jettisoning parts of their personality they liked. Discussions with your teen as they talk through their feelings will help you both. It can clarify and deepen their reflections and help you understand and appreciate their perspective. My conversation with Kai as we drove to New York for chest surgery strengthened our relationship and allayed my fears. He had obviously considered the losses and gains and was not acting impulsively. I was proud of his self-awareness and depth.

Puberty can be a precarious time when your teen may feel a sense of urgency to start hormones and explore surgery. Responding to their need to act can protect your child's safety since teens can often find street hormones when medical treatment is denied. Some transgender adolescents feel the urgent need for cross-gender hormones and/or surgery by age fifteen or sixteen but since they are still minors, they need parental consent for these irreversible interventions. This can create considerable tension between transgender teens and their parents. Many parents are reluctant to make such life-altering medical decisions on behalf of their child. Some may consent to hormones but not gender reassignment surgery.

Often our own life experiences inform our parenting. I made a hasty decision to marry as a teen and eventually got divorced. "You can get out of a marriage," I told Kendra when she asked about chest surgery at sixteen, "but you can't undo surgery." I didn't want her to make a mistake similar to mine. While this was a totally different situation, I still felt Kendra was too young to be absolutely certain. I'd have trouble forgiving myself if we got it wrong.

After the reading and research I have done for this book, I now feel differently. Kendra had always been gender nonconforming and with age, it became more pronounced. Gender dysphoria was negatively impacting her life on every level: academic achievement, relationships with peers, emotional affect, and self-esteem. In her sixteen-year history, there was not one shred of evidence that she was going to wake up one day feeling like, and happy to be, a young woman. The only indications otherwise were the ones I grasped at: she had been a darling little girl, she liked some "feminine" activities, she could be warm and affectionate, she had more female than male friends. It was an unconvincing list.

Kai's arguments for medical intervention were much stronger. He had already spent his entire life in the wrong gender and knew it was not a match for how he felt inside. He had missed out on many developmental and life experiences in the wrong gender and didn't want to miss any more. His twenties were crucial for making educational, professional, and relationship decisions that would forever impact his adult life and he wanted his future to be better than his past. I see now that my reasons for hesitating despite his compelling and cogent arguments were based on my own life experiences, not Kai's. What was finally the most undeniable evidence that Kai was the best one to decide his future and not me, was how happy and confident he became moving about in the world shortly after beginning testosterone.

Making decisions for our minor children is a weighty responsibility. If you find yourself disagreeing with your teen over what's best for them, explore what's informing your reasons. Write your reasons down so you can see them in black and white. Which ones are based on your life and which are based on your child's? While it may be reasonable to want more time so you can feel confident that you and your teen are making the best decision for their future, you cannot take forever. Make a plan with your teen listing all of the activities or decisions required as she or he moves toward medical interventions. Create a realistic timeline for when each will occur and discuss who needs to be involved. This will give you a sense of how much time you have to prepare and it will give your teen hope for their future.

Supporting the Whole Child

LGBTQ children run the risk of falling behind their peers in developmental milestones partly because so much internal energy is taken up with coming to terms with their feelings, worrying there is something wrong with them, working for acceptance from family and friends, and dealing with social stigma. What other issues or concerns are there in your child's development that, if addressed, will help them achieve more self-confidence and independence? For example, getting his driver's license was a huge boost to Kai's self-esteem that rippled over into every other facet of his life. What are realistic milestones that might do the same for your child and how can you help them accomplish some of them?

Until your child or teen achieves some sense of gender congruity, gender may be all they can think about. It's up to parents to hold the longer view for our children since we have the perspective of time. Our children may be desperate for us to see them for who they really are today. We may be desperate for our children to think about who they will become tomorrow. Neither needs to be exclusive of the other. The sooner your child feels comfortable in the present, the more attention they can turn to the future. Helping them prepare for their future by not only addressing their gender concerns but keeping them on track academically, socially, emotionally, spiritually, and vocationally, you give them something to work toward and dream of during times of despair.

Telling

Building a supportive community for your child and your family is critical in helping everyone move forward. Deciding how, who, when, and what to tell is something you may want to discuss with your gender specialist. Carefully thinking through how you will disclose to others can impact their ability to hear and reach acceptance. You may decide to start with those you know will be most supportive regardless of whether or not they are immediate family. Anticipating questions or concerns and considering how you will respond will help you feel more prepared. Being on the frontlines of change in any family can be difficult. You may be able to predict and prevent some skirmishes but others may be unexpected and from startling sources. No parent, however strong and committed to the well-being of their child, can take this journey alone so if your family is not supportive, you will do well to find others outside your family who are.

It's best not to disclose during a crisis when you are emotionally distressed, though sometimes the truth erupts out of the urgency of the moment. For example, when my father asked a routine question, "How is Kendra?" the truth escaped unbidden and the outcome, though unplanned, was not adversely affected. For most, there is a natural period of concealment while you go through your own steps of transition before disclosing to others.[115] In my case, there were months when I couldn't speak about it without crying so I waited until I could maintain my composure.

Grandparents can be especially valuable allies for you and your family. With all that you are balancing, knowing there are grandparents in your corner to turn to for advice, a listening ear, a shoulder to cry on, or childcare for an evening out can lighten your load and brighten your spirits. There is probably no one else who loves your children as much as you and their grandparents. Grabbing hold of all the love possible for your entire family will help sustain and nurture you.

A celebration or blessing that involves family and friends marking your child or teen's transition and emergence in a new gender can be very affirming. A coming out or naming ceremony that brings together cherished items from your child's past with those from their present and/or future symbolizes and honors their wholeness before a circle of supportive witnesses.

Balancing what others might need to know, with your child's need for privacy, is a matter for thoughtful consideration. If your child is socially transitioning in school and you don't want parents and teachers to find out by surprise, you may decide to discreetly tell several key administrators, teachers, guidance counselors, or parents rather than all the teachers or every family in the entire grade.

Your Other Children

Proactively plan who and when to disclose to in order to guard the safety and privacy of your family. Work with the gender specialist on your team to prepare your other children for how to respond to questions about their transgender sibling during and after gender transitioning. Help all the children in your family know what to say if peers or adults ask them questions about their sibling. Role-play age-appropriate responses with each child to help them handle invasive questions and build protective boundaries. Asking children to keep secrets is usually inadvisable. Secrets are confusing for children since they have difficulty knowing the difference between appropriate and inappropriate secrets. The best way to protect children from sexual predators is to teach them never to keep secrets since secrecy is how predators conceal their abuse. Teaching your child to tell you if they are ever asked to keep a secret will help protect them.

As a family of introverts we did not participate in camps and conferences for families with transgender children but these events and gatherings can be important places of support, acceptance, and community for the entire family. If your other children attend events like these to support their gender nonconforming sibling, create equal time for your transgender child to attend events of interest to their cisgender siblings. As much as possible try to balance the time and attention the family spends on activities of interest to each child. Encourage rather than require participation of your children in one another's activities and celebrate those moments when mutual support occurs.

Continue attending to the emotional needs of your other children as they transition from relating to their sibling as one gender to another gender. Like you, they may need time to mourn the loss of the brother or sister they thought they had while experiencing conflicting feelings such as sadness, confusion, fear, and protectiveness. They may feel angry and resentful about how this is changing their family and their sibling relationship, while having little or no control themselves. Continuing the same family outings, activities, and celebrations will help stabilize everyone while adjusting to the affirmed gender of your child.

Gender conforming brothers and sisters hold a great deal of power over their transgender sibling because in a word, they can out them at any time, especially if your transgender child's gender history is hidden. The sibling of a transgender child can be their best friend and ally, or biggest threat and persecutor. Since siblings are likely to be in one another's lives longer than anyone else, it behooves you to help them build the healthiest, most supportive, and mutually compassionate relationship possible. This requires that everyone's needs must be openly and respectfully explored and discussed. Creating a standard of fairness, consistency, and mutual respect is critical in setting the right tone and negotiating feelings of rivalry.[116] Staying actively involved with each child, attending to unique needs, and doing things as a family that honor your differences, demonstrates that your love is equally shared and that there is enough for everyone.

7

Amazement and Advocacy

Your children are not your children.
They are the sons and daughters of Life's longing for itself.
They come through you but not from you.
And though they are with you yet they belong not to you.[117]

KAHLIL GIBRAN, *THE PROPHET*

RECOLLECTIONS

Trans-Welcoming Environments

Kai graduated with a bachelor of science in biology from Tufts University on his twenty-third birthday. We had worried this day might never come. For too many transgender teens it doesn't. We had all worked hard for this important occasion and no one worked harder than Kai. With so much pain and struggle behind us, the joy tasted that much sweeter and we celebrated Kai's many successes. Despite having one more course before actually receiving his diploma he was able to walk with his class. And to top it off, he received highest thesis honors for his senior research project, attended a national conference with his advisor, and was one of the authors on a paper accepted for publication. His science and lab skills were finally being recognized. He was beaming that day.

We were proud and impressed with all he'd accomplished given everything he was juggling. Our friends Lisa and John invited us to their house for a birthday and graduation celebration that afternoon, and the following Sunday we had a graduation party at our house. Char flew in from Florida and my sister Donna came from Maryland. About forty friends—many of whom had been key supporters of us on our journey including Carol, Joanna, and Mike—joined us for the celebration.

Kai's initial faith in Tufts' commitment to creating a trans-welcoming environment was broken his senior year when Keith Ablow, a high profile psychiatrist affiliated with Tufts Medical School and member of the Fox News Medical A-Team published an editorial on the Fox website warning parents not to let their kids watch Chaz Bono on *Dancing with the Stars*. In part, Ablow stated:

> It would be wrong to think that gender dysphoria cannot be kindled by celebrating those who have undergone sexual reassignment surgery. . . . By broadcasting, applauding and mainstreaming the journey of a very disordered person who endured, and likely will continue to endure, real suffering based on extraordinarily deep psychological problems, we suggest that that journey is a smart—even heroic—one to take.[118]

Chaz Bono had recently received wide media attention as the TV daughter of Sonny and Cher who was transitioning to become male. Ablow was suggesting that children might question their own gender identity by watching the show and that:

> It's a toxic and unnecessary byproduct of the tragic celebration of transgender surgery that millions of young people who do watch *Dancing with the Stars* will have to ponder this question: Maybe my problems really stem from the fact that I'm a girl inside a boy's body (or a boy inside

a girl's body). . . . Maybe all the angst and suffering I'm
feeling as I emerge into puberty and pass through it isn't
just because I'm changing, but because I should change
completely—and have my breasts removed or my penis
amputated! [119]

Tufts LGBTQ students, allies, and parents, along with the executive director of the Massachusetts Transgender Political Coalition,
demanded that the school publicly denounce these comments. The
university posted a statement on the university president's webpage
distancing itself from Ablow but never countered the misinformation
or supported its transgender students. To Kai and other LGBTQ
students this felt like a very public slap in the face by a place that had
initially welcomed them. Had this incident occurred while Kai was
considering colleges, he would never have applied to Tufts.

Information about nonconforming gender identities and
exposure to transgender people does not cause others to become
transgender. No one "catches" a transgender identity, just as transgender children don't "catch" a conforming gender identity, despite
considerable pressure to do so. Left-handedness was once suppressed
as deviant and abnormal and everyone with a natural inclination to
write left-handed was forced to write with their right. Right-handed
people didn't suddenly switch hands when left-handed people were
finally allowed to do what came naturally.

For those already questioning their gender identity, exposure to
others who are gender nonconforming or transgender can replace
myths with facts on an issue they have been wondering about in
secret. For others, it can foster awareness, understanding, and acceptance. There was a time when I worried that being transgender was a
fad since it seemed to have taken recent generations by storm—like
piercing and tattoos. Body morphing is a huge industry today, much
more so than when I was growing up. Liposuction, tummy tucks,
nose jobs, breast implants, and hair plugs are all commonplace. I
too, had the impulse to fence my child in and keep the world out

because peers can influence what is considered acceptable and what is outlandish. I now understand this reaction as transphobic, my own version of what my mother worried about in her generation: that information about sex would encourage sexual activity.

As parents of gender nonconforming and transgender children we know how affirming and reassuring it is for our children to see and meet others like themselves. Gathering information, discussing feelings, asking questions, and working through fears about the future, can end isolation, create hope, and literally save lives. It is beneficial and even life changing, for children and parents to see transgender people pursuing their dreams and going about their lives like everybody else. As the research indicates, gender identity is rooted in a person's core since before birth, often manifesting at a very young age, strengthening or emerging during puberty, and enduring over time.

The impulse to isolate transgender people and to keep children sheltered and apart so as not to "give them any ideas," is not a defensible position. Shunning transgender people perpetuates the shame and secrecy that threatens not only their safety and self-esteem but their very lives. Like other segregationist ideologies based on race, religion, sexual orientation, ethnicity, or any of the myriad ways in which humans differ from and judge one another, forcing transgender people into hiding harms us all. Segregation can only be maintained by intolerance, and history has repeatedly shown the human toll that bigotry and dehumanization exacts on everyone—victims, bystanders, and perpetrators alike.

Granted, seeing other transgender people pursuing fulfilling lives may give a person who is suffering with gender dysphoria in silence and isolation the courage to be true to oneself and to take some action, but the questions and longing had to have already been there just under the surface. To see Chaz Bono and other trans people on TV and elsewhere in the world sends a much needed message of hope to trans youth that life can go on pretty normally; that recognizing the truth of one's dilemma and pain is not the end of the world but just the beginning. For others it will hopefully contribute to greater awareness, understanding, and compassion.

It takes more than adding a check box for a school, workplace, or other institution to open doors and create an atmosphere of acceptance for transgender people. It will take all of us to confront and dismantle the many uninformed but widely held notions about the transgender experience. This incident with Ablow highlighted the unfortunate reality that even places with proud histories of inclusivity, can fall short when it comes to accepting those outside generally accepted norms. In many ways gender is the last frontier of our human capacity to embrace diversity.

Life on Kai's Terms

After graduation, Kai gave up his apartment and came home to live for several months while he looked for jobs in his field. In December he was offered a position at a research laboratory in Maine. He knew Maine well since we frequently vacationed there, a tradition he continued once he had his own vehicle. It was a welcome break from the congestion of the city and nature always cleared his head. I accompanied him the weekend before Christmas to find an apartment so he could begin the job in early January. It was the winter solstice, the longest night of the year, and the rain came down in sheets across the windshield. My little car was buffeted from side to side on twisting wet roads up the Maine coastline. It was so tiring I asked Kai to take over driving. He did so with ease. Here we were again on another December night on our long journey together. Four years earlier he had taken an overdose. Two years earlier we were driving to Manhattan for top surgery. Now we were driving to Maine so he could launch his own future, a career in science. Just like the road outside, the road we had taken to get here had been winding, filled with obstacles, blown around by a swirl of emotions, and clouded by poor visibility.

We stopped at a store to buy a newspaper just out of curiosity since there were so few apartments listed online. Kai thought he'd stepped back in time when he realized he needed to actually call ads listed in the newspaper's classifieds rather than click through apartment photos online. Cold calls were not Kai's forte and finding my way around a new area was not mine. So in the morning, I got on the phone while he navigated the wet, branch-strewn roads. The first day was discouraging as Kai shot down each apartment we viewed. He had something specific in mind yet I feared he'd ever find it.

We spent the second night at John and Lisa's house in Belfast. To avoid cranking up the furnace to heat so large a house, we opted to start the wood stove and slept on couches in the living room. It felt like camping in the old days as firelight flickered on the ceiling and we laughed over the day's events. We listed the pros and cons of each apartment, assessed each landlord, hoped to hear back from several the next day, and worried if he'd have a place to live in time to start work in a week. Many were busy or away for the holidays and didn't return calls. Kai considered passing up the job if the right place didn't emerge. I kept my hopes up and fingers crossed. The next morning we got three calls in a row with three more apartments to see. Each was as good as the next so now the decision was Kai's.

He went with the landlord he liked best (a woman) and a two-bedroom ranch with a yard. I took one trip with him to help unpack the few items he had and organize his kitchen—cleaning cabinets, unpacking dishes, buying household supplies and food. On January 3, he packed up one last load in his truck and officially moved out to begin his new life in Maine. After kissing and hugging goodbye, I went downstairs to the room where he'd lived for the past seven months. I was proud, relieved, tired, thankful, and nostalgic. I'd learned how to sit and hold this stew of emotions.

Kai had three separate bedrooms in our house. First, the big front bedroom upstairs when we moved in. He'd kept all his geckos in his bedroom then. And as usual, it was always in a state of disarray. Since some of the geckos ate live crickets, it was not uncommon to find a cricket escapee in the bathroom. Once, when my sister Debbie stayed in his room, he assured her the crickets couldn't escape. On her flight back to Bolivia, when she noticed her bag had been inspected and was half open coming down the carousel, a cricket sat staring at her as she went to zip it closed. True to Kai's wishes she let the cricket go. When he left for college, we brought his geckos downstairs so I could feed them and he moved into a smaller bedroom. That first Christmas home from college the new bedroom was a harder adjustment than he'd let on. He referred to it as his Harry Potter room—as in under the stairway. When he came home after graduating he moved into the basement studio. It was a spacious room with its own outside entrance, and the wood stove where he and I sat during the blizzard after his surgery when the power went out. It was large enough for his geckos and he could keep his own hours without waking us coming up and down stairs.

While I sat in this room sorting through the few remaining items—textbooks, tools, reptile supplies—I realized with a pang I'd never taken a picture of it the whole time he lived here. Most of the time I caught a glimpse on the way past to the washer. It was usually in chaos: clothes piled on the floor, a collection of half-empty glasses and coffee mugs, a jumble of aquariums, beer bottles, plants, and projects in various stages of completion. But every once in awhile he cleaned it up nicely. The day of his graduation party, it looked very inviting. He and several friends sat talking, drinking, and relaxing. Those times were now gone for good and I never captured them. How had I overlooked it? As much as I loved this room when it was clean, I already missed Kai's telltale chaos. It was a bittersweet feeling the afternoon that he left. He was ready to go. So many times when he complained about living at home—in the basement no less—and Tony's insistence on tidiness when that is constitutionally impossible for Kai, I simply responded: "Yes, Kai. The sooner you move out to a place of your own, the better. It's time. You deserve that. You've worked hard for it." I meant every word of that. It was time. And now it was here. I was happy for him and for us. But I missed him already.

I want to make medical progress in sex reassignment surgery.
My hope is that sometime in the near future the process will not be
looked at as plastic surgery, but as something that is necessary for
the physical and psychological health of an individual.

I also hope that each generation brings new characteristics,
which we can learn to accept, realizing individuals don't always
carry the assumptions of strangers.

KAI, AGE 18

Kai hopes to someday become a surgeon so he can help other teens
the way he was helped. Transitioning during college, he has his
whole life ahead of him unlike those on whose shoulders he stands
who waited well into adulthood to transition. Children coming
after Kai are transitioning even earlier, and why not? Every year
growing up in the wrong body means developmental lessons and
life experiences lost. Kai never made the male friends in childhood
he might have. He never played sports, engaged in the rough and
tumble play of boys, or got lessons from his feminist mom about
how to be a sensitive, conscious man—though living twenty years as
a girl was as good a start as any. Kai is now free to live his own life.
He has taught me much and our connection is strong. I love this son
as much as I ever loved my daughter. I admire his courage, tenacity,
intelligence, perception, and skill. I trust his wisdom. I know he has
what it takes to make his dreams come true. After all, look at what
he has managed to make happen so far!

Gratitude

Home, childhood, belonging, memories, coming of age: every aspect
of a person's life is influenced by the body they are born with and
how that carries them during their journey in this life. Mind and

body along with the spirit that ignites and unites them are what we are given. Like a book's cover our packaging defines us. People make assumptions based on gender, skin color, hair color, height, weight, beauty, build, ability, nationality, age, and so on. And the assumptions of others have an impact on us—particularly when we are young and just learning about our place in the world. And without a welcome, a place in society, we are adrift.

Most of us don't worry about being singled out and humiliated in a public restroom. We can share childhood memories without having to disguise the gender we were living as and hide or destroy childhood pictures to protect our safety. Few of us have to avoid beaches and swimming in the sweltering heat because our bathing suit would be considered socially inappropriate. We don't worry which of two gender boxes to check and if we'll be accused of deception either way. Few of us worry about ridicule when disrobed for a healthcare visit. Most of us don't wonder how someone we're dating feels about transgender people and when to share our gender history.[120] No wonder transgender children and teens are susceptible to anxiety and depression. Every social interaction is fraught with landmines.

Love is a catalyst for change. Parents go to great lengths out of love for their children. And children, too, protect that love, even when it means hiding for a time or coming back again and again looking for love's full acceptance when its expression is imperfect and limited by the fear and shortsightedness of "parents. Most parents do all we can to help when our child is hurting. Many childhood conditions are intractable leaving parents few options but to bear witness to their child's suffering. Parents of transgender children are fortunate in that we can actually do something to help our children. This is powerfully good news so who wouldn't choose to act?

And what really is gender anyway other than a complicated and nuanced set of rules for sorting, valuing, and separating people? Few cultures or successive generations agree on what constitutes masculine and feminine. And yet gender remains one of the most defining and confining aspects of a person. Much of what people assume about someone is framed by their gender and since gender is seen as synonymous with anatomical sex we make assumptions before a child is even born. When we ask an expectant woman, "Is it a boy or a girl?" what we're really asking is, "What will this child be like?" as if by finding out the sex, the qualities and images that come to mind will be predictive. But what is a boy? What is a girl? When does a person know they are a boy or a girl? How and when did you know your own gender? If your anatomy changed overnight would it change how you feel about your gender?[121]

Gender roles are broadening to be sure, thanks to a century of struggle mostly by women but there are still many diehard biases. Given what we now know, a healthcare provider's response to an expectant couple's question about the gender of their child should be "Your baby's anatomical sex is female (or male) and you'll learn their gender from them over time." We owe it to prospective parents to inform them that their child may not be the gender they think based on their anatomical sex. It is the only just and responsible approach so that parents will not be unaware, uninformed, and unprepared. Letting parents know this possibility during prenatal visits, childbirth classes, in pregnancy books, and well-baby visits will help both parents and children as their gender identity emerges.

Transgender people are the world travelers of gender. They have been to the frontiers of gender and offer a wealth of knowledge as a result. They are the only ones who know firsthand the differences between how one feels and is treated as first man and then woman, or woman and then man. They have had to unlearn and then learn whole new ways of moving, speaking, dressing, taking or giving up space, expressing or hiding feelings. They have experienced both sides of the gender binary world we have created over millennia, and they can make informed comparisons. Others who try only fabricate and presume. Transgender people have seen and walked both coastlines after traveling across the great divide. The mere fact that this can be done, and has been done by so many, is evidence that the divide is not as great as we have been led to believe. Trans people are bilingual in gender, bigender, able to bridge one of humanity's greatest rifts at a time when we need expanded awareness, understanding, and compassion. They have walked in another's shoes and have rare and valuable knowledge as a result. We would do well to listen and learn.

We hear a lot about raising resilient children. Gender nonconforming and transgender children and teens are some of the most resilient youth out there. Their ability to withstand the pressure to conform and to still fight for their own authentic self-expression is nothing short of amazing. Trans children and teens have courage, tenacity, strength, sensitivity, and honesty—in addition to their other gifts, abilities, and academic interests. Their transgender identity is not all of who they are, but it can become most of what they think about, without our assistance and advocacy. It is our job as parents to help them over this huge and unfair hurdle so they can get on with their creative and gifted lives.

As a parent of a gender nonconforming or transgender child or teen you deserve our deepest respect and support. In many communities, you find yourselves at the frontlines of a heated debate you never sought or expected. Your only goal is to love and raise your child to be as healthy and happy as possible. Supporting your child's inner truth today, knowing it could change tomorrow, is a daunting task. With your love, help, and hope your child can reach their highest and best.

Almost a year to the day after Kai's surgery and a year before he moved on to his adult life, I dreamed he and I had climbed up onto a hill overlooking a rushing stream. We could see others just below. Suddenly the height scared me. It was narrow with steep drop-offs on all sides. I asked Kai if he could see where we had come from since it was almost impossible to get down from where we were standing. I couldn't imagine how we'd gotten up there. Every direction looked as frightening and as impossible as the next. I was happy that he was with me and I relied on his resourcefulness. Once, when the bumper of my car got loose a couple of days after a minor fender bender and began to drag along the highway, Kai told me to pull over. He jumped out, removed the shoelace of his sneaker, and tied the bumper up so we could continue home from school. In my dream, I knew he'd think of something—and would calm me down in the meantime. Then suddenly, we were down from that hill. When I looked up at what I'd been afraid of it was nothing really; not high at all. Fear can be a trick—more perception than reality. Much suffering is mental.

I've learned much on this journey with my son. I too have transitioned. I am more conscious than before, more aware of my privilege and committed to social change for LGBTQ people. Journaling throughout the process helped me make sense of my feelings and resistance. Writing and researching for this book has added knowledge and perspective. I am happy to have known Kendra. She was a blessing to me from the universe at a time when I needed her most. I am just as happy to know Kai. I don't really distinguish the two of them anymore. They are simply two of the many sides of the multifaceted person that is my unique and gifted son.

RESEARCH

Transforming Schools

Among students who expressed a transgender or gender noncon-forming identity during grades K-12, the *National Transgender Discrimination Survey* (*NTDS*) found alarming rates of harassment (78 percent of respondents), physical assault (35 percent), and sexual violence (12 percent), creating so harsh an environment that almost one-sixth (15 percent) left a school in grades K-12 or college.[122] Adding to these devastating figures is the fact that 31 percent of respondents reported harassment by teachers or school personnel and students of color experienced even higher rates of harassment and violence across the board.[123] In addition to harassment, 15 percent had to interrupt school due to financial reasons related to gender transition.[124] Yet despite these considerable barriers, 47 percent of respondents received a college or graduate degree, compared to 27 percent of the general population, by returning to school later in life.[125] Mistreatment in school had a lasting negative impact on the lives of respondents. More than half (51 percent) of those reporting harassment attempted suicide. A staggering three-quarters (76 percent) of those who were assaulted by teachers or staff reported having attempted suicide, compared to attempted suicide prevalence for the general population of 1.6 percent.[126] Those mistreated in school were half as likely as the general population to earn incomes of $50,000 a year, had higher rates of drug and alcohol abuse, and smoking. Nearly half (48 percent) of those who had to leave school as a result of abuse and harassment, experienced homelessness, and were eight times more likely to be HIV positive than the general population.[127]

School is where children spend the bulk of their time when they're not at home so the environment of your child's school is of paramount importance. Unfortunately research points to a high degree of bullying against LGBTQ students at all age levels, mostly due to gender nonconformity rather than sexual orientation. According to a 2003 survey by the National Mental Health Association, 75 percent of adolescents witnessed bullying against classmates who were LGBT or were considered to be LGBT.[128] Daily ostracism, ridicule, and harassment have an impact on school engagement and achievement.[129] With the prevalence of social media, bullying can continue well after the school day and beyond school grounds, virtually permeating and poisoning a teen's entire life. A study by the National Gay and Lesbian Task Force found that LGBTQ youth of color often confront a "tricultural" experience: homophobia from their respective racial or ethnic group; racism from LGBTQ people from other racial or ethnic communities; and a combination of the two from society as a whole.[130]

The effects of bullying can range from withdrawal, depression, aggression, lowered self-concept, poor academic achievement, and dropping out of school, to suicide and homicide. For these reasons, parents sometimes have no recourse but to move to other school districts to ensure the safety and well-being of their transgender or gender nonconforming child. Recognizing the devastating impact of bullying, some state legislatures have passed laws to protect the safety of schoolchildren. Because of the explicit targeting of gender nonconforming students, some of these laws explicitly protect the rights of LGBTQ youth. Even without specific state laws, a legal basis for the rights of gender nonconforming children to receive fair and equal protections while in school are based on a combination of First and Fourteenth Amendment principles in federal law that protect "a right to express an identity and a right to be treated equally as a result of expressing this identity."[131] Based on court decisions, state, and federal statutes, the right to be "out" includes "disclosure of one's race, ethnicity, religion, sexual orientation, gender identity, political views, medical conditions, past experiences, present involvement, and future plans."[132]

At the time of publication eighteen states and the District of Columbia have safe schools laws that protect transgender as well as gay and lesbian students. These states are: Arkansas, California, Colorado, Connecticut, Illinois, Iowa, Maine, Maryland, Massachusetts, Minnesota, New Hampshire, New Jersey, New York, North Carolina, Oregon, Rhode Island, Vermont, and Washington. Twenty-five states have no laws protecting LGBTQ students; five states have regulations protecting gay, lesbian, and transgender students and two states have regulations protecting gay and lesbian students only.[133] For specific information about policies and practices in your child's public school, visit the website for your state's Department of Education or call your local school superintendent. Private schools are not always governed by public school policies but the same social and parental pressures that brought about public policies to protect students from bullying can be used to advocate for safety in private schools.

Areas of greatest concern for protecting the safety and rights of LGBTQ children include: policies and procedures for changing your child's name and pronoun in the classroom and on school records; privacy matters with regard to disclosure of assigned gender; school transfers for a conducive learning environment; bathroom and locker room use; participation in gender-segregated athletics; lodging on overnight field trips; LGBTQ-welcoming clubs such as a Gay-Straight Alliance; policies related to dating events such as prom; and school safety policies to prevent bullying. LGBT-inclusive practices in these matters are outlined in *Best Practices for Serving Transgender and Gender Non-Conforming Students in Schools*, by the Massachusetts Transgender Political Coalition summarized below:[134]

Names and pronouns: Preferred names and pronouns should be used by school personnel and reflected in official school records without requirement of a court order or medical diagnosis. Student information systems should make a reasonable effort to include a preferred name instead of or in addition to the student's legal name.

Official records: Upon receipt of a legal name change, the student's school should be required to make the necessary corrections to the student's official record for both current and former students. High schools should also provide an updated copy of a former student's high school diploma with the student's new name.

Confidentiality: Unless the student has given informed written consent, school personnel should not discuss or disclose a student's transgender status with anyone other than parents or legal guardians unless that information is necessary to accommodate the student or ensure their safety.

Transfers: Transgender or gender nonconforming students desiring to transfer to a school with a more conducive learning environment should be accommodated.

Bathroom and locker room use: Transgender students should have access to bathrooms and locker rooms that correspond to their affirmed gender. Available accommodation that best meets the needs and privacy concerns of all students should be used including a private, curtained area within the locker room, a separate changing schedule or use of a nearby private area.

Participation in athletics: Transgender and gender nonconforming students should be allowed to play on sports teams based on their affirmed gender and be permitted to wear clothing and uniforms that correspond with their gender identity and expression. They should have access to equal instruction, training, and coaching as well as facilities, equipment, and practice opportunities and be called by their preferred name and pronoun. They should be able to participate in a safe environment without exposure to harassment or derogatory, homophobic, or transphobic comments or behaviors by team members, parents, or coaches.

Lodging on overnight field trips or athletic events: Efforts should be made to include and not isolate transgender or gender nonconforming students on overnights and room assignments should take into account the student's comfort level, privacy, and consent.

LGBTQ-welcoming clubs: School-based Gay-Straight Alliances (GSA's are also called Gender and Sexuality Alliances today) should be encouraged since clubs and their faculty/staff advisors send the message that LGBTQ students are important members of the community and have the right to a safe place to discuss issues, interests, and concerns.

Dating events and formals: LGBTQ-welcoming proms, dances, and events help counteract the prevailing heteronormative culture and send the message that all students are valued and welcome. They also allow LGBTQ students the same opportunities to develop social skills as non-LGBTQ peers.

School safety policies: Schools with specific safety policies to prevent bullying and other forms of abuse often require routine professional education on LGBTQ issues as well as appointing a safety leader to foster initiatives that support a positive, collaborative, and inclusive school climate.

Identification Documents

Identification documents that are congruent with one's appearance and consistent with one another are required for social and economic functioning in today's world. Access to a job, a place to live, education, health care, travel, some office buildings, the right to vote, even a bar, often require photo identification. Obtaining identity documents that match one's affirmed gender can be costly, confusing, time consuming, and sometimes impossible. Yet living with incongruent documents not only forces some to live on the margins of society, it can endanger one's safety. Documents are governed by state or federal agencies, with state requirements varying widely. Some require proof of surgical procedures a person may not choose or cannot afford, thereby creating an insurmountable barrier for obtaining accurate and congruent identification documents. There are nine common documents to alter when one changes their gender: driver's license; social security record; passport; birth certificate; work ID; student records; military discharge papers; health insurance records; professional license or credentials.

Changing one's name is usually done at the family court level in most states, and court documents are required for name changes on other legal documents. Changing one's gender marker on a driver's license is done at the state motor vehicle department, and while many states no longer require proof of surgery, the *National Transgender Discrimination Survey* (*NTDS*) found that those who had not had surgery had a more difficult time obtaining a license with their affirmed gender.[135] Of those who were denied a gender change on a driver's license, 67 percent reported being disrespected and harassed in the process.[136]

Changing one's birth certificate is also done at the state level, with twenty-eight states and the District of Columbia issuing new birth certificates, preferable for privacy and safety consideration reasons, while other states amend an original birth certificate thereby outing the person as transgender. Many states still require proof of surgery, and some even require a court order, adding to the inconvenience and cost.[137]

Social security records (cards do not have gender markers) are revised at the federal level, and require proof of legal name change and medical documentation of gender surgery. Passports are also handled at the federal level by the U.S. Department of State, and in 2010 the department eliminated the surgery requirement.[138]

Updating health insurance records is fraught with the complication that doing so may prevent one from obtaining medical care for reproductive systems that don't match one's gender. For example, a male is likely to be denied coverage for a hysterectomy because it is seen as gender transition, which most insurers don't cover. Updating school records of a legal name change and gender transition is critical to ensure that references and transcripts sought after graduation reflect one's affirmed gender, rather than assigned gender, thereby protecting one's privacy and hopefully preventing employment discrimination.

The *NTDS* found that most people who have transitioned their gender live with some degree of incongruity with their identity documents. About half (46 percent) reported success in changing some of their documentation and only 21 percent reporting success in changing all of them. One third (33 percent) of respondents reported living with none of their documents matching their current gender identity[139] and 41 percent live with a driver's license or state identification that does not match their gender.[140]

With more states requiring identity documents for voting, transgender people are becoming increasingly disenfranchised. Asked about their experiences when presenting identity documents that do not match their gender expression or name, 40 percent reported harassment; 15 percent reported being asked to leave an establishment; and 3 percent reported being physically assaulted. People of color and gender nonconforming people reported higher rates of harassment and assault.[141] People living with incongruent identification documents live with the stress of knowing that everyday experiences can become opportunities for them to be outed and subjected to "disrespect, harassment, discrimination or violence."[142] Some have had employment offers withdrawn when government issued ID forms don't match one's gender expression.[143] Using two documents together, such as a license and passport when one has been changed and the other has not, can also create difficulties.

Health Care

To protect their long-term health and because of the possible negative effects of a gonadectomy (removal of ovaries or testes) early in life, and long-term, high-dose cross-gender hormone therapy, people who have medically transitioned need health care providers knowledgeable, in primary care and transgender health. Regular communication among a team of providers may be necessary if one practitioner is unable to provide the full range of care. Endocrinologists and surgeons are important members of a team during medical transition but primary care providers are critical for health care over the lifespan.

Health education to prevent sexually transmitted infections and promote safe sex is important, as are preventive screening procedures. Organ systems that are not impacted by cross-hormone therapy can follow the same screening guidelines as the general public. Since feminizing and masculizing hormones may adversely affect particular organ systems, special screening guidelines for transgender patients are recommended to protect against cardiovascular risk, osteoporosis, and certain cancers (breast, cervical, ovarian, uterine, and prostate).

There are also special considerations in the urogenital health of transgender patients. Gynecologic care is necessary for female to male patients who have not had genital surgery, and male to female patients may have anatomic differences that affect intercourse and urination.[144] Knowledgeable and supportive health care providers for transgender people are critical since these procedures and discussions may be emotionally charged. With increasing numbers of people medically transitioning, the demand for experienced and compassionate health care providers is also on the rise, as is the need for specialized medical knowledge to protect and promote the health and longevity of transgender people.

Family Equilibrium

Balance does eventually return to families with transgender children, as surprising as this may seem when family members are in the turmoil phase of their mutual transitions. There comes a time when the gender of your child is no longer uppermost in your mind but just one aspect of who they are as a person.[145] Through the process, the full circle of family and friends can become more informed, aware, knowledgeable, and accepting of the gender difference that was hidden until someone they love came forward. Then there is the realization that there is nothing wrong with the child, but instead with a social structure designed to deny that child's truth. The community of acceptance around the child is strengthened, often nurtured and inspired by the child's own wisdom and bravery. Family and friends become crucial allies in moving society toward acceptance and appreciation of gender nonconformity and diversity. Over time fear vanishes, and hope for a happy and fulfilling future for your child and others like him or her flourishes. There is gratitude for what has been learned along the way and amazement for the multitudinous ways in which humans express their essence and contribute to the growth and expansion of one another when fear is vanquished and the heart is opened.

REFLECTIONS

Safety Concerns

Learn what policies your child's school has in place for name and pronoun changes, how these are reflected in school records, and whether the policy protects your child's privacy—bathroom and locker room use; participation in gender segregated athletics; lodging on overnight field trips; LGBTQ affirmation clubs such as a Gay-Straight or Gender and Sexuality Alliance; dating events such as prom; and the enforcement of school safety measures. Advocate as needed to ensure your child's safety and full participation in activities. Speak to teachers and administrators if any of your children experience bullying or harassment due to gender nonconformity since it's not only the gender nonconforming child who may be targeted but their siblings as well. Learn what school district and statewide policies are in place to protect your children from bullying based on gender identity, and appeal to appropriate officials and institutions if the school does not adequately address these issues. Talk to your children about how to handle bullying and pay attention to whether they are being harassed online. If they refuse to attend school or have decided to drop out, pursue the reasons why and address the causes. Visit websites to learn what legal resources are available if needed.

Role-play proactive responses if your child is publicly outed so they don't resort to hiding or lying but can be honest, confident, and instructive. A simple statement like, "Yes—I was a boy but now I'm a girl. My name is _____. That can happen you know," can deflect the intent to harm.[146] At the outset, discuss with your child the safety reasons why it might be necessary at times to conceal their true gender feelings because of how others still think. If they can exert conscious control over protective strategies for when and how they express their gender nonconformity in the world, with supportive and accepting people in their inner circle, it can become an important step in guarding their safety long-term.[147]

Your Own Transformation

Parenting is a transforming experience. Our children change us. We learn about ourselves with each stage of our child's life—our own strengths and weaknesses. Love for our children can awaken feelings we never knew we had, require sacrifices we didn't consider possible, and open us to new experiences. But we also hold great power over our children. The seeds we plant in their young, tender souls take root and flower for the rest of their lives. When your child is gender nonconforming or transgender, your ability to join and support them on the path less traveled will forever influence them for the better.

If you have embarked on this journey alongside your child you have probably made some changes yourself. Perhaps you know more now about gender identity development and have let go of feeling responsible for the cause, and therefore the fix, of your child's nonconformity. If you look back at where you started you may see some of the following: a fuller, more accurate understanding for who your child is; more knowledge and information about gender and the transgender experience; movement through some of your own fears and negative feelings; greater ability to respond to your child with acceptance; efforts to improve communication with your partner to better support your gender nonconforming or transgender child; helping your other children and family members work through their feelings; protecting the safety of your children; increased knowledge of social and medical transitioning options to address gender dysphoria.

It can be difficult if not impossible to be totally accepting of your gender nonconforming or transgender child from the start, given the culture we live in and the norms we were raised with. You may need to grieve your lack of understanding and support early on as well as your uninformed, even detrimental parenting responses. For example, my resistance to having a son or when I told Kai I considered gender reassignment surgery mutilation. Forgiving yourself and, depending on their age, asking for your child's forgiveness, may be in order to help you let go of the past and celebrate your loving bond with your child and your own transformation. Acknowledging the pain, anxiety, and loneliness of our children can inspire understanding, acceptance, and protectiveness. Parents who do not or cannot engage in their own change process run the risk of being forever estranged and alienated from their child.

As you reflect back on the weeks, months, or years that have transpired since your child disclosed their transgender identity, ask yourself some of the following: Is your family back on level ground? Were threads in the family tapestry dropped along the way that are in need of mending? Is forgiveness in order? What have you learned about yourself, your children, your partner, your family that you didn't know before? Celebrate your capacity to learn and grow and your willingness to open your heart to your own child and others like her or him. Bring this knowledge about yourself to the next phase of your own transition with the confidence that you will get through those challenges as well.

Becoming an Advocate

You probably already know that one of the most important tools in your toolbox has been courage. You have had to call upon courage to face your own feelings, support your child in breaking norms you were taught to conform to, learn new concepts, revisit your values, educate others, talk to school personnel, and possibly even end relationships.

More than anyone, you know what it takes to create a village for gender nonconforming and transgender children. And you also know what happens when there is no safe village out there. As children disclose their transgender identity earlier, parents' roles as decision makers require us to examine all that blocks us from being our child's best advocate. Turning our backs on them can have life and death consequences. Considering all the ways you have been called upon to support and advocate for your child, imagine for a moment how a child traverses this terrain without a caring adult by their side. How do they advocate for themselves, gather information, make appointments with providers, access transportation, obtain economic resources, and healthcare coverage? It's a daunting journey, particularly when you are alone, so many give up. We all need to work to change that.

Parents have a front row seat for witnessing the devastating impact of labels, ridicule, and shunning on our otherwise cheerful, creative, and vibrant children. We have the best vantage point for seeing the health, strength, and resilience of transgender and gender nonconforming children despite outmoded theories that try, even today, to label them deviant and disordered. How many times have you dreamed of whisking your gender nonconforming child away from the sea of judgment to live on a welcoming island of gender fluidity so you can watch how they thrive when not being tamped down by confining views of how they should feel and act? Every time you host a play date, a conference, a camp, or a welcoming classroom for gender unique children you create these havens. And as these oases of understanding and support expand and link, a great web of safety and acceptance is created that protects our gender nonconforming children from the damage of intolerance.

It is personal rejection, social ostracism, and political marginalization that hamper the mental and physical health of transgender people, not their gender identity. Social acceptance, early and accurate information, and a cultural expectation that parents and communities stand beside our children, will reduce the number who are abandoned and endangered on their journey toward authentic self-expression. Parents of transgender children are coming together to ensure that our children, like all children, have a place to belong in this world. Many parents and family members have become passionate advocates, and allies are essential if we're going to make lasting changes in social perceptions, public policy, and acceptance of gender nonconforming and transgender people. See Appendix D for social change activities you may want to join when you are ready. Together we can work to tilt the balance in favor of love, acceptance, and healthy lifelong family relationships that will launch all transgender and gender nonconforming children on the bright and creative futures they have every right to expect and experience.

Kai, Twenty-five

Endnotes

INTRODUCTION

1. See Diane Ehrensaft, *Gender Born, Gender Made: Raising Healthy, Gender-Nonconforming Children* (New York: The Experiment, 2011), 1.

CHAPTER ONE

2. Marion Zimmer Bradley, *The Mists of Avalon* (New York: Ballantine Books, 1982), 275.

3. Susan Stryker, *Transgender History* (Berkeley: Seal Press, 2008), 9.

4. Will Roscoe, *Changing Ones: Third and Fourth Genders in Native North America* (New York: St. Martin's Griffin, 2000), 14–15. See also Ehrensaft, *Gender Born, Gender Made*, 243.

5. Stryker, *Transgender History*, 11.

6. Joan Roughgarden, *Evolution's Rainbow: Diversity, Gender and Sexuality in Nature and People* (Berkeley: University of California Press, 2004), 241. See also D. R. Abramovich et al., "Sex Differentiation of the Human Midtrimester Brain," *European Journal of Obstetrics and Gynecology and Reproductive Biology* 25, no. 1 (1987): 7–14.

7. Roughgarden, *Evolution's Rainbow*, 241.

8. Ibid., 244.

9. Ibid.

10. Ibid.

11. John Colapinto, *As Nature Made Him: The Boy Who Was Raised as a Girl* (New York: Harper Perennial, 2001), 34.

12. See Phyllis Burke, *Gender Shock: Exploding the Myths of Male and Female* (New York: Doubleday, 1996).

13. Colapinto, *As Nature Made Him*, 32.

14. Ibid., 44.

15. Milton Diamond and Keith Sigmundson, "Sex Reassignment at Birth: Long-term Review and Clinical Implications," *Archives of Pediatric and Adolescent Medicine* 151, no. 3 (1997): 298–304.

16. Mildred L. Brown and Chloe Ann Rounsley, *True Selves: Understanding Transsexualism: For Families, Friends, Coworkers and Helping Professionals* (San Francisco: Jossey–Bass, 1996), 22–23.

17. Ibid., 23.

18. The Boston Women's Health Book Collective, *Our Bodies, Ourselves* (New York: Simon and Schuster, 2011), 626.

19. Andrew Solomon, *Far from the Tree: Parents, Children, and the Search for Identity* (New York: Scribner, 2012), 607.
20. The Boston Women's Health Book Collective, *Our Bodies, Ourselves*, 738.
21. Ibid., 739.
22. Solomon, *Far from the Tree*, 607–608.
23. Brown and Rounsley, *True Selves*, 23.
24. Genny Bremyn and Susan Rankin, *The Lives of Transgender People* (New York: Columbia University Press, 2011), 74.
25. Anatomical sex is used instead of biological sex throughout this book because it is more accurate.

CHAPTER TWO

26. Norman Spack, MD, quoted in Stephanie Brill and Rachel Pepper, *The Transgender Child: A Handbook for Families and Professionals* (San Francisco: Cleis Press, 2008), 3.
27. Ibid., 62.
28. Ibid., 16.
29. World Professional Association for Transgender Health (WPATH), *Standards of Care for the Health of Transsexual, Transgender, and Gender Nonconforming People (SOC)*, 7th version, 11. See http://www.wpath.org for a downloadable copy.
30. Ibid, 12.
31. Brill and Pepper, *The Transgender Child*, 62–63.
32. Ehrensaft, *Gender Born, Gender Made*, 85.
33. Brill and Pepper, *The Transgender Child*, 3.
34. Ibid.
35. Roughgarden, *Evolution's Rainbow*, 265.
36. Brill and Pepper, *The Transgender Child*, 62.
37. Ibid., 17.
38. Solomon, *Far from the Tree*, 608.
39. Brill and Pepper, *The Transgender Child*, 16.
40. Ehrensaft, *Gender Born, Gender Made*, 89.
41. See Lori Duron, *Raising My Rainbow: Adventures in Raising a Fabulous, Gender Creative Son* (New York: Broadway Books, 2013) for an engaging presentation of negotiating limits with your young gender nonconforming child. Duron also has a blog at http://www.raisingmyrainbow.com.

CHAPTER THREE

42. Ehrensaft, *Gender Born, Gender Made*, 96.
43. Brill and Pepper, *The Transgender Child*, 33.

44. Ehrensaft, *Gender Born, Gender Made*, 13–14.
45. WPATH, *SOC*, 16.
46. See American Psychiatric Association, *Diagnostic and Statistical Manual of Mental Disorders, Fifth Edition,* (Washington, D.C.: American Psychiatric Publishing, 2013) 452–53 (*DSM-5*).
47. WPATH, *SOC*, 11.
48. Ibid., 12.
49. Ibid., 13.
50. Gianna E. Israel and Donald E. Tarver II, MD., *Transgender Care: Recommended Guidelines, Practical Information and Personal Accounts (*Philadelphia: Temple University Press, 1997), 8.
51. Summarized from WPATH, SOC, 13–14. See http://www.wpath.org to download complete text.
52. Ibid., 15.
53. Gary, J. Gates, *How Many People are Lesbian, Gay, Bisexual, and Transgender?* The Williams Institute, UCLA School of Law, 2011, 6. http://williamsinstitute.law.ucla.edu.
54. WPATH, *SOC*, 7.
55. Olyslager, Femke and Lynn Conway, *On the Calculation of the Prevalence of Transsexualism.* Paper presented at the WPATH 20th International Symposium, Chicago, Illinois, September 5–8, 2007, 2.
56. WPATH, *SOC*, 7.
57. Solomon, *Far from the Tree*, 602.
58. Olyslager, Femke and Lynn Conway, *On the Calculation of the Prevalence of Transsexualism*, 23.
59. Roughgarden, *Nature's Rainbow*, 286–87.
60. Roscoe, *Changing Ones,* 127.
61. Ibid., 8. *Berdache* was the word used by Europeans to describe third and fourth gender Native Americans in early writings. Over time in Europe it came to mean male homosexual, which was not accurate for what it described in the Americas. By 1902 the term had become part of standard anthropological terminology pertaining to cross-dressing and gender nonconforming work or behavior.
62. Roscoe, *Changing Ones,* 111–12.
63. Ibid., 204. See also Roughgarden, *Nature's Rainbow*, 329–66.
64. Ehrensaft, *Gender Born, Gender Made*, 37.
65. Ibid., 210.
66. Ibid., 208.
67. Ibid., 211–12.
68. Ibid., 229.
69. Ibid., 231.

CHAPTER FOUR

70. Roscoe, *Changing Ones*, 15.
71. Brill and Pepper, *The Transgender Child*, 65.
72. Ibid., 18.
73. Ibid., 32 and 63.
74. Ibid., 65.
75. Diana Fosha, *The Transforming Power of Affect: A Model for Accelerated Change* (New York: Basic Books, 2000), 40.
76. Caitlin Ryan, *Supportive Families, Healthy Children: Helping Families with Lesbian, Gay, Bisexual and Transgender Children*, San Francisco State University, 2009, 12. See http://www.familyproject.sfsu.edu.
77. Arlene Istar Lev, *Transgender Emergence: Therapeutic Guidelines for Working with Gender-Variant People and Their Families* (New York: Hawthorn Press, 2004), Kindle edition, Box 7.1.
78. Ibid., Box 8.1.
79. Brill and Pepper, *The Transgender Child*, 45.
80. Ibid., 48.
81. Ibid., 49.
82. Brill and Pepper, *The Transgender Child*, 44–45.
83. Ehrensaft, *Gender Born, Gender Made*, 222.

CHAPTER FIVE

84. Carol Gilligan, *In a Different Voice: Psychological Theory and Women's Development* (Cambridge: Harvard University Press, 1982), 23.
85. Israel, *Transgender Care*, 21.
86. American Psychiatric Association, *DSM-5*, 457–58, and Ryan, *Supportive Families, Healthy Children*, 5–7.
87. Israel, *Transgender Care*, 21.
88. Ibid., 133.
89. Brown and Rounsley, *True Selves*, 102.
90. See Ehrensaft, *Gender Born, Gender Made*, 141–59 for an overview of treatment considerations for teens.
91. WPATH, *SOC*, 10–21. Go to http://www.wpath.org to download the 7th version of the *SOC*.
92. Ibid., 17.
93. Ibid., 19.
94. Ibid., 18.
95. Ibid., 21.
96. Sofia Pazos, "Social Work Practice with Female-to-Male Transgender and Gender Variant Youth," in *Social Work Practice with Transgender and Gender Variant Youth*, ed. Gerald P. Mallon (New York: Routledge, 2009), 98.

97. Jaime M. Grant, Lisa A. Mottet, and Justin Tanis, *Injustice at Every Turn: A Report of the National Transgender Discrimination Survey* (National Center for Transgender Equality and National Gay and Lesbian Task Force, 2013), 126.

98. WPATH, *SOC,* 18.

99. Kevin Jennings with Pat Shapiro, *Always My Child: A Parent's Guide to Understanding Your Gay, Lesbian, Bisexual, Transgendered or Questioning Son or Daughter* (New York: Simon and Schuster, 2003), 172–75. See also Brill and Pepper, *The Transgender Child*, 49–57.

100. Ehrensaft, *Gender Born, Gender Made*, 226.

CHAPTER SIX

101. *The American Heritage Dictionary*, Second College edition (Boston: Houghton Mifflin Co., 1985), 1287.

102. Solomon, *Far from the Tree*, 2.

103. Ibid.

104. Grant, Mottet, and Tanis, *Injustice at Every Turn*, 126.

105. Ibid., 3.

106. Ibid., 8.

107. Ibid., 82.

108. Ryan, *Supportive Families, Healthy Children, 10. Family Acceptance Project* brochure, downloadable at http://www.familyproject.sfsu.edu.

109. Center for American Progress, *Gay and Transgender Youth Homelessness by the Numbers*, June 21, 2010 at http://www. americanprogress.org/issues/2010/06/homelessness_numbers.html.

110. Grant, Mottet, and Tanis, *Injustice at Every Turn*, 94.

111. Ibid., 179.

112. Ibid., 103.

113. Ibid., 7.

114. Brill and Pepper, *The Transgender Child*, 105. Used with permission.

115. Ibid., 39.

116. Ehrensaft, *Gender Born, Gender Made*, 177–80. See also Brill and Pepper, *The Transgender Child*, 53–57.

CHAPTER SEVEN

117. Kahlil Gibran, *The Prophet* (New York: Alfred A. Knopf, 2005), 18–19.

118. Keith Ablow, "Don't Let Your Kids Watch Chaz Bono on 'Dancing with the Stars,'" *Fox News*, September 9, 2011, http://www.foxnews.com/opinion/2011/09/02.

119. Ibid.

120. See Evin Taylor, "Cisgender Privilege: On the Privileges of Performing Normative Gender," in *Gender Outlaws: The Next Generation*, Kate Bornstein and S. Bear Bergman (Berkeley: Seal Press, 2010), 268–72.

121. Brill and Pepper, *The Transgender Child*, 7.

122. Grant, Mottet, and Tanis, *Injustice at Every Turn*, 3.

123. Ibid., 33.

124. Ibid., 42.

125. Ibid., 33.

126. Ibid., 45 and 72.

127. Ibid., 33.

128. Stuart Biegel, *The Right to Be Out: Sexual Orientation and Gender Identity in America's Public Schools* (Minneapolis: University of Minnesota Press, 2010), 116.

129. Ibid., 114.

130. Ibid., 125.

131. Ibid., xiii.

132. Ibid.

133. Transgender Law Center, *Equality Maps and Safe Schools Laws in Issues and Publications*, http://www.transgenderlawcenter.org.

134. Massachusetts Transgender Political Coalition Policy Committee, *Best Practices for Serving Transgender and Gender Non-Conforming Students in Schools* (Boston: Massachusetts Transgender Political Caucus, 2012), 1–30. See http://www.masstpc.org to download.

135. Grant, Mottet, and Tanis, *Injustice at Every Turn*, 140.

136. Ibid., 126.

137. Ibid., 143.

138. Ibid., 150.

139. Ibid., 152.

140. Ibid., 5.

141. Ibid., 153.

142. Ibid., 154.

143. Ibid., 154.

144. WPATH, *SOC*, 65–67.

145. Brill and Pepper, *The Transgender Child*, 39–42.

146. Ehrensaft, *Gender Born, Gender Made*, 190–91.

147. Ibid., 90.

Appendices

APPENDIX A

Glossary of Terms

Below are some frequently used terms in the literature addressing transsexuality, transgenderism, and the LGBTQ community. These terms have developed and evolved over the last century in a variety of disciplines including medicine, psychiatry, the courts, academia, and more recently LGBTQ people themselves and their allies. The terms continue to expand and evolve as they come closer to reflecting the lived experience of the people they refer to.

Affirmed gender: the gender with which one identifies.
Ally: a person who works to understand their own privileges whether related to gender, sexual orientation, race, class, able body, language, religion, and age; and who works in solidarity with others understanding that everyone benefits when all forms of oppression end.
Anatomical sex: visible physical characteristics of the body used to determine sex. Anatomical males have a penis and testicles. Anatomical females have a vagina, vulva, clitoris, and later, breasts. In this book I use anatomical sex when referring to assigned gender instead of biological sex because it is more precise.
Androgyne: presenting with a balance of masculine and feminine characteristics.
Asexual: attracted to neither men nor women.
Assigned gender (assigned sex; birth gender; natal gender): Gender given by others (usually medical providers) at a baby's birth based on the visible appearance of genitalia.
Bigender: a person who identifies as both male and female.
Biological sex: includes external genitalia, gonads, chromosomes, genes, hormones, and secondary sex characteristics. Assigned gender is

based solely on external genitalia since all other components of one's biological sex are invisible to the naked eye or not present until puberty.

Birth sex (natal sex): primary sex characteristics present at birth that form the basis for assigning sex on the birth certificate (penis and scrotum for males; vulva, labia, clitoris, and vagina for females).

Bisexual: attraction to people irrespective of sex.

Bottom surgery: genital surgery.

Cisgender: people whose assigned gender and affirmed gender fit traditional gender norms; "cis" meaning "on this side of" and "trans" meaning "across from; on the other side of."

Closeted: a person who does not disclose their gender identity or sexual orientation. Partially closeted people disclose to only a select few.

Coming out: disclosing one's gender identity or sexual orientation to others.

Crossdresser: (formerly transvestite) a person who dresses in the clothing of the gender opposite to that considered appropriate for their anatomical sex. Most crossdressers do not want to change gender.

Cross-gender (cross-sex) hormones: prescribed for transgender teens and adults who decide to alter some aspects of their body to better conform to their affirmed gender. Testosterone taken by a female masculinizes the body and estrogen taken by a male feminizes the body over time.

DBT: dialectical behavior therapy encourages patients to accept uncomfortable thoughts, feelings, and behaviors and develop coping skills such as mindfulness and relaxation to deal with self-destructive responses and make better choices.

Female-to-male (FTM): a person born or assigned at birth as female who identifies as male and takes the gender and identity of a man by socially transitioning through name, pronoun, dress, mannerisms, and behavior, and possibly medically transitioning through hormone therapy and/or surgery.

Gay (men)/lesbian (women): (formerly homosexual) attraction to people of the same sex.

Gay-Straight Alliance (GSA): in-school clubs or groups for LGBTQ students usually with faculty/administrator advisors. More recently called Gender and Sexuality Alliance.

Gender: a psychosocial construct used to classify a person as male, female, both or neither; behaviors, cultural characteristics, and psychological traits that are associated with a specific sex.

Gender binary (dual; twofold): refers to the widely held notion that there are only two genders that stand in opposition to one another and individuals are either one or the other: boy or girl; man or woman.

Gender conforming: acting within the culturally prescribed gender expression/role for people of one's anatomical sex.

Gender dysphoria: a medical term for internal feelings of discomfort, dissonance, anxiety, or unhappiness as a result of the gender incongruity between one's body and one's internal sense of self. Not all gender nonconforming people experience gender dysphoria.

Gender expression (or presentation): the way a person moves in the world to communicate one's gender to others through name, clothing, mannerisms, body language, speech patterns, voice, hairstyle, and behavior.

Gender fluidity: the understanding that the human experience of gender identity, expression, and roles range along a continuum rather than being confined to two opposite genders.

Gender identity: a person's innate, deeply felt sense of self as: girl or boy; woman or man; both; neither; or somewhere in between. Awareness of the anatomical differences between boys and girls occurs by age three and a person's gender identity begins in childhood and may continue through adolescence into adulthood.

Gender identity disorder (GID): a diagnostic term used by the medical and psychiatric professions to describe the condition whereby one's internal gender identity does not conform to one's anatomical sex (or assigned gender). A GID diagnosis was required up until May 2013 to receive cross-gender hormones or sex reassignment surgery.

Genderism: advocacy of a binary gender system.

Gender nonconforming (gender variant; gender creative): acting outside of the culturally prescribed gender expression/role for people of one's anatomical sex.

Genderqueer: a person whose gender identity exists outside of the traditional gender binary of opposites between man and woman. A person who blurs, rejects, or transgresses gender norms. Other related terms include gender-variant, intergender, gender bender, bi-gender, beyond binary, third gender, gender fluid, gender outlaw, pan gender, two spirit.

Gender role: the socially determined set of attitudes and behaviors that are expected based on anatomical sex.

Gender transitioning: a multi-step process of moving toward living in one's affirmed gender rather than one's assigned gender when the two are incongruent. Transitioning often includes changing one's name, pronoun, dress, body language, speech, and hairstyle and may, but does not always, include physical changes such as hormone therapy and medical procedures to modify one's body to better conform to one's gender identity.

Gonadectomy: surgical removal of ovaries or testes.

Heteronormative: the assumption or expectation that everyone is heterosexual; that it is normal to be heterosexual; that any other sexual orientation is deviant.

Heterosexism: the belief that heterosexuality is the norm; the presumption that all people are (or should be) heterosexual; that people attracted to members of the same sex are abnormal.

Heterosexual: emotional and physical attraction to people of the opposite sex.

Homophobia: negative feelings, attitudes, and behaviors toward people who are lesbian, gay, or bisexual.

Homosexual: outdated term for emotional and physical attraction to people of the same sex. See gay/lesbian.

Hormone blockers (puberty suppressants): GnRH analogues that suppress testosterone in males and estrogen and progesterone in females thereby preventing the body's biological progression toward puberty; prescribed to children in Tanner Stage 2 of puberty (ages eleven to sixteen) as a way to buy time until further decisions are made about gender identity and transitioning options.

Intersex (formerly hermaphrodite): people born with ambiguous genitalia or with primary sex characteristics of both sexes. It was once the practice that doctors assigned the infant's sex and conformed the child's body surgically. The recommended practice today is to wait until the child is old enough to self-identify. Intersex births occur in approximately 1 in 2,000 births.

LGBTQI: an acronym for lesbian, gay, bisexual, transgender, queer or questioning, intersex.

Male-to-female (MTF): a person born or assigned at birth as male who identifies as female and takes the gender and identity of a woman by socially transitioning through name, pronoun, dress, mannerisms, and behavior, and possibly medically transitioning through hormone therapy and/or surgery.

Mastectomy (top surgery; chest surgery): surgical removal of breasts.

NTDS: National Transgender Discrimination Survey.

Out: living openly as lesbian, gay, bisexual, transgender, queer, or intersex. Being outed is when someone purposely or accidentally discloses another person's sexual orientation or gender identity without the person's knowledge or permission.

Passing: for a transsexual person, the ability to be seen and accepted by others as one's affirmed gender instead of one's assigned gender (or anatomical sex). Also refers to closeted gay, lesbian and bisexual people passing as straight; or people assuming a different racial/ethnic or cultural identity.

Penectomy: surgical removal of the penis.

Phalloplasty: surgical creation of a penis.

Preferred gender pronouns (PGPs): he/him/his; she/her/hers with some gender queer youth preferring they/them/theirs.

Preferred name: name with which a person identifies or chooses to use. In schools, since some states require parental consent or age of eighteen before petitioning for a legal name change, transgender students may choose to use a name different from their legal name, as with the common practice of using a nickname.

Pre/post-op: before/after sex reassignment surgery.

Privilege: unearned ways in which members of dominant groups benefit at the expense of minority groups including access to resources, respect, social acceptance, freedom of expression and setting the norm. Those with privilege are often unaware of it or take it for granted while those without it are acutely aware that it's denied to them.

Queer: refers to people who are lesbian, gay, bisexual, transgender, and questioning. Formerly used as a slur, now reclaimed and used by LGBTQ people as an expression of pride and unity.

Questioning: being uncertain of one's gender identity or sexual orientation.

Read (being read): being perceived by others as a gender different than the one being presented.

Real-life test: the period of time in which a person lives full time in their affirmed gender instead of their assigned gender. Recommended by the SOC for one year prior to irreversible treatment.

Secondary sex characteristics: physical traits associated with anatomical sex such as skin texture, body fat distribution, patterns of hair growth, overall body size; socially significant bodily signs that others read to guess one's sex and attribute gender.

Sex: a biological classification based on reproductive physiology with four main components: 1) primary sex characteristics (penis and scrotum for boys; vulva, labia, clitoris and vagina for girls) which form the basis for assigning sex at birth; 2) genetic sex or chromosomes (typically XX for females and XY for males; however, there is much greater variation in chromosomal combinations than this simple formula suggests); 3) gonads (ovaries for females and testes for males); 4) secondary sex characteristics (not present at birth and developing during adolescence) including chest and facial hair for males, breasts for females, and pubic hair for both.

Sexual identity: how a person views and internally identifies oneself in terms of sexual orientation or behavior based on who they are attracted to.

Sexual orientation: a feeling of attraction to others—romantic, emotional, physical, and sexual—categorized by the sex of the person to whom one is attracted. Transgender people can be heterosexual, gay, lesbian, or bisexual. See heterosexual, gay/lesbian, and bisexual, above.

Sex reassignment surgery (SRS; also called gender reassignment or gender confirmation surgery): surgical modification of the primary (genitals) and/or secondary sex characteristics (breasts, Adam's apple) to conform more closely to one's affirmed gender. May include penectomy and vaginoplasty in an anatomical male and mastectomy and/or phalloplasty in an anatomical female.

SOC: Standards of Care, the internationally accepted recommendations for transgender people seeking medical care to transition their gender. Revised periodically by the World Professional Association for Transgender Health (WPATH).

Social transitioning: includes changing one's gender presentation in ways that are reversible. A partial social transition includes wearing clothing and hairstyles that conform to one's affirmed gender. Complete social transitioning includes using a name and pronoun congruent with one's affirmed gender and communicating one's transition to others.

Stealth: not sharing one's gender identity, experience, or past history.

Straight: synonymous with heterosexual.

Tanner Stage 2: a five-stage scale for physically measuring the development of primary and secondary sex characteristics in children and adolescents, identified by James Tanner, a British pediatrician.

Stage 2 in girls is when breast buds appear and in boys, when the skin on the scrotum thins and reddens but before the penis elongates. Stage 2 is the point at which hormone blockers are prescribed to prevent the progression of puberty.

Top surgery (chest surgery): surgical removal of breasts.

Transgender: people whose gender identity does not match their anatomy; the generally accepted umbrella term for those who do not accept or conform to the social expectations of their anatomical sex including transsexuals, crossdressers, two spirit people, drag performers, and people who do not identify with their biological sex. Many transgender people report experiencing conflict over their assigned gender and their innate self-identity from early childhood. Transgender people may have any sexual orientation.

Transitioning: see gender transitioning.

Transman: a person whose birth sex and assigned gender were female but who identifies and presents his gender as male.

Transphobia: negative feelings, attitudes, and behaviors toward transgender people.

Transsexual: an older term used in the medical profession for a person who experiences dissonance between their assigned gender and their internal gender identity. Some transsexuals undergo medical treatment to bring their body into conformity with their gender identity. Procedures can include modification of secondary sex characteristics such as surgical breast removal, permanent hair removal, hormone therapy to feminize or masculinize the body, and sex reassignment surgery (SRS; also called gender confirmation surgery) of the genitalia.

Transvestite: outmoded term; see crossdresser.

Transwoman is a person whose birth sex and assigned gender were male but who identifies and presents her gender as female.

Two Spirit: from some Native American cultures that viewed transgender people as having "two spirits," born into one sex but taking on the dress and gender roles of the other.

Vaginoplasty: surgical creation of a vagina.

WPATH: World Professional Association for Transgender Health. See SOC.

Appendix B

REFERENCES

Ablow, Keith. "Don't Let Your Kids Watch Chaz Bono on 'Dancing with the Stars.'" *Fox News*, September 9, 2011. http://www.foxnews.com/opinion/2011/09/02.

Abramowich, D. R., I. A. Davidson, A. Longstaff, and C. K. Pearson. "Sex Differentiation of the Human Midtrimester Brain." *European Journal of Obstetrics and Gynecology and Reproductive Biology* 25, no. 1 (1987): 7–14.

American Psychiatric Association. *Diagnostic and Statistical Manual of Mental Disorders, Fifth Edition*. Washington, D.C.: American Psychiatric Publishing, 2013.

Biegel, Stuart. *The Right to Be Out: Sexual Orientation and Gender Identity in America's Public Schools*. Minneapolis: University of Minnesota Press, 2010.

Bono, Chaz. *Transition: The Story of How I Became a Man*. New York: Dutton, 2011.

Bornstein, Kate and S. Bear Bergman. *Gender Outlaws: The Next Generation*. Berkeley: Seal Press, 2010.

Boston Women's Health Book Collective. *Our Bodies, Ourselves*. New York: Simon and Schuster, 2011.

Boylan, Jennifer Finney. *She's Not There: A Life in Two Genders*. New York: Broadway Books, 2004.

Bradley, Marion Zimmer. *The Mists of Avalon*. New York: Ballantine Books, 1982.

Bremyn, Genny and Susan Rankin. *The Lives of Transgender People*. New York: Columbia University Press, 2011.

Brill, Stephanie and Rachel Pepper. *The Transgender Child: A Handbook for Families and Professionals*. San Francisco: Cleis, 2008.

Brown, Mildred L. and Chloe Ann Rounsley. *True Selves: Understanding Transsexualism: For Families, Friends, Coworkers and Helping Professionals*. San Francisco: Jossey–Bass, 1996.

Bullough, Bonnie, Vern Bullough and James Elias, eds. *Gender Blending*. Amherst, NY: Prometheus Books, 1997.

Burke, Phyllis. *Gender Shock: Exploding the Myths of Male and Female.* New York: Doubleday, 1996.

Califa, Pat. *Sex Changes: The Politics of Transgenderism.* San Francisco: Cleis Press, 1997.

Center for American Progress. *Gay and Transgender Youth Homelessness by the Numbers.* June 21, 2010, http://www.americanprogress.org/issues/2010/06/homelessness_numbers.html.

Colapinto, John. *As Nature Made Him: The Boy Who Was Raised as a Girl.* New York: Harper Perennial, 2001.

Diamond, Milton and Keith Sigmundson. "Sex Reassignment at Birth: Long-term Review and Clinical Implications." *Archives of Pediatric and Adolescent Medicine* 151, no. 3 (1997): 298–304.

Dohrenwend, Anne. *Coming Around: Parenting Lesbian, Gay, Bisexual, and Transgender Kids.* Far Hills, NJ: New Horizon Press, 2012.

Duron, Lori. *Raising My Rainbow: Adventures in Raising a Fabulous, Gender Creative Son.* New York: Broadway Books, 2013.

Ehrensaft, Diane. *Gender Born, Gender Made: Raising Healthy, Gender-Nonconforming Children.* New York: The Experiment, 2011.

Evelyn, Just. *Mom, I Need to be a Girl.* Imperial Beach, CA: Walter Trook Publishing, 1998.

Feinberg, Leslie. *Trans Liberation: Beyond Pink or Blue.* Boston: Beacon Press, 1998.

Feinberg, Leslie. *Transgender Warriors: Making History from Joan of Arc to Dennis Rodman.* Boston: Beacon Press, 1997.

Fosha, Diana. *The Transforming Power of Affect: A Model for Accelerated Change.* New York: Basic Books, 2000.

Gates, Gary, J. *How Many People are Lesbian, Gay, Bisexual, and Transgender?* The Williams Institute, UCLA School of Law, 2011.

Gibran, Kahlil. *The Prophet.* New York: Alfred A. Knopf, 2005.

Gillespie, Peggy, ed. and Gigi Kaeser, photographer. *Love Makes a Family: Portraits of Lesbian, Gay, Bisexual, and Transgender Parents and their Families.* Amherst: University of Massachusetts, 1999.

Gilligan, Carol. *In a Different Voice: Psychological Theory and Women's Development.* Cambridge: Harvard University Press, 1982.

Grant, Jaime M., Lisa A. Mottet, and Justin Tanis. *Injustice at Every Turn: A Report of the National Transgender Discrimination Survey.* National Center for Transgender Equality and National Gay and Lesbian Task Force, 2011.

Huegal, Kelly. *GLBTQ: The Survival Guide for Lesbian, Gay, Bisexual, Transgender and Questioning Teens.* Minneapolis: Free Spirit Publishing, 2011.

Israel, Gianna E and Donald E. Tarver II, M.D. *Transgender Care: Recommended Guidelines, Practical Information and Personal Accounts.* Philadelphia: Temple University Press, 1997.

Jennings, Kevin with Pat Shapiro. *Always My Child: A Parent's Guide to Understanding Your Gay, Lesbian, Bisexual, Transgendered or Questioning Son or Daughter.* New York: Simon and Schuster, 2003.

Jorgensen, Christine. *Christine Jorgensen: A Personal Autobiography.* San Francisco: Cleis Press, 1967.

Kailey, Matt. *Just Add Hormones.* Boston: Beacon Press, 2006.

Lev, Arlene Istar. *The Complete Lesbian and Gay Parenting Guide.* Berkeley: Berkeley Books, 2004.

Lev, Arlene Istar. *Transgender Emergence: Therapeutic Guidelines for Working with Gender-Variant People and Their Families.* New York: Hawthorn Press, 2004. Kindle edition.

Mallon, Gerald, P. ed. *Social Work Practice with Transgender and Gender Variant Youth.* New York: Routledge, 2009.

Massachusetts Transgender Political Coalition Policy Committee. *Best Practices for Serving Transgender and Gender Non-Conforming Students in Schools.* Boston: Massachusetts Transgender Political Caucus, 2012. See http://www.masstpc.org to download.

Meyerowitz, Joanne. *How Sex Changed: A History of Transsexuality in the United States.* Cambridge: Harvard University Press, 2002.

Miller, Jean Baker. *Toward a New Psychology of Women.* Boston: Beacon Press, 1976.

Morris, Jan. *Conundrum: An Extraordinary Personal Narrative of Transsexualism.* New York: Harcourt Brace Jovanovich, 1974.

Olyslager, Femke and Lynn Conway. *On the Calculation of the Prevalence of Transsexualism.* Paper presented at the WPATH 20th International Symposium, Chicago, Illinois, September 5–8, 2007.

Pazos, Sofia. "Social Work Practice with Female-to-Male Transgender and Gender Variant Youth." In *Social Work Practice with Transgender and Gender Variant Youth,* edited by Gerald P. Mallon, ed., 87–103. New York: Routledge, 2009.

Pepper, Rachel, ed. *Transitions of the Heart: Stories of Love, Struggle and Acceptance by Mothers of Transgender and Gender Variant Children.* Berkeley: Cleis Press, 2012.

Perrotti, Jeff and Kim Westheimer. *When the Drama Club is Not Enough: Lessons from the Safe Schools Program for Gay and Lesbian Students.* Boston: Beacon Press, 2002.

PFLAG, *Welcoming Our Trans Family and Friends: A Support Guide for Parents, Families and Friends of Transgender and Gender Non-Conforming People.* Washington, D.C. http://www.pflag.org.

Richards, Renee. *No Way Renee: The Second Half of My Notorious Life.* New York: Simon and Schuster, 2007.

Roscoe, Will. *Changing Ones: Third and Fourth Genders in Native North America.* New York: St. Martin's Griffin, 2000.

Roughgarden, Joan. *Evolution's Rainbow: Diversity, Gender and Sexuality in Nature and People.* Berkeley: University of California Press, 2004.

Rudacille, Deborah. *The Riddle of Gender: Science, Activism and Transgender Rights.* New York: Anchor Books, 2006.

Ryan, Caitlin. *Supportive Families, Healthy Children: Helping Families with Lesbian, Gay, Bisexual and Transgender Children.* San Francisco State University, 2009. http://www.familyproject.sfsu.edu.

Solomon, Andrew. *Far from the Tree: Parents, Children, and the Search for Identity.* New York: Scribner, 2012.

Stryker, Susan. *Transgender History.* Berkeley: Seal Press, 2008.

The American Heritage Dictionary, Second College edition. Boston: Houghton Mifflin Co., 1985.

Transgender Law Center. *Equality Maps* and *Safe Schools Laws* in *Issues and Publications.* http://www.transgenderlawcenter.org.

World Professional Association for Transgender Health (WPATH), *Standards of Care for the Health of Transsexual, Transgender, and Gender Nonconforming People (SOC)*, 7th version. http://www.wpath.org.

FICTION

Beam, Chris. *I am J.* New York: Little Brown and Company, 2011.

Beam, Chris. *Transparent: Love, Family and Living the T with Transgender Teenagers.* New York: Harcourt Books, 2007.

Peters, Julie Anne. *Luna.* New York: Little Brown and Company, 2004.

Wittlinger, Ellen. *Parrotfish.* New York: Simon and Schuster, 2007.

MOVIES

Ma Vie en Rose (My Life in Pink), 1997.

Appendix C

RESOURCES AND SUPPORT

ADVOCACY

American Civil Liberties Union, www.aclu.org

Advocates for Youth, www.advocatesforyouth.org

Amplify, www.amplifyyourvoice.org

Anti-Violence Project, www.avp.org

Camp Aranu'tiq, www.camparanutiq.org

Camp Pride, www.campuspride.org

Eyes on Bullying, www.eyesonbullying.org

Family Acceptance Project, www.familyproject.sfsu.edu

Gay and Lesbian Medical Association, www.glma.org

Gender Odyssey, www.genderodyssey.org

Gender Spectrum Education and Training, www.genderspectrum.org

GLAAD, Gay and Lesbian Alliance Against Defamation, www.glaad.org

GLBT National Help Center, www.glnh.org

GLSEN, Gay, Lesbian and Straight Education Network, www.glsen.org

Human Rights Campaign, www.hrc.org

Intersex Society of North America, www.isna.org

It Gets Better, www.itgetsbetter.org

Jim Collins Foundation, www.jimcollinsfoundation.org

Lambda Legal, www.lambdalegal.org

Laura's Playground, www.lauras-playground.com

Massachusetts Transgender Political Caucus, www.masstpc.org

Matthew Shepard Foundation, www.matthewshepard.org

My Princess Boy website, www.myprincessboy.com

National Bullying Prevention Center, www.pacer.org/bullying

National Center for Transgender Equality, www.transequality.org

National Gay and Lesbian Task Force, www.thetaskforce.org

PFLAG, Parents, Families, and Friends of LGBTQ People,
        www.pflag.org/transgender

Teaching Tolerance, www.tolerance.org

The Point Foundation, www.pointfoundation.org

The Trevor Project, www.thetrevorproject.org

StopBullying.Gov, www.stopbullying.gov
TransActive Education and Advocacy, www.transactiveonline.org
TransFaith Network, www.transfaithlonline.org
Transforming Family, www.transformingfamily.org
Transgender Law and Policy Institute, www.transgenderlaw.org
Transgender Law Center, www.transgenderlawcenter.org
Trans Kids Purple Rainbow, www.transkidspurplerainbow.org
Transgender Faith and Action Network, www.tfaan.org
Transsexual Roadmap, www.tsroadmap.com
TransYouth Family Allies, www.imatyfa.org
Welcoming Schools, www.welcomingschools.org
World Professional Association for Transgender Health, www.wpath.org
UCLA School of Law, The Williams Institute,
        http://williamsinstitute.law.ucla.edu

MEDICAL

Children's Hospital Los Angeles, www.chla.org
        Center for Transyouth Health and Development
Children's National Medical Center, Washington, D.C.,
        www.childrensnational.org/gendervariance
Dimensions Clinic San Francisco, www.dimensionsclinic.org
Fenway Health Center, www.fenwayhealth.org
GeMS Gender Management Services Clinic, Boston,
        www.childrenshospital.org
Sidney Borum Junior Health Center, Boston, MA., www.sidneyborum.org
World Professional Association for Transgender Health, www.wpath.org

CRISIS LINES

The National Suicide Prevention Lifeline 1-800-273-TALK (8255)
The Trevor Project 1-866-4-U-TREVOR (866-488-7386)
The GLBT National Help Center Hotline 1-888-THE-GLNH
        (888-843-4564)
The GLBT National Youth Talkline 1-800-246-PRIDE (800-246-7743)

Appendix D

ADVOCACY ISSUES

You may decide to continue the change work you've begun by moving it out into the world. Some of the most dedicated allies in the LGBTQ community are family members who have witnessed the brave journeys of transgender children and youth. When and if you are ready, consider asking yourself what you have learned that can help other families? What will it take to make the world a more welcoming and accepting place for children like yours? Are there specific changes needed that you can see yourself working toward? The following are just some of the possible issues to consider:

- Education of school personnel to create safe, gender inclusive school environments

- School policies that are established and enforced to protect transgender and gender nonconforming students of all ages from harassment, bullying, and violence

- Education of health care providers on medical care for transgender people across the lifespan

- Inclusion of medical treatment for transgender people in health insurance policies

- Education of mental health professionals in addressing the needs of transgender and gender nonconforming people of all ages and their family members

- Education of family court judges in protecting the care and custody needs of transgender and gender nonconforming children

- Employment and housing policies that prevent discrimination against transgender and gender nonconforming people

- Professional education and equal, respectful public accommodation in health care settings, police departments, government agencies, retail stores, restaurants, hotels, public transportation, etc.

- Participation in efforts that enhance diversity and cultural competency and reduce personal prejudice and societal patterns of inequality with the goal of reducing racial disparities in accessing services and resources

Along your journey you have hopefully been surprised and pleased to find that there is a larger supportive public out there than you first imagined. Many are rooting for our children to thrive and succeed. Adding your voice and experience as a parent lends authenticity to the pressing need for these changes to enhance the future for your child and others like him or her.

Index

About the Author

Photo: Cheryl Crotty

Candace Waldron, MDiv, is an educator, administrator, and public policy advocate in violence prevention and women's health. She has served as executive director of a domestic violence agency, director of women's health in a community hospital and the Massachusetts Department of Public Health, and coordinator of a rape crisis center. Gender equality has been foundational in Waldron's professional pursuits yet even so, she felt unprepared when her adolescent daughter disclosed being transgender. She wrote *My Daughter He* to help other parents be better equipped and more informed when parenting their nonconforming or transgender children and currently cofacilitates PFLAG support groups for parents in the Boston area.

Thank you for reading *My Daughter He.* I hope you found it helpful and inspiring for wherever you are on your journey and invite you to tell a friend, share a post, or write a review on Amazon or Goodreads. Sharing stories of love for our nonconforming and transgender children, adolescents, and adults, can educate others, change attitudes, and make safer schools and communities for everyone.

If you would like to continue the conversation about how best to support our unique and creative children, connect with other parents, or find more in-depth suggestions about working with schools or advocating for policies, please visit my website at **www.candacewaldon.com**.

Thanks and best wishes,
Candace Waldron